W9-COT-404

# BRITISH AUTHORS

*Introductory Critical Studies*

General Editor: ROBIN MAYHEAD

# JANE AUSTEN

In this series

*John Keats* by ROBIN MAYHEAD
*William Wordsworth* by GEOFFREY DURRANT
*George Eliot* by R. T. JONES

# JANE AUSTEN

BY

YASMINE GOONERATNE

*Senior Lecturer in English*
*University of Ceylon*

CAMBRIDGE
AT THE UNIVERSITY PRESS
1970

Published by the Syndics of the Cambridge University Press
Bentley House, 200 Euston Road, London N.W.1
American Branch: 32 East 57th Street, New York, N.Y.10022

© Cambridge University Press 1970

Library of Congress Catalogue Card Number: 75–123669

Standard Book Numbers
521 07843 1    clothbound
521 09630 8    paperback

Printed in Great Britain
at the University Printing House, Cambridge
(Brooke Crutchley, University Printer)

# GENERAL PREFACE

This study of Jane Austen is the third in a series of short introductory critical studies of the more important British authors. The aim of the series is to go straight to the authors' works; to discuss them directly with a maximum of attention to concrete detail; to say what they are and what they do, and to indicate a valuation. The general critical attitude implied in the series is set out at some length in my *Understanding Literature*. Great literature is taken to be to a large extent self-explanatory to the reader who will attend carefully enough to what it says. 'Background' study, whether biographical or historical, is not the concern of the series.

It is hoped that this approach will suit a number of kinds of reader, in particular the general reader who would like an introduction which talks about the works themselves; and the student who would like a general critical study as a starting point, intending to go on to read more specialised works later. Since 'background' is not erected as an insuperable obstacle, readers in other English-speaking countries, countries where English is a second language, or even those for whom English is a foreign language, should find the books helpful. In Britain and the Commonwealth, students and teachers in universities and in the higher forms of secondary schools will find that the authors chosen for treatment are those most often prescribed for study in public and university examinations.

The series could be described as an attempt to make available to a wide public the results of the literary criticism of the last thirty years, and especially the methods associated with Cambridge. If the result is an increase in the reading, with enjoyment and understanding, of the great works of English literature, the books will have fulfilled their wider purpose.

ROBIN MAYHEAD

*For Brendon*

---

This book was completed during the
tenure of a research fellowship
awarded by the American Association
of University Women

# CONTENTS

# 1

# INTRODUCTORY

About thirty years ago, Miss Maria Ward of Huntingdon, with only seven thousand pounds, had the good luck to captivate Sir Thomas Bertram of Mansfield Park, in the county of Northampton, and to be thereby raised to the rank of a baronet's lady, with all the comforts and consequences of an handsome house and large income. All Huntingdon exclaimed on the greatness of the match, and her uncle, the lawyer, himself, allowed her to be at least three thousand pounds short of any equitable claim to it. She had two sisters to be benefited by her elevation; and such of their acquaintance as thought Miss Ward and Miss Frances quite as handsome as Miss Maria, did not scruple to predict their marrying with almost equal advantage. But there certainly are not so many men of large fortune in the world, as there are pretty women to deserve them.     *Mansfield Park*, Chapter 1 (1814)

These are the opening sentences of a novel, the third published by Jane Austen, that appeared in the year that saw the publication of Sir Walter Scott's *Waverley*. The interest aroused by *Mansfield Park* was a mere ripple beside the tide of enthusiasm that met Scott's historical fiction. Yet her reputation has risen steadily; in our own times it has been written of her, that

she not only makes tradition for those coming after, but...creates the tradition we see leading down to her. Her work, like the work of all great creative writers, gives a meaning to the past.[1]

And while that part of Scott's enormous output that deals with the heroism and humanity of common people in a familiar setting shares today something of the critical acclaim accorded to Jane Austen's work, the reputation of his historical novels (so great in his and Jane Austen's time) has been seen to dwindle into comparative insignificance.

Such changes in literary taste serve a useful function, for though they might seem for a time unfair, they focus attention on different aspects of a writer's quality and sensibility. Sometimes they betray a good deal about the *readers*, and the ideas that are common in their generation. Readers of fiction today do not care

---

[1] F. R. Leavis, *The Great Tradition* (1948).

as much for historical novels as did those of a century and a half ago; the loss of interest in a part of Scott's work and its revival in another is a symptom of this fact. But the view that Jane Austen's writing gives 'a meaning to the past' does not merely illuminate some part of her work that had been shadowed by public neglect. It gives her a special and honoured place in the centre of the great tradition of the English novel, and pays tribute to her achievement in creating a fictional world whose values have a real relevance to universally experienced human dilemmas.

Can this really be so? Jane Austen refers, with some casualness, to 'all the comforts and consequences of an handsome house and large income', but a reader of her novels today could probably not, without some specialised information, estimate Sir Thomas's income at all accurately. Jane Austen's contemporaries would, by virtue of their accumulated experience, have been able to grasp her exact meaning better than we can. More important than mere calculation of pounds, shillings, and pence, they would have understood the nature of those accompanying 'comforts', appreciated the advance in rank and importance (or *consequence*) made by the lucky Maria, and the irony implicit in Jane Austen's use of the plural could not have escaped them, knowing as they did that her marriage would bring Maria luxury and a pleasant sense of her own importance, the usual rewards or *consequences* of such an elevation in society. New readers of Jane Austen's novels cannot, for obvious reasons, bring experience of quite this kind to the enjoyment of her writing. The world we know well, whether Ghanaian, Canadian, or Ceylonese, is very different from the world she knew, in externals at least. The social customs she takes for granted are so different from those obtaining even in Britain today that British readers might feel, quite as much as those of any other country or nation, that the fluctuations of the Huntingdon marriage market as described in the passage above have nothing to do with them. We might all prefer to believe that the pressures exerted upon young women to win security for themselves by exploiting their physical attractions as deliberately as hunters bait traps (for what else are we to understand by Jane Austen's delicate, yet devastating use in this context of the oldfashioned word *captivate*?) belong to an imaginary country-town world of the nineteenth century that has become with time quite remote from our own lives and from contemporary problems.

How, then, does it happen that though Jane Austen's characters move strictly within a framework fashioned upon the social milieu of Regency England, the reader of her novels is continually led to make fresh discoveries about himself, about other people, and about the hitherto uncontested values of his world?

Let us look again at the last sentence of the quoted passage:

But there certainly are not so many men of large fortune in the world as there are pretty women to deserve them.

Do we accept this statement? *Can* we assent to its implications? It is amusing, certainly; but only superficially, for the authoritative manner in which it is phrased compels serious consideration, seems to declare that easy laughter is not enough. Acceptance of it implies a willingness to believe physical beauty as admirable an attribute as moral integrity or good sense, and a rich husband as being necessarily one worth striving to acquire: a readiness, in fact, to condone society's tendency to judge men according to their incomes, and women according to their faces. Any kindly satisfaction the unwary reader may have felt at Maria's unexpected good fortune—*she* thinks herself lucky, too!—must be shattered when such subtly ambiguous phrasing unites with an (apparently) matter-of-fact tone to point the irresponsibility of attitudes such as these. We may deny that the sentence voices our personal point of view, but we must acknowledge the existence of people who think and act in apparent obedience to it, and admit the universality with which these 'principles' operate in the society we know. Jane Austen's power to speak clearly to our generation, and to readers in any English-speaking society, springs from our admiration of her deft use of language, from the alertness and uncertainty that it awakes in us, successfully removing any complacency created earlier by the deceptive tranquillity of her style—*and from our acknowledgment of the relevance and fidelity of her ironic vision to life as we know it to be in our own world.*

Jane Austen quite deliberately excluded from her work all sensational or decorative material, however intrinsically interesting or historically important, concentrating her attention upon the thoughts and feelings, motives and prejudices of men and women. Her choice of a setting for them was sensible: by placing them in the world she knew best, she gave them the solidity they must have to convince us of their truth to life, and spared herself the laborious creation of an unfamiliar milieu. We have only to compare the casual gesture that indicates the wealth and elegance of Mansfield ('all the comforts and consequences of an handsome house and large income') with the brilliantly detailed fragment that follows it, to see how her method allows her to go swiftly through and beyond the social externals of her novels to what really interested her:

All Huntingdon exclaimed on the greatness of the match, and her uncle, the lawyer, himself, allowed her to be at least three thousand pounds short of any equitable claim to it.

Are these people really enthusiastic about the marriage? Their 'exclamations' at its *greatness*, and its *advantage* to Maria and her sisters suggest an open, probably uncharitable discussion of the match, for the emphasis seems to be on *surprise* rather than on pleasure or joy at Miss Maria's happiness. This impression is reinforced by the mercenary calculations of her uncle. The word that sets this briefly glimpsed character apart from the rest as worthy of special attention—*himself*—prepares the reader for some important opinion. As an elder relation of the lady's his views are to be respected, and as a lawyer presumably experienced in money transactions and marriage settlements, his words carry some weight. And what are those words? Maria, he considers, has done very well; the property she has acquired is worth far more than she has had to pay for it. She has made an excellent business investment! This judgment, based on a careful estimation of the current market prices, shows us that social recognition of the match is by no means denied, but clearly discernible in the chorus of congratulation are envious, spiteful overtones, and a habitual application of market terms to human relationships such as those of love and marriage. In a single sentence that captures the very tones and phrases of 'polite' conversation, Jane Austen lays bare the moral chasms in elegant and respectable society.

Avoiding the sensational, the melodramatic, and the unfamiliar, she is able by means of fine discrimination in the matter of choice of setting and subject-matter, to draw character in its true proportions, as revealed in the thoughts and actions of people so vividly realised that they seem to become real persons.

This is not to say that Jane Austen's settings serve merely as suitable backgrounds for her characters. On the contrary, although the details of a landscape or an interior are never dwelt on for their own sake, the country-houses, towns and fields of her novels take on a vivid life because they live in and through the characters. Let us consider the passage below, for example, taken from *Northanger Abbey*:

An abbey! yes, it was delightful to be really in an abbey! but she doubted, as she looked round the room, whether any thing within her observation, would have given her the consciousness. The furniture was in all the profusion and elegance of modern taste. The fire-place, where she had expected the ample width and ponderous carving of former times, was contracted to a Rumford ...The windows, to which she looked with peculiar dependence, from having heard the General talk of his preserving them in their Gothic form with reverential care, were yet less what her fancy had portrayed. To be sure, the pointed arch was preserved—the form of them was Gothic—they might be even casements—but every pane was so large, so clear, so light! To an imagination which had hoped for the smallest divisions, and the heaviest stone-work, for painted glass, dirt and cobwebs, the difference was very distressing.

Catherine Morland's feelings range from delight to distress as she looks about her, and Jane Austen's description of Northanger Abbey tells us a great deal about the mood of the young woman through whose eyes we see it. Visiting a country house that is larger and more impressive than any she has ever seen, Catherine is disappointed—not because it is oldfashioned or badly kept, but because each new sign of cleanliness and modernity strikes at her hopes that she will be living in a romantic ruin. Her imagination has been inflamed by the sensational fiction she has been reading, and she must be helped through many similar disappointments and disillusionments by her friends' sympathy and her own good sense and courage before she is able to appreciate that real life is very different from Gothic novels, and a good deal more interesting. Jane Austen's description of the Abbey becomes in this way much more than a sketch of an appropriate background for the action of the novel; it is an exposition of an important stage in Catherine's journey to maturity, and as such it contributes to the novel's main theme.

While the organic nature of writing such as this and those elements that illustrate the relation of her art to tradition have attracted much praise from modern critics of Jane Austen's work, there are many other reasons for the high opinion in which her novels are held. She has been commended for her fine control of language, her mastery of the art of ironic exposure, for her discrimination in rejecting eighteenth-century fashions in fiction, for her deliberate limitation of the scope of her novels in order to produce great art, her habit of constant, painstaking revision; and for the subtlety with which she handles point of view to mark the developing relationships between her characters. Her genius for comedy has delighted readers of each succeeding age, but perhaps the modern critic has been above all impressed by her power to externalise personal problems in those of her heroines, her ability to discipline herself through the act of writing creatively, and by her 'moral concern, perplexity, and commitment'.[1]

The truth of these judgments and the value of their contribution to our appreciation of Jane Austen's writing do not, unfortunately, outweigh their tendency to make of her a writer's writer, or worse, a critic's writer. The terms used are those of academic criticism, and the general reader tends to be wary of them. The great admiration Jane Austen has aroused at another level, too, does not encourage a new reader, for much more of it is affectionate than serious, or even sober. Enthusiasts who have labelled her work 'quaint', 'charming', 'whimsical', and 'delightful' have done Jane Austen a disservice by severely limiting the numbers and quality of her readers; the myth of her lightweight attractions has sent some serious readers elsewhere, in the belief that her novels hold pleasure only for the romantic and the sentimental. Nothing could be further from the truth:

But there certainly are not so many men of large fortune in the world, as there are pretty women to deserve them.

[1] Andrew H. Wright, *Jane Austen's Novels. A Study in Structure* (1953).

Only a superficial reading could create or support the impression
that Jane Austen is a harmlessly amusing purveyor of romantic
social comedy. On the contrary, she cannot be completely enjoyed
or even partly understood, except by readers who bring the most
alert and critical attention to her novels. Those who take the
above and similar sentences at their face-value can read and
re-read the six novels, and never cease to praise the gentle charm
of 'dear Jane'. But a careful reader cannot miss the irony
implicit in the maxim that only the fair deserve the rich, with its
criticism of a society that provided no satisfactory alternative to
marriage for portionless women, pretty or plain. Jane Austen's
tone is exquisitely poised between ironic detachment and protest
at the immorality and injustice of accepted social values. To miss
this is to miss an element in her writing that has been called
'subversive', a continual flow of critical perceptiveness beneath
the smooth, socially 'acceptable' surface of her tone.

Who was Jane Austen? The facts of her quiet, uneventful life can
be very simply stated. Born in 1775 in Steventon, a village in
southern England, the younger daughter of a country clergyman,
Jane Austen distributed the greater part of her life between visits
to Bath, London, and Kent. She had six brothers, all older than
herself, with whose families she and her elder sister, Cassandra,
enjoyed a close and affectionate relationship. With some of her
nieces and nephews, besides Cassandra, she maintained an intimate correspondence. Until she was twenty-five years old, Jane
Austen lived in her father's rectory. In 1800 she went with her
parents and Cassandra Austen to Bath, and five years afterwards,
on the death of the Rev. George Austen in 1806, the family
moved to Southampton. In 1809 the three ladies moved to Chawton, in Hampshire, where Jane Austen lived until within a few
weeks of her death. Of the six published novels, *Sense and Sensibility* appeared in November 1811, when Jane Austen was
thirty-six years old, *Pride and Prejudice* in January 1813,
*Mansfield Park* in May 1814, *Emma* in December 1815, and
*Northanger Abbey* with *Persuasion*, posthumously, in December
1817. Her characteristic method of writing was to make an initial

draft, which she would work upon for varied lengths of time afterwards, and subject before publication to a thorough revision. Although all her novels were published within seven years—and those the seven last of her life—three of them (the first versions of *Northanger Abbey*, *Sense and Sensibility*, and *Pride and Prejudice*) were already in the form of initial drafts, and had been, perhaps, partially worked on, when Jane Austen left Steventon for Bath in 1800. She did not marry. Between 1816 and 1817 her health failed, and on 18 July 1817 she died, at the age of forty-two.

It does not surprise us that the surface of the novels Jane Austen wrote presents the smooth pattern of social life in the country, as led by a leisured English middle class at the beginning of the nineteenth century. Ladies go walking, distribute charity to the poor, pay morning calls on one another, and delight in occasional balls or impromptu country dancing. Gentlemen hunt, shoot, read widely and converse well, and improve their property. Jane Austen's gaze penetrates, however, through the externals of the social customs and behaviour she knew so well, to the bases of human conduct.

Her partner now drew near, and said, 'That gentleman would have put me out of patience, had he staid with you half a minute longer. He has no business to withdraw the attention of my partner from me. We have entered into a contract of mutual agreeableness for the space of an evening, and all our agreeableness belongs solely to each other for that time. Nobody can fasten themselves on the notice of one, without injuring the rights of the other. I consider a country-dance as an emblem of marriage. Fidelity and complaisance are the principal duties of both; and those men who do not chuse to dance or marry themselves, have no business with the partners or wives of their neighbours.'

'But they are such very different things!'

'—That you think they cannot be compared together.'

'To be sure not. People that marry can never part, but must go and keep house together. People that dance, only stand opposite each other in a long room for half an hour.'

'And such is your definition of matrimony and dancing. Taken in that light certainly, their resemblance is not striking; but I think I could place them in such a view. You will allow, that in both, man has the advantage of choice, woman only the power of refusal; that in both, it is an engagement between man and woman, formed for the advantage of each; and that when once entered into, they belong exclusively to each other till the moment of its dissolution; that it is their duty, each to endeavour to give the other no cause for wishing that he or she had bestowed themselves elsewhere, and their best interest to keep their own imaginations from wandering towards the perfections of their neighbours, or fancying that they should have been better off with any one else. You will allow all this?'

'Yes, to be sure, as you state it, all this sounds very well; but still they are so very different. I cannot look upon them at all in the same light, nor think the same duties belong to them.'     *Northanger Abbey*, Vol. I, Chapter 10

Catherine Morland's definition of marriage is characteristically childish but sound, placing its emphasis on the idea of a permanent union; as she is a person who brings 'fresh feelings of every sort' to each new experience, her definition of dancing is equally innocent and unsophisticated. Between people who 'stand opposite each other in a long room for half an hour' a relationship must necessarily be so fleeting—and mutual understanding so superficial—that Henry Tilney's witty analogy is rejected by her. Yet, though Catherine does not have the sophistication to perceive it—and Tilney too much delicacy to point it out to her—dancing with each other is not only comparable with marriage, but a socially permitted preliminary to it. The 'duties' of dancers to each other as described by Tilney, and the conventions of the socially acceptable custom according to which Catherine and her partner have met and are moving, even as they speak, provide a framework for this and many other exchanges in Jane Austen's novels. In *Pride and Prejudice*, Mr Bingley's fondness for dancing is considered 'a certain step towards falling in love'; and his dancing twice with Jane Bennet at the Meryton assembly ball inspires hopes in her mother that Jane will soon be happily settled at Netherfield. The single occasion on which Mr Darcy and Elizabeth Bennet dance together—at the Netherfield ball—provides this pair who so rarely meet with an opportunity to explore each other's mind and motives in a situation of intimacy and privacy impossible to procure outside the ballroom, but made possible within it by the marriage-like conventions that surround dancing itself and by the very presence of other dancers in the set and the lookers-on in the crowded room who represent for this couple the society of which they are themselves a part: '...One must speak a little, you know. It would look odd to be entirely silent for half an hour together...' Elizabeth's final words to Darcy—'if I do not take your likeness now, I may never have another opportunity'—illuminate the difficulties in the way of their achieving a true understanding of each other, and demonstrate at the same time the importance of dances and balls to Jane Austen's faithfully accurate picture of country living. In *Mansfield Park*, Mr Rushworth and Maria Bertram become engaged to be married 'after dancing with each other at a proper number of balls'. The rules that have grown up around dancing—that it is a 'charming amusement for young people' particularly, although supervised and respectably chaperoned by responsible adults, that to dance twice with the same person denotes unusual interest in that person, and so on—are so generally known and adhered to, that to defy or deliberately break them becomes an act of some significance. Thus, the experienced Isabella Thorpe protests to James Morland, in *Northanger Abbey*, that to dance together a second time 'is a most improper thing, and entirely against the rules'. The speed and willingness with which she immediately breaks these 'rules' reveals her eagerness to become permanently associated with Morland in marriage. When, later in the novel, Isabella breaks her resolution of not dancing in Morland's absence, she neatly demonstrates the aptness of Henry Tilney's comparison of dancing with marriage and gives it a deeper ironic truth; her action shadows forth her future infidelity to Morland, and the ultimate breaking of their engagement to marry.

Jane Austen's use of the country dance to reveal hidden feelings and motives in her characters is matched by her use of other social diversions familiar in the everyday life of her world (such as card-games like 'Speculation' and whist in *Mansfield Park* and *Sense and Sensibility*, the riddles and anagrams in *Emma*, and expeditions to places of interest in all the novels) for similar purposes. But the occasions on which lovers meet or withdraw from one another in the setting and the special atmosphere of a dance are themselves distributed so as to balance with each other within *Emma* and *Pride and Prejudice* in particular, creating by this means a formal grace and symmetry that is very like the patterning of the movements in a country dance, giving a 'rightness' to the convention by which each novel ends with a wedding, the novelist's equivalent of the dancers' bow and curtsy. The subtle uses to which the minutiae of ordinary life are put in her work illustrate the intensity of the gaze Jane Austen directed at the values beneath their smooth refinements, showing how her quality of 'moral concern' can be understood to include and permeate all important aspects of her total achievement, her gift for comedy, her talent for drawing characters that evince a lifelike energy and a society whose existence we never doubt, the perception that leads her to concentrate her critical attention on just those matters that are relevant to human societies of every age and country. To appreciate Jane Austen's quality as an artist and a moralist in the fullest sense, we must go to her writing itself, to her letters, the juvenilia, the unfinished work in manuscript, and the six famous novels.

The problem of assigning accurate dates to the novels is a difficult one, even now. All that is certain is that every novel could have been, and probably was, the result of varying periods of elaborate and drastic revision. *Northanger Abbey* was published nineteen years after Jane Austen wrote the first draft, *Sense and Sensibility* fourteen years after, *Pride and Prejudice* sixteen. *Mansfield Park* apparently occupied two years and *Emma* one between first draft and publication, but there is excellent reason to believe that Jane Austen based these two novels on pieces written much earlier, *Lady Susan* and *The Watsons* respectively; if this is so, *Mansfield Park* took eight years in the writing, and so did *Emma*. *Persuasion* can be regarded as a special case, having been written very late in Jane Austen's life, and subjected to less careful scrutiny and revision than the others: its writing occupied a year. Much space has been expended on attempts to date the novels satisfactorily, but when all is said, we are left with the following facts:

It was this author's invariable practice to recast most carefully before publication. For this reason, it is unhelpful and misleading in the case of *Northanger Abbey*, *Sense and Sensibility*, and *Pride and Prejudice*, to talk of 'early' and 'mature' work, because in each of these novels writing which, for various reasons, strikes the reader as 'mature' in theme and quality exists side by side with material that has obvious connections of one kind or another with Jane Austen's juvenilia. All the novels having been published within or after the last seven years of her life, we cannot ignore the fact that a mature Jane Austen revised each one before publication (except *Persuasion* and *Northanger Abbey*, whose titles were chosen by her brother Henry Austen when publishing them posthumously). It follows that, whatever the source may have been from which the germ of each novel sprang—from Jane Austen's reading, for instance, or from some event in her family history that engaged her interest and her deepest feelings—the final version has been shaped by the interests of a mature or maturing personality and the skills of an experienced artist. Of *Sense and Sensibility* alone, perhaps, can the word 'immaturity' be used with any real meaning; it was the first novel that she published, and it bears many marks of its author's inexperience— notably a certain crudeness in characterisation and an unevenness of texture that betrays uncertainty and a flagging interest. And yet, even here, so unified does the novel seem that such weaknesses appear only when we compare it with her later work.

In each of the three novels whose first drafts were completed in Jane Austen's youth, the remarkable poise of her manner and the apparent composure of her tone combine to cover inequalities under a surface so deceptively smooth that we are given an impression of settled standards and firmly grasped artistic and moral values:

Where people wish to attach, they should always be ignorant...A woman especially, if she have the misfortune of knowing any thing, should conceal it as well as she can.                           *Northanger Abbey*

The whole of Lucy's behaviour in the affair, and the prosperity which crowned it, therefore, may be held forth as a most encouraging instance of what an earnest, an unceasing attention to self-interest, however its progress may be apparently obstructed, will do in securing every advantage of fortune, with no other sacrifice than that of time and conscience. *Sense and Sensibility*

It is a truth universally acknowledged, that a single man in possession of a good fortune, must be in want of a wife.                    *Pride and Prejudice*

The epigrammatic ease of these statements, linking Jane Austen with her eighteenth-century predecessors, is striking when we find it in work we regard as 'early', although it is likely that the smooth surface of her prose hides a good many doubts, uncertainties, possibly even personal dismay, towards the resolution of which she was finding her way as she wrote.

When we come to *Emma* and to *Mansfield Park*, we can at last talk of 'maturity', for although these novels, like the two published earlier, may have had their beginnings in an early sketch, *they were revised and rewritten in their published form in the last few years of Jane Austen's life*. *Persuasion*, her last-written complete work, also comes of this period, but here we cannot talk of 'finish' in any artistic sense. Its theme and central interests relate to Jane Austen's maturity, but the inequalities it contains can only be adequately accounted for by the probability that it was but partly subjected to careful revision.

Is this matter of dating the novels absolutely essential to the reader's enjoyment of them? Fortunately, it is not. But as a great part of the pleasure of reading Jane Austen comes from our appreciation of her control of the written word, the novels afford an extended demonstration of how that control was achieved. Quite apart from such natural gifts as her wit, her intelligence, and her powers of observation, Jane Austen's development as an artist derived from her ability to submerge her personal concerns in the fulfilment of an artistic intention, from her power to use constructively and creatively the materials that her reading and her social experience presented her with, and from her understanding of the ironic uses of language. In the discussion that follows, *Northanger Abbey* has been taken up immediately after the minor works, with a view to emphasising the connection that exists between Jane Austen's juvenilia and the major themes of the novels; and the rest succeed in the order of their publication, *Sense and Sensibility* first, *Persuasion* last. Perhaps, by this means of proceeding, we shall be able to obtain some insights into the development of Jane Austen's personality, which will complete the impression of the novelist yielded by the letters we examine in our next chapter. We shall also, it is hoped, follow more easily by this means the steadiness with which her literary interests and her vision of life spread wider and penetrated deeper with the writing of each novel. Changing interests shape the themes of each; and since Jane Austen's judgment was maturing rapidly even as her literary skills were gaining precision through continuous experiment, each novel differs from every other in intention, in atmosphere, and in the quality of its final achievement. For these reasons each novel deserves to be read as an individual work of art that bears incidental signs of the author's growing skill, her ceaseless experimentation in matters of technique, and her maturing view of life and of society.

As we shall concentrate our attention on Jane Austen's achievement as a *writer*, that is, on her use of language, we shall not concern ourselves in this study with such matters as the furniture of the parlour at Chawton Cottage in which she revised her novels and wrote some of them, the English country houses that are reputed to have provided her with settings, or with such impressions of the Austens' tastes in food and clothing as can be garnered from her writings. Neither, although recent criticism and scholarship has done much to uncover the processes by which Jane Austen's early drafts could have become the novels that we know today, and by which she transformed what she borrowed from earlier or contemporary writers into something original and unique, will we refer very much to this body of important work. The present study owes much to them, but it does not set out to tread the same ground. We can try to establish some idea of the kind of person Jane Austen was, *in so far as such an impression of her helps us to understand her reasons for writing novels, and to appreciate more fully the novels she wrote*, but it is wise to beware of romantic speculation built on the facts of her life as we know them. The novels may yield a little help in deciphering the mind and heart of their author, but we should bear in mind that all the evidence on the subject indicates that Jane Austen drew nothing from life that she did not change or split up in the process of her writing to a point almost beyond recognition, according to the requirements of her artistic intention. Besides, her novels probe the concerns of other, fictional people, and these need not necessarily have been identical with her own. In attempting to explore the sensibility from which the novels sprang, Jane Austen's letters are the only material that can be safely used. Censored and unrepresentative as they are, we must accept their limitations.

# 2

# THE LETTERS

With few exceptions, letters written by Jane Austen that survive today are addressed to her sister Cassandra or to some other member of the Austen family, and were probably intended for reading aloud to a circle of relations and intimate friends, in much the same way that Frank Churchill's letters to Mrs Weston are circulated among a small number of chosen people, in *Emma*. The letters describe new acquaintances as they are introduced to Jane Austen, and provide details of her daily life in the country or as a guest in the houses of her relatives, accounts of visiting, of housekeeping, and of neighbourhood gossip. Asked for her advice from time to time, she gives her opinion of novels that her nieces have submitted to her in manuscript, and of certain young men that they are thinking of marrying. A great deal of her correspondence we know to have been destroyed by the scrupulous hand of Cassandra Austen, who probably feared for the family's privacy, as well as for her sister's public reputation when the letters came to be read by persons outside the Austens' circle. What she did not destroy she censored, and many passages that probably relate to the novelist's personal life have been deleted. Even in their unsatisfactory form and numbers, however, Jane Austen's letters have a very special value for the critic and the reader of her work.

To begin with, there emerges from them a solid picture, made up of a thousand little details, of a country-town milieu; and of a woman of unusual sensitivity and discernment busy making the best of the world she has been born into. It is clear from the letters that Jane Austen was not in complete harmony with her society, despite the fact that her whole life long she was a social creature, visiting and being visited. Total rebellion was, for her, out of the question (as it was not, incidentally, for George Eliot or for Shelley). For those who wished to live in society, the rules had already been formulated. Etiquette demanded of a woman that

part of the hours appropriated to relaxation must, of necessity, be less agreeably taken up in the paying and receiving visits of mere ceremony and civility; a tribute, by custom authorized, by good manners enjoined: in these...the great art of pleasing is to appear pleased with others: suffer not then an ill-bred absence of thought, or a contemptuous sneer, ever to betray a conscious superiority of understanding, always productive of ill-nature and dislike.[1]

Reading Jane Austen's letters, with their incisive comments about other people and the social activities that filled the passing days, we can understand something of the difficulties an apprenticeship to 'the great art of pleasing' must have imposed on a person of her intelligence and sensitivity. They give us a glimpse of the feelings she could not express in public, or to any one outside her own circle. They suggest that her immediate (and perhaps, unending) problem was how to conform, outwardly at least and without hypocrisy, to the requirements of polite, civilised behaviour. A consciousness of a double responsibility—to society and to high personal standards of her own—can be clearly seen in a passage such as the following, in which Jane Austen writes to Cassandra of Lord Craven's pleasant manners:

The little flaw of having a Mistress now living with him at Ashdown Park seems to be the most unpleasing circumstance about him.     (1801)

Her attitude appears at first reading to be extraordinarily uninhibited, even permissive; and the passage has been frequently quoted to illustrate Jane Austen's ability to take life (even in the raw) as it came. But it must not be forgotten that here she reports, not her own personal impressions of Lord Craven, *but the reactions of her sophisticated sister-in-law who had met him.* The word *seems* would have conveyed to her sister's ear an ironic reflection upon the difference between their shared standards and those held by Elizabeth Austen. The letters, read carefully, provide instances of many similar occasions, when Jane Austen has presumably displayed the polite tolerance expected of her in social life, but reserved the right to comment upon them more freely to her

[1] Lady Sarah Pennington, *An Unfortunate Mother's Advice to Her Absent Daughters* (1761).

sister. It becomes clear that part of her compulsion to write novels was the need to extend the area of freedom she enjoyed in her letters; the personal need to find 'some mode of existence for her critical attitudes',[1] to create a world in which her own beliefs and ideals need be no longer disguised and could assert themselves in the characters of 'real' people, influencing 'human' behaviour.

Jane Austen's letters reflect the society she knew, which contributed, through her experience of it, to the making of the novels. What was her opinion of provincial society? 'Not even Death itself can fix the friendship of the World' she wrote in 1801, and despite their gaiety, the letters reveal an acute awareness of the ill-nature that world was capable of. The brief histories of their acquaintances retailed for Cassandra's information are frequently those of persons slandered, envied, spied upon, ridiculed, or in some other way victimised by a polite neighbourhood. Jane Austen's unqualified praise is rare, and tends to be given chiefly to personalities in or connected with her intimate circle, as in the following reference to the ailing father of a particular friend:

Poor man! his life is so useful, his character so respectable and worthy, that I really believe there was a good deal of sincerity in the general concern expressed on his account.

The assumption of insincerity and ill-nature in those outside her own circle is characteristic, and sometimes finds indirect expression in the novels, as in Henry Tilney's ambiguous rebuke to the over-imaginative Catherine (who, in *Northanger Abbey*, has been secretly suspecting his father of murder):

'Could [such atrocities] be perpetrated without being known, in a country like this...*where every man is surrounded by a neighbourhood of voluntary spies*? (My italics.)

The picture of Jane Austen that emerges from her letters is similar in one important particular to those of her heroines: for her as well as for each of them, the experience of living involved a continual process of adaptation of character and personality to an unfriendly social environment.

[1] D. W. Harding, 'Regulated Hatred: an aspect of the work of Jane Austen', *Scrutiny* (1940).

By presenting in her novels a social world that undergoes no change of heart, Jane Austen proves herself a realist. Her heroines marry men who appreciate their virtues and their moral (and sometimes, intellectual) superiority to their immediate world, but never does that world recognise their superiority, seldom does it even wish them well. 'Only a small band of true friends' are really happy on the occasion of Emma's wedding to Mr Knightley. Elinor Dashwood is slighted by her husband's relations, Elizabeth Bennet misunderstood and undervalued even by her own. To Marianne Dashwood in London, to Fanny Price in her parents' home at Portsmouth, and to Anne Elliot entering her father's new lodgings at Bath, life becomes a burden, creating a sickness of heart that agonises and seems almost like death. Jane Austen allows each of them to change their habitat for pleasanter, more congenial surroundings; but their contentment is won through self-discipline and selfcontrol *in the world they know*, before they find means of escape into another. They learn to avoid selfpity, and to accept society for what it is, giving credit to its virtues and uses even as they suffer from its defects and injustices. Above all, they learn to conduct themselves in a way that contributes positively to those social virtues, maintaining at the same time their own selfrespect and their integrity as individuals.

And so, as Elinor and Marianne Dashwood guard their unhappiness from the curiosity of outsiders, and struggle to subdue their emotions; as Elizabeth Bennet learns that her judgment is fallible, and Emma Woodhouse repents her arrogant benevolence; as Fanny Price puts up with indifference, persecution, and neglect, and Anne Elliot strives towards greater confidence in her own judgment; they display or achieve a selfcontrol and a grasp of the social virtues that are, in the context of their lives, heroic. It becomes possible to see how attributes that we might have considered purely social graces, such as tact and politeness, win moral victories in the world of Jane Austen's novels. Sustained by the sympathetic understanding of a small circle of intimate friends, the young women who possess them are 'heroines' by virtue of their efforts to discipline their personalities according to the standards of good sense, and their outward behaviour to the requirements of the polite world outside their special circle. So it is that Emma Woodhouse calls on her neighbour Miss Bates, reluctant to be bored and irritated, but resigned to doing her duty with the best possible grace; and Anne Elliot provides the music to which Louisa Musgrove dances with her own former lover, Captain Wentworth. It is the weak character who fails these tests, runs away from them, or affects to despise them. We learn of John Willoughby, in *Sense and Sensibility*, that 'in slighting too easily the forms of worldly propriety, he displayed a want of caution that Elinor could not approve'. Jane Austen's life was shaped by those 'forms of worldly propriety', and although they presented her with obstacles, irritations, and matter for resentment, it is evident from the spirit of her acceptance of them that she appreciated their usefulness in regulating the otherwise uncontrollable jungle of the human emotions.

The letters go far, therefore, to establish a dependable impression of Jane Austen's personality, and of the environment that gave her a framework for her novels. They dissolve those difficulties, stemming from her relation to a particular period and locality, that might have made her appear remote from the modern world. We perceive that her life was, in its details (and it is from these details that she created a great art) rather similar to our own, wherever we may live. She had to learn, as we all must, to get on with other people, and to accept certain rules and customs as patterns for her own conduct. Jane Austen was very much of her age, and her work reflects the accumulated traditions of a settled way of life; but in her application of civilised principles to the problems of daily living she transcends the limitations of place and time, to present the modern reader with material that he recognises as relevant to immediate and universal dilemmas.

Her characters feel deeply, and their greatest efforts go towards controlling their emotions and regulating their outward behaviour. The calm composure, the fortitude, and the resolution that her heroines show under stress have made some readers impatient with Jane Austen. Charlotte Bronte's view that she had no acquaintance with the 'stormy sisterhood' of the passions implied that Jane Austen's picture of life is not a true one, either because she knew nothing of life outside her quiet, chosen sphere, or because she lacked the courage and the ability to depict it.[1] Yet her letters bear witness to the variety of her experience:

He went to inspect a gaol, as a visiting magistrate, and took me with him. I was gratified, and went through all the feelings which people must go through, I think, in visiting such a building.

These 'feelings', however, she chose not to dwell on in her fiction. Jane Austen knew very well of the existence of such unhappy couples as the Gunthorpes—

He swears, drinks, is cross, jealous, selfish and Brutal;—the match makes *her* family miserable, and has occasioned *his* being disinherited. (1807)

but she knew also (and in this the Scott of the 'Scottish' novels resembles her) that provincial life could afford instances of virtue, endurance, and bravery that were not less heroic for being unknown and unspectacular.

In defining the values that provide the indispensable framework for her novels, the letters are of the greatest assistance. They establish, for instance, that Jane Austen was no romantic in her attitude to marriage. Her life, spent in a yearly increasing family of nephews and nieces, in continual and irksome familiarity with domesticity, and perfectly understanding the dangers and difficulties of childbirth, kept Jane Austen from sentimental imaginings about the state which, above all others, affords a happy hunting ground for writers of romantic and mawkish fiction.

She is not tidy enough in her appearance...things are not in that comfort and style about her which are necessary to make such a situation an enviable one

she wrote, after a visit to a sister-in-law and her new baby. In her letters Jane Austen states her minimum requirement of married life, which was, that a wife should be able to respect her husband. His mind might sometimes move in spheres beyond her knowledge or interests, but his behaviour to her and to others in their circle must be important, because it provides the clue to his character:

[1] Charlotte Bronte, letter to W. S. Williams (1850).

And now, my dear Fanny [she writes to a favourite niece], I shall entreat you not to commit yourself further, and not to think of accepting him unless you really do like him. Any thing is to be preferred or endured rather than marrying without Affection; and if his deficiencies of manner &c &c strike you more than all his good qualities, if you continue to think strongly of them, give him up at once.

Nothing less does she trust to as a source of true happiness in marriage, and as compensation and justification for the trials of married life, than that mutual respect for the partner's personality that she calls *esteem* in her novels. Every one of her fictional heroines, even the poorest and the silliest, adopts it as the foundation of her married life. We could usefully compare Jane Austen's advice, here given to a doubting and uncertain young woman who looked to her for guidance, with the 'only rule of conduct' ever bestowed on Fanny Price by her Aunt Bertram in *Mansfield Park*:

'No, my dear, I should not think of missing you, when such an offer as this comes in your way. I could do very well without you, if you were married to a man of such good estate as Mr Crawford. And you must be aware, Fanny, that it is every young woman's duty to accept such a very unexceptionable offer as this.'

Novel after novel explores as a major interest, the adjustments of personality and outlook that must take place before young people can safely enter upon marriage, involving an abandonment of romantic illusions and of vanity, initiating attempts to assess a lover's character rationally and responsibly that might seem surprisingly prosaic to lovers of sentimental fiction who come to Jane Austen's novels in the belief that her work is of the same kind. It is equally far removed, however, from the squalid morality which produces the opinion that Miss Maria Ward was 'at least three thousand pounds short of any equitable claim' to the honour of marriage with Sir Thomas Bertram of Mansfield Park.

A similar good sense characterises Jane Austen's attitude to money. She was too much of a realist to affect to despise it in her novels. Like other good housekeepers she knew its value, and spent it carefully, as her letters show. Such an ironic comment as the following indicates that she had personal experience of the pride and selfishness that sometimes accompanies wealth:

I suppose they must be acting by the orders of Mr —— in this civility, as there seems no other reason for their coming near us. They will not come often, I dare say. They live in a handsome style and are rich and she seemed to like to be rich, and we gave her to understand that we were far from being so; she will soon feel therefore that we are not worth her acquaintance.

And so, although Elizabeth Bennet marries a man of great wealth in *Pride and Prejudice*, Jane Austen's personal attitude of sturdy independence that refuses to be cowed or even impressed by a display of wealth alone finds an echo in the fact that Mr Darcy's great estates in Derbyshire do not impress Elizabeth until she has discovered that his character, too, is worth her respect and 'esteem'. Alone among the party admitted by Lady Catherine de Bourgh to the grandeur of Rosings, Elizabeth 'found herself quite equal to the scene, and could observe the three ladies before her composedly'. It would seem that great wealth and high social status were not, in Jane Austen's view, necessary (or even conducive) to happiness. In a letter to Cassandra, joyfully announcing her imminent return home from a visit to her wealthy relations, she wrote:

Luckily the pleasures of Friendship, of unreserved Conversation, of similarity of Taste and Opinions, will make good amends for Orange Wine

and a similarly harmonious setting, together with an income adequate for their position in society, are all that Jane Austen's heroines ask of life. To ask or to settle for less would have been, from her point of view, extremely foolish and eventually destructive of happiness and respectability. 'Earle and his wife live in the most private manner imaginable at Portsmouth, without keeping a servant of any kind', she wrote once to her sister, adding, 'What a prodigious innate love of virtue she must have, to marry under such circumstances!'

Elinor Dashwood is practical and sensible in her attitude to money in marriage. Neither she nor Edward 'were...quite enough in love to think that three hundred and fifty pounds a-year would supply them with the comforts of life'. Elinor's good sense contrasts with the wild irresponsibility of Lydia Bennet, which leads to an elopement that is justified neither by rational respect for Wickham nor by the dictates of common prudence.

Lydia and Wickham are a pair who are 'only brought together because their passions were stronger than their virtue' and neither Elizabeth Bennet nor Jane Austen could be optimistic about their chances of achieving 'permanent happiness'.

The letters reveal Jane Austen's attitude to real-life Lydia Bennets and Maria Rushworths:

I am proud to say that I have a very good eye at an Adultress, for. . .I fixed upon the right one from the first. . .She is not so pretty as I had expected. . . She was highly rouged, & looked rather quietly & contentedly silly than any thing else. (1801)

The casual, amused manner in which Jane Austen describes this counterpart of Maria Rushworth as appearing more foolish than guilty (or even interesting) contrasts strikingly with the deep horror felt by Edmund Bertram in *Mansfield Park* at his sister's elopement with Henry Crawford. Edmund's revulsion is perhaps intensified by the fact that he has been ordained a clergyman, and we need not believe that Jane Austen's own views were identical with his. The novel, like her letter to Cassandra, shows us on the contrary that she could see every aspect of the situation quite clearly; for there, though she allows Edmund to express his appalled indignation—'Guess what I must have felt. . .No harsher name than folly given!'—she gives equal weight to Mary Crawford as she resourcefully plans the strategy that could reinstate Maria in society—

when once married, and properly supported by her own family, people of respectability as they are, she may recover her footing in society to a certain degree. In some circles, we know, she would never be admitted, but with good dinners, and large parties, there will always be those who will be glad of her acquaintance; and there is, undoubtedly, more liberality and candour on those points than formerly. . .

and even records the emotions of Crawford and Maria themselves, which become 'so like hatred, as to make them for a while each other's punishment, and then induce a voluntary separation'.

Such insight as this into human behaviour and feeling indicates, not that Jane Austen's standards were flexible but that her view of life was comprehensive. The moral code according to which Maria Rushworth is punished for her elopement with Crawford, by permanent exile from Mansfield Park and from respectable society, is not Jane Austen's own, if we can judge by the tone of her description of 'an Adultress' in her letter to Cassandra Austen. It is a stricter code than that of her time, as Mary Crawford's remarks about 'liberality and candour' indicate—it is, in fact, the code of the old-fashioned Sir Thomas Bertram, Maria's father, and the severity of the punishment is heightened by his own disappointment at his daughter's moral weakness. The fate of Maria Rushworth has been thought to show that Jane Austen's sexual *mores* had stiffened at the time she wrote *Mansfield Park* to the point of rigidity, shutting out sympathy and compassion. It is unfortunate that Maria's moral fault of selfish vanity, in which her creator is primarily interested, is carried by the plan of the novel to an act that outrages social morality, because the punishment society exacts is a drastic one and administered in a public manner; and though it is in this unlike the more subtle *moral* punishment of private wretchedness, it has been confused and identified with it. Jane Austen does not involve herself in discussing the penalty exacted by society from those who break its laws, apart from briefly expressing her conviction that a price—if it is to be paid publicly at all in a case such as Maria's—should be shared between both culprits and not borne by one alone ('In this world, the penalty is less equal than could be wished'). Her concern is with Maria's *moral* weakness, originating in vanity; according to Jane Austen's scheme of values, Maria has fallen from the superior position in which she was once considered (and taught to think herself) 'indeed the pride and delight of them all—perfectly faultless—an angel'. Crawford, who escapes a public punishment, cannot however elude 'self-reproach, and...wretchedness', and this private and self-created hell (shared by Maria with Mrs Norris, her companion in exile) is their true and equal punishment, rather than their unequal shares of public disgrace.

While Maria Rushworth's physical fate is decreed by a social code that is stricter than her creator's, her moral fall carries wider implications than, for example, Lydia Bennet's, involving the people who educated her and the society she has been accustomed to lead, as well as reflecting upon her own principles and character. She should have known better. With her excellent education and her social advantages, it is implied, she should have had more Sense.

I use a capital letter for the word *Sense*, because it is very important in any discussion of Jane Austen's ideas about life. It occurs again and again in her letters, as she comments on her acquaintances:

A handsome young man certainly, with quiet, gentlemanlike manners.—I set him down as sensible rather than Brilliant.

The absence of this attribute often provides the basis for discriminating portraits of insincere, silly or pretentious people, showing how sense, commonsense, and reason extended their range as Jane Austen matured, to include moral virtue as well as social tact and an active intelligence. Turning to the novels, we find Catherine Morland in *Northanger Abbey* finally achieving a *sensible* grasp on real life, after her earlier *sense*-less inclination to confuse it with the extravagances of Gothic fiction. When she began work on *Susan*, the first version of *Northanger Abbey*, Jane Austen was evidently using the criterion of Good Sense as a means of judging literature. But with each novel she wrote, Good Sense applies to more than literature, it becomes the foundation, in the words of Elinor Dashwood in *Sense and Sensibility*, 'on which every thing good may be built'.

The letters provide ample evidence that Jane Austen's familiar world was, socially and emotionally, much less circumscribed than that of her novels; and that her experience of life was wider, her attitudes to it more various, than some biographical and critical accounts would lead us to imagine. The calmness with which, for example, she comments on the character of Don Juan as she saw it represented at Covent Garden as an 'interesting... compound of cruelty and lust', the tactful good humour that answers a courtier's compliments on her writing, the composure with which she visits a gaol, are proofs of an unexpected poise and knowledge of the world, and not of a lax morality. The fact that she could call *adultery* and *lust* by their proper names, and recognised their activity in her own world and the world at large, did not make her any readier to take them as her subjects or her themes, or to describe them in any detail in her novels except in so far as their entry into a plot contributed to or illustrated her exploration of a larger, more interesting theme. In the last chapters of *Persuasion*, for example, Jane Austen scatters with care the clues that will lead to Mrs Clay's elopement with Mr Elliot, but it is evident that her chief artistic interest is elsewhere. Her letters are evidence that the limitations of scope in Jane Austen's novels are deliberate and self-imposed, dictated as much by a fastidious moral taste as by sound artistic judgment.

The letters are evidence, too, of the way the novels took shape. As some detail is tossed in, described with a confident brevity that relies on shared experiences and familiar opinions for its impact, we sense the origins of that intimacy every reader of Jane Austen experiences, that sense of being treated by the novelist as an appreciative friend and fellow-conspirator: 'The C.s are at home, and are reduced to read.' Compare with this scrap, indicative of an idle, unintellectual way of life that obviously amused the Austens, the astonishment of Mr Hurst in *Pride and Prejudice* at Elizabeth's liking for books: 'Do you prefer reading to cards?' said he; 'that is rather singular.' The interference of Mrs Norris and of Lady Catherine de Bourgh in the domestic economies of Mrs Grant and of Charlotte Collins find frequent echoes in the letters, illustrating Jane Austen's amused awareness that the Great House liked to see frugality practised at the Parsonage. Personalities and events are described with a wit and liveliness that is called forth by the appreciative pleasure of her familiar audience, and the characteristic manner evolved in this way is transferred to the novels, where Jane Austen addresses herself habitually to a co-operative and sympathetic reader.

Her artistic development was possible partly because she could read nothing uncritically, not even light fiction. 'There is very little story, and what there is told in a strange, unconnected way', she commented once in a letter, upon a novel she was reading. 'There are many characters introduced, apparently merely to be delineated.' Her criticisms of her nieces' attempts at fiction urge them continually towards greater precision and discrimination in the choice and management of language, greater fidelity to the rules of etiquette and of probability, greater consistency of characterisation:

> Devereux Forester's being ruined by his Vanity is extremely good; but I wish you would not let him plunge into a 'vortex of Dissipation'. I do not object to the Thing, but I cannot bear the expression;—it is such thorough novel slang—and so old, that I dare say Adam met with it in the first novel he opened.

We know from her letters that Jane Austen's censorship in the matter of improbability was very strict, for in her remarks on a niece's manuscript novel we find this:

> I have scratched out Sir Tho: from walking with the other Men to the Stables &c the very day after breaking his arm, for though I find your Papa *did* walk out immediately after *his* arm was set, I think it can be so little usual as to *appear* unnatural in a book.

Her preference was for what was in her experience so *usual*, so intimately known and experienced that doubt and uncertainty must become impossible. Her characteristic method is defined in a letter written in 1814:

> You are now collecting your People delightfully, getting them exactly into such a spot as is the delight of my life;—3 or 4 Families in a Country Village is the very thing to work on.

Such words indicate that Jane Austen had a clear conception of what she wanted to do, and confidence that she had selected the method most appropriate to her intention and her talents. The Reign of Terror in France, the naval experiences of her sailor brothers, are examples of contemporary phenomena that touched her own life, and would have provided most novelists with a staple source of incident and action for transformation into fiction. But, as we noted in Chapter 1, these matters figure in Jane Austen's novels (when they do so at all) in a casual and incidental manner, never in any indispensable or significant way. Her characters too are restricted, tending to 'keep the middle state' in English social life, drawn chiefly from among the smaller country gentry, but disposed in groups that include the local parson and touch the respectable tradesman on the one hand, and the wealthy landowner on the other. The craftsmanlike manner in which Jane Austen approached her task and selected her materials makes itself evident in her courteous reply to a misguided admirer of her work, who advised her to take advantage of current tastes and ensure her own popular success with a historical romance. She was aware, she wrote, that such a venture as he proposed might bring her greater wealth and reputation

than such pictures of domestic life in country villages as I deal in. But I could no more write a romance than an epic poem...No, I must keep to my own style and go on in my own way; and though I may never succeed again in that, I am convinced that I should totally fail in any other.

When she wrote this letter, Jane Austen was in full control of her powers. She had evolved her individual style and her characteristic method, and she had written and published novels that satisfied even her own high standards.

It has been pointed out with justice that the letters present the material of Jane Austen's novels in 'a preliminary stage, halfway between life and art'.[1] The lightning sketches in the letters ('My Aunt...looks about with great diligence and success for Inconvenience and Evil'; 'Miss Beaty is good-humour itself, and does not seem much besides'; 'Miss Holder and I adjourned after tea into the inner Drawing room to look over Prints and talk pathetically') demonstrate the novelist's mental alertness and her acuteness of ear and eye, but they have still to undergo her characteristic process of refinement through revision. There is much in common between these swiftly composed portraits and a picture such as that, in *Persuasion*, of

thick-headed, unfeeling, unprofitable Dick Musgrove, who had never done any thing to entitle himself to more than the abbreviation of his name, living or dead

much to suggest that this character, like the personages in the letters, is still in 'a preliminary stage, halfway between life and art'.

She was continually reading, constantly writing, and her critical faculty operated as actively on her own creations as on

[1] Q. D. Leavis, 'A Critical Theory of Jane Austen's Writings', *Scrutiny* (1941).

those of other people. 'How ill I have written,' she exclaimed in a letter of 1796, of her performance in that very letter, 'I begin to hate myself.' We can do no less than pay such a serious artist the due of critical attention as we read the novels she wrote. And through their successful evocation of a personality and a milieu, by their definition of Jane Austen's moral and artistic standards, her letters provide a background of fact against which we may trace the progress of a youthful talent that steadily attains the level of great, the very greatest, literature.

# 3

# THE MINOR WORKS

> The Uncle of Elfrida was the Father of Frederic; in other words, they were
> first cousins by the Father's side.
>   Being both born in one day & both brought up at one school, it was not
> wonderfull that they should look on each other with something more than
> bare politeness. They loved with mutual sincerity but were both determined
> not to transgress the rules of Propriety by owning their attachment, either
> to the object beloved, or to any one else.    *Frederic and Elfrida* (1790–3)

Jane Austen's family, as we learn from her letters, were 'great
Novel-readers & not ashamed of being so', and the popular
fiction of her day provided plenty of exercise for lively minds that
delighted in the ridiculous and the silly. Her first attempts at
writing creatively were directed to fabricating jokes for the
amusement of her family and her friends, at the expense of
different kinds of contemporary literature. Frederic and Elfrida
in the fragment from 'a novel' quoted above, for instance, act in
obedience to 'rules of Propriety' in not confessing their love,
rules of a surely false modesty that may have begun in decorum
but had been carried by the fashions of romantic fiction to
extravagant limits. In *Northanger Abbey*, the novel that the
mature Jane Austen based on similar excesses in popular fiction,
Catherine Morland transgresses the laws of just such a question-
able 'morality' by proving herself a normal, healthy, and innocent
young woman:

> ...for if it be true, as a celebrated writer has maintained, that no young lady
> can be justified in falling in love before the gentleman's love is declared,
> it must be very improper that a young lady should dream of a gentleman
> before the gentleman is first known to have dreamt of her.

By falling in love with Henry Tilney, and by probably dreaming
of him, Catherine shows her innocence—of the affectations and
false modesty idealised in the sentimental novel. Jane Austen's
guiding rule of good sense gave her much to criticise in the
situations and incidents common in the popular fiction of her day.

She makes her own attitude clear in *Frederic and Elfrida* and in *Northanger Abbey* by mock-seriously carrying to its logical conclusion some romantic notion that had been given currency by Richardson, Anne Radcliffe, and certain less reputable writers, displaying by this means its absurdity and its false values.

For such is the virtuous modesty, the *propriety* of Frederic and his cousin that they speak of their love to nobody—not even to one another! Their marriage takes place twenty years after the story opens, having been delayed so long by their shy reluctance—and then it is brought about by jealousy on her part and pity on his, for their mutual affection has long since evaporated. Since it is part of human experience that affection can change its character with time to become its own opposite, Jane Austen aims here at the irresponsible writer who projects false and overstrained ideas in the guise of heroic virtues, when common sense should make it plain that they can only create havoc and unhappiness in the lives of those who adopt them. The piece introduces another interesting character, a young woman so good-natured that she cannot bear to 'make any one miserable'; Charlotte Drummond accordingly accepts every proposal of marriage that comes her way, drowning herself at last because she cannot keep all her promises and because

the reflection of her past folly, operated so strongly on her mind, that she resolved to be guilty of a greater.

We meet three families whose neighbourly intimacy

daily increased till at length it grew to such a pitch, that they did not scruple to kick one another out of the window on the slightest provocation.

Love can turn to pity, kindheartedness be carried to extremes, familiarity breed contempt. To common sense such facts must be obvious, but the readers of sentimental fiction and the writers who cater to their tastes prefer romantic fantasy to everyday reality.

The placing of love and courtship at the centre, not only of a heroine's consciousness, but of the hero's and of every other person's in a novel's fictional world, Jane Austen recognises as being itself such a fantasy; a fiction pleasing to the vanity of

feminine readers and sweetening for them a bitter truth, profitable
to the writers of novels, but dangerous if mistaken for the reality
that it is not and cannot be. Jane Austen's own view of marriage
is steadily, uncompromisingly, realistic. It is as a social reality and
as a source of disciplining, morally and emotionally enriching
experience, that marriage is presented in her novels. At its best,
where affection and talent are equal or complementary between
the partners, a happy marriage could be

> an union that must have been to the advantage of both; by her ease and liveli-
> ness, his mind might have been softened, his manners improved, and from his
> judgment, information, and knowledge of the world, she must have received
> benefit of greater importance.

At its worst, where they were not, marriage could still serve a
social purpose, being the community's

> only honourable provision for well-educated young women of small fortune,
> and however uncertain of giving happiness, must be their pleasantest pre-
> servative from want.                                        *Pride and Prejudice*

A steady determination to see and present life in true perspective
gives a moral strength to Jane Austen's earliest satires at the
expense of romanticism and sentimentality.

*Frederick and Elfrida* anticipates *Northanger Abbey* in its
comic exploitation of the melodramatic situations and unnatural
language commonly found in sentimental and sensational novels.
Similarly, the efforts of Marianne Dashwood in *Sense and Sensibility* to 'gain' an increase of sadness, 'court' misery, and feed
on the 'nourishment' of affectionate memories echo the 'determination' of Frederic and Elfrida to create their own ultimate
unhappiness. The brisk precision with which 'romantic' preconceptions are systematically destroyed by Jane Austen in these
early sketches points forward to many aspects of her later work;
to a scene such as that in *Pride and Prejudice*, where Mrs Bennet's
vow that she 'will never see' Elizabeth again if she refuses Mr
Collins's proposal of marriage (a familiar cliche of sentimental
fiction, and one upon which an entire plot was frequently made to
turn) is exposed to ridicule; and even in the method that creates
the sustained structural perfection of *Emma*, as the heroine falls

into trap after trap of her own making. *Frederic and Elfrida* hardly rates as a work of genius—unlike *Emma*, which we acknowledge to be one—but it helps to indicate what Jane Austen and her circle found comic or worth criticising in fiction, and in doing so it points forward to her development through and out of literary satire to the more complex and difficult task of depicting real life.

Jane Austen's juvenilia, for the most part comic fragments of lighthearted satire, take as their starting point her conviction that reason and good sense are more reliable guides for living than the ideas circulated by popular fiction. Her attitude in this matter is summed up in *Persuasion*; Anne Elliot, talking about poetry with a young man who has been disappointed in love, recommends, in the manner of a good dietician, 'a larger allowance of prose in his daily study'. Anne's words indicate that Jane Austen saw literature as a food on which the imagination grows, so that literary diets should be sensibly balanced, containing nutritive elements in just proportion. Captain Benwick, like a patient who prolongs his illness by eating the wrong food, has been poisoning his mind by reading too much literature of a type that does not have the ability to sustain and strengthen him. Anne, who reads widely, and whose lonely, loveless situation and emotional nature expose her equally with Benwick to the 'dangers' of romantic poetry, prescribes for this sufferer from literary malnutrition

such works of our best moralists, such collections of the finest letters, such memoirs of characters of worth and suffering, as occurred to her at the moment as calculated to rouse and fortify the mind by the highest precepts, and the strongest examples of moral and religious endurance.

The passage indicates the practicality of Jane Austen's approach to life and to literature, and shows how natural it was that she should have found comic, unreal, and dangerous the sentimental elements in popular novels and plays that moved her contemporaries to tears.

We might note, in passing, that the poems discussed by Anne Elliot and Benwick were not contemporary versified trash but the work of Scott and Byron, the most popular poets of the age.

Anne and Benwick *compare* opinions, *debate* the rival claims of specific poems, and *judge* the rank of others. This, from Anne's point of view, is good conversation; but it is also a sound way of treating literature, and it helps to indicate that Jane Austen's literary loyalties lie with the eighteenth century. Her perception of the faults in the popular literature of her time stems from her appreciation of traditional patterns of behaviour as much as from her reading, which has been shown to have included the work of historians, moralists, and experts on design, all of which taught her the value of a keen sense of proportion, in literature as in life. Like Johnson and other critics she admired, it is evident that Jane Austen had a scale of values in mind that she applied to whatever came under her eye.

Let us consider, for example, a passage from another early piece, *Love and Freindship*:

'In the society of my Edward and this Amiable Pair, I passed the happiest moments of my Life; Our time was most delightfully spent, in mutual protestations of Freindship, and in vows of unalterable Love, in which we were secure of being interrupted, by intruding and disagreeable Visitors, as Augustus and Sophia had on their first Entrance in the Neighbourhood, taken due care to inform the surrounding Families, that as their Happiness centered wholly in themselves, they wished for no other society'  (1790)

The unreal relationships of the sentimental novel are traced directly to their origins in selfishness, and when put to the test of normal social behaviour are found to be both comic and offensive. This method Jane Austen was to use with greater skill and naturalness in her portrayal of Marianne Dashwood in love, believing any attempt to conceal her straightforward emotions from the public gaze both wrong and unreasonable: she

abhorred all concealment where no real disgrace could attend unreserve; and to aim at the restraint of sentiments which were not in themselves illaudable, appeared to her not merely an unnecessary effort, but a disgraceful subjection of reason to common-place and mistaken notions.

Their absorption in each other makes Marianne and Willoughby 'most exceedingly laughed at'. The lovers in *Love and Freindship* presumably afforded their neighbours equal amusement and offended them even more. Their story is presented in broader outline than Marianne's, and conveniently indicates a beginning

35

in the development of an ironic method that brings Jane Austen's work into the sphere of satire. The tension generated by playing off a crisp, matter-of-fact tone against wildly romantic and silly material reminds us that she ranks with and learned her art from such masters of satire as Henry Fielding, Alexander Pope, and Samuel Johnson. Like her eighteenth-century predecessors, Jane Austen found much in society that offended general standards of good sense and morality, and much that struck her personally as insensitive, heartless, and wrong.

Already, in these early pieces, we soon see her venture beyond literary jokes, to probe human motives. Some of the portraits she draws are too serious in their implications to be mere lighthearted nonsense. 'He is quite an old Man,' writes Mary Stanhope of her future husband, in *The Three Sisters*,

'about two & thirty, very plain, *so* plain that I cannot bear to look at him. He is extremely disagreeable & I hate him more than any body else in the world. He has a large fortune & will make great Settlements on me; but then he is very healthy. In short I do not know what to do.'     (1790–3)

How is the reader to take this? With amusement, to begin with, at the romantic, inexperienced child to whom thirty-two appears *very old*, at the exaggeration that declares itself in *I cannot bear to look at him* and *I hate him more than any body else in the world*. Even the word *Settlements*, which introduces a more worldly note, suggests that Mary is merely quoting her elders' conversation, which she only partly understands. Up to this point her situation invites sympathy as well as amusement. But what of *but then he is very healthy*? Has she, in fact, resigned herself to the marriage, and can she be already hoping for an early release from it into widowhood?

'If I refuse him, he as good as told me that he should offer himself to Sophia and if *she* refused him to Georgiana, & I could not bear to have either of them married before me...I believe I shall have him. It will be such a triumph to be married before Sophy, Georgiana & the Duttons.'

There are many hints here of future effects in *Pride and Prejudice*; we may perceive a shadowy outline of Mr Collins, the transference of whose affections from Jane Bennet to her sister Elizabeth 'was soon done—done while Mrs Bennet was stirring the fire', and of

Lydia Wickham's 'anxious parade' on her return to Longbourn: 'Ah! Jane, I take your place now, and you must go lower, because I am a married woman.' But there is more than that. Jane Austen communicates the selfish agony of mind her subject experiences. As Mary Stanhope changes and shifts her position, progressing from dislike to prudent calculation, through indecision to a settled resolve, there can be seen already a foreshadowing of the masterly study of selfishness and disloyalty Jane Austen was to undertake later in her portrayal of the Bertram sisters in *Mansfield Park*. Her ability to draw character advances steadily through exercises of this kind, and her interest in this aspect of her art has an important effect on the structure of her novels, in which development of incident seems more and more to arise out of what is natural to the characters, not out of mere chance nor in response to the author's whim.

We see this demonstrated in *Lady Susan*, a novel written in the form of letters (Jane Austen used this form, once popular, for her first drafts of *Sense and Sensibility*, and—it is very likely—of *Pride and Prejudice*):

'It has been delightful to me to watch [Mr de Courcy's] advances towards intimacy, especially to observe his altered manner in consequence of my repressing by the calm dignity of my deportment, his insolent approach to direct familiarity. My conduct has been equally guarded from the first, & I never behaved less like a Coquette in the whole course of my Life, tho' perhaps my desire of dominion was never more decided'     (1805)

Jane Austen concentrates here on the subtle stages by which a relationship between two people develops, regulated by the motives and temperaments of the two concerned. We shall find this interest maintained and the technique immeasurably developed in her treatment of Darcy and Elizabeth in *Pride and Prejudice*, of Wentworth and Anne Elliot in *Persuasion*, and especially in *Mansfield Park* (a novel considered with some justification to have been partially based on *Lady Susan* according to Jane Austen's characteristic methods of elaborating and rewriting first drafts), where Edmund Bertram's alternate moods of attraction and disgust towards the charming, worldly Mary Crawford are a principal source of interest:

37

They had talked—and they had been silent—he had reasoned—she had ridiculed—and they had parted at last with mutual vexation.

Lady Susan enjoys 'the pleasure of triumphing over a Mind prepared to dislike' her, Mary Crawford's insensitivity denies her a clear view into Edmund's disturbed thoughts. Between Jane Austen's bold, clear outline of a siren and her subtle shading of Miss Crawford, whose worldly outlook and damaging experience are her misfortunes rather than her crimes, lie years of rethinking and rewriting with a purpose—that the succession of stages by which people are drawn to each other or driven apart, together with the novel's conclusion, should seem to arise naturally, directed by their temperaments and desires. While Lady Susan is 'unmasked' at last and her guilt 'discovered' by de Courcy by sheer accident, Mary Crawford uncovers the deep-rooted corruptions in her way of thinking *by her own words* to the startled Edmund, who laments to Fanny,

'She saw it only as folly, and that folly stamped only by exposure...it was the detection in short—...not the offence which she reprobated...Could you have believed it possible? '

Jane Austen's early and incomplete later work contains many original ideas that she later improved upon and used in writing her novels, and themes that never ceased to interest her, displaying, too, early trials of certain important features of her characteristic technique. Consider the following passages:

'Two Gentlemen most elegantly attired but weltering in their blood was what first struck our Eyes—we approached—they were Edward and Augustus—. Yes dearest Marianne they were our Husbands. Sophia shrieked and fainted on the Ground—I screamed and instantly ran mad—. We remained thus mutally deprived of our Senses, some minutes, and on regaining them we were deprived of them again. For an Hour and a Quarter did we continue in this unfortunate Situation—Sophia fainting every moment and I running Mad as often.'                                                *Love and Freindship*

'A little before she came my Mother had given us an account of it, telling us that she certainly would not let him go farther than our own family for a Wife. "And therefore (said she) If Mary wont have him Sophy must, & if Sophy wont Georgiana *shall*." Poor Georgiana!—We neither of us attempted to alter my Mother's resolution, which I am sorry to say is generally more strictly kept than rationally formed'.                                *The Three Sisters*

Although the wit in these passages is rudimentary and their effects laboured in comparison with the graceful precision of later work, Jane Austen has begun to take up the themes of excessive emotionalism and petty tyranny that she later explores more fully in her portraits of Marianne Dashwood and of Mrs Bennet. The third of *A Collection of Letters* (1790–2) sketches a character named Lady Greville, combining some characteristics of Mrs Norris in *Mansfield Park* with an incident from *Pride and Prejudice*, in which Lady Catherine de Bourgh calls Charlotte Collins out of the Parsonage at Hunsford and keeps her talking on a windy day:

'"Why I think Miss Maria you are not quite so smart as you were last night— But I did not come to examine your dress, but to tell you that you may dine with us the day after tomorrow...There will be no occasion for your being very fine for I shant send the Carriage—If it rains you may take an umbrella ...an horrible East wind...I assure you I can hardly bear the window down—But you are used to be blown about by the wind Miss Maria and that is what has made your Complexion so ruddy and coarse...Drive on—" And away she went, leaving me in a great passion with her as she always does'.

These scraps show how Jane Austen husbanded her material. Some everyday incident, situation or conversation, translated into fictional form—perhaps as a vent for irritated exasperation—could serve her many times over at different times and in different ways. When we come to the novels we find that the themes she takes up there are not abstractions, but similarly very much of this world.

In a setting of artistically contrived, smoothly flowing social activity, a heroine is introduced who is about to make the major choice in marriage which will decide her future life. We see her journey from a state of uncertainty to one of clearsighted confidence. Each novel can be seen without distortion as a full-length study, based on such a plan, of the possible alternatives presented by different standards of morality and social behaviour, by different habits of thinking and feeling, and by human personalities of various kinds. Central characters and groups of individuals are so disposed that they illustrate and embody these alternatives as aspects of major themes, which are developed through the intermingling of the characters in the day-to-day life of the country town.

In *The Watsons*, an early novel of which only a fragment has survived, and which has been thought to have provided the basis upon which Jane Austen later constructed *Emma*, this technique has already begun to emerge:

Emma was the first of the females in the parlour again; on entering it she found her brother alone.—'So Emma, said he, you are quite the Stranger at home...A pretty piece of work your Aunt Turner has made of it!—By Heaven! A woman should never be trusted with money. I always said she ought to have settled something on you, as soon as her Husband died.' 'But that would have been trusting *me* with money, replied Emma, & *I* am a woman too.' 'It might have been secured to your future use, without your having any power over it now.—What a blow it must have been upon you!— To find yourself, instead of heiress of 8 or 9000 £, sent back a weight upon your family, without a sixpence.—I hope the old woman will smart for it.' 'Do not speak disrespectfully of her—She was very good to me; & if she has made an imprudent choice, she will suffer more from it herself, than *I* can possibly do.' 'I do not mean to distress you, but you know every body must think her an old fool...Pity, you can none of you get married!—You must come to Croydon as well as the rest, & see what you can do there.'

(1803 or later)

This dialogue, besides sketching in past and present events with much greater economy and interest than could have been gained by narrative, has Emma Watson discussing her situation with her brother in the course of a family visit. We thus learn of her aunt's remarriage and of her own return home, to be regarded (by her brother, at any rate) as 'a weight upon her family'. But we learn a great deal about the speakers, too. Robert Watson shows himself to be selfish and revengeful, insensitive to his sister's feelings, contemptuous of feminine intelligence, and persistent in placing a mercenary value on all human relationships. Emma's single attempt at goodnatured raillery—'But that would have been trusting *me* with money...'—misses its target, for only verbal assault of a more direct kind could penetrate Watson's thick hide of insensitivity. She is too polite to protest further, and so has no effect upon him. If Watson were presented merely as a comic fool, in the spirit of Sir Walter Elliot in *Persuasion* for instance, his opinions would not matter much, but we sense—and Emma *knows* —that his words express the generally accepted views of society.

If we compare this passage with the picture in *Sense and Sensibility* of Mr John Dashwood discussing with his sister Elinor the chances she and Marianne have of marrying well, certain similarities appear at once. Elinor, like Emma Watson, makes a lonely stand for the values of taste and good sense against the attacks of vulgarity and moral coarseness. John Dashwood resembles Robert Watson, as he delivers his considered opinion of his sisters' respective market value; ironically, he cannot perceive the qualities of mind and character that set them both far above *him*! He also calls to mind a grocer pricing the fruit in his shop window:

'At her time of life, any thing of an illness destroys the bloom for ever! Her's has been a very short one! She was as handsome a girl last September, as any I ever saw; and as likely to attract the men. There was something in her style of beauty, to please them particularly. I remember Fanny used to say that she would marry sooner and better than you did; not but what she is exceedingly fond of *you*, but so it happened to strike her. She will be mistaken, however. I question whether Marianne *now*, will marry a man worth more than five or six hundred a-year, at the utmost, and I am very much deceived if *you* do not do better'.

*As likely to attract the men*; *I question whether Marianne now, will marry*... John Dashwood imagines Elinor to be complimented by his estimate of her superior attractions. In fact his words are not only thoughtlessly cruel, but actually destructive of the feminine delicacy he would have doubtless rated high among the attributes 'likely to attract the men'. Marianne's illness has destroyed her 'bloom', and (as buyers judge by appearance) so her price must fall. The passage does more than characterise an insensitive man; it is a bitter indictment of society itself, and suggests that at the age of thirty-six, when she revised *Sense and Sensibility* for publication in 1811, Jane Austen was very much at odds with her world, and unhappy about the helplessness in it of intelligent women of modest means, such as herself.

Like Emma Watson, Elinor Dashwood can only politely discourage her brother's benevolent cruelties, for the laws of custom and of family loyalty forbid attack. Yet Emma and Robert Watson, and Elinor and John Dashwood (although contrasting, in their respective encounters, insensitivity and selfishness with true generosity of heart) are characters in their own right, not merely mouthpieces for their creator. They talk, especially the men, as though the thoughts they express had only just come into their heads. What they say, and their oracular manner of saying it seems brutal and tactless, and the reader senses, from his own involuntary irritation, that the two young women are finding it extremely difficult to keep a retort in check. In passages such as this it is possible to see how Jane Austen's characters begin to fulfil their parts in a structural pattern, remaining at the same time wholly convincing human personalities.

*The Watsons* reveals preliminary stages in the development of what was to become Jane Austen's ironic method:

'Have you been walking this morning?' 'No, my Lord. We thought it too dirty.' 'You should wear half-boots.' After another pause, 'Nothing sets off a neat ankle more than a half-boot...Do not you like Half-boots?' 'Yes—but unless they are so stout as to injure their beauty, they are not fit for Country walking.'—'Ladies should ride in dirty weather.—Do you ride?' 'No my Lord.' 'I wonder every Lady does not.—A woman never looks better than on horseback.' 'But every woman may not have the inclination, or the means.' 'If they knew how much it became them, they would all have the inclination, & I fancy Miss Watson—when once they had the inclination, the means wd soon follow.' 'Your Lordship thinks we always have our own way.—*That* is a point on which Ladies & Gentle[me]n have long disagreed—But without pretending to decide it, I may say that there are some circumstances which even *Women* cannot controul.—Female Economy will do a great deal my Lord, but it cannot turn a small income into a large one.'

Emma has at last reached a point of such exasperation at masculine selfsatisfaction and insensitivity that she refuses to give the coquettish reply invited by Osborne's heavy gallantry and patronising compliments to her sex. She reminds him instead of women's helplessness and economic dependence, and hints at their insecurity and unhappiness. Her reply is neither impertinent nor unfeminine, but it silences Lord Osborne, and makes 'his Lordship think'. This is because Emma's words, while giving a general impression of politeness, are in fact made up of disparate, one could even say contradictory, elements. A proud intelligence coexists with caution as to its free display in public; an intimate knowledge of women's lot in life (her remarks about 'Female Economy' are deeply felt) with resentment at Osborne's persistence in talking of them as decorative toys; and, on the author's part, an interest in the working of Emma's intelligent

and sensitive mind is accompanied by the recognition of the fact
that such moral fastidiousness as hers rarely survives unaltered or
unhurt in the school of social experience. Reconciliation of such
opposites is possible for Jane Austen through her use of irony,
an approach usually possible only to the writer who shares his
standards with an audience that can be relied upon to see some
things at least from his point of view.

Now Jane Austen, although convinced of the moral justification for certain of her personal ideals, had often to see them rudely
subverted by that very society which constituted her reading
public and her own immediate world. Emma Watson's tone
produces a superficial gloss of detachment that recalls the polite
urbanity of tone achieved by eighteenth-century satirists who
were more at one with their society than Jane Austen was with
hers. In the poetry of Pope, in Swift's prose pamphlets and in
Fielding's novels, the writer's tone creates an atmosphere of
intimacy and understanding; the reader becomes one of that
group of friends whose support these authors could depend on
enlisting, whether in laughter at the follies they described, in
battle with the evils they perceived in contemporary society and
attacked in their writings, or in appreciation of their skill in the
use of language and of established literary techniques. In Jane
Austen's work, on the other hand—and we sense this in her
characterisation of John Dashwood, for example, quoted on
page 41—there are strong undercurrents of passionate feeling,
even of personal uncertainty, that have their source in a sense of
isolation. Despite the outward poise of her manner, the reader
feels sometimes that Jane Austen is clinging to her ideals rather
than calmly stating them, and that the final triumphs of her
heroines are so many challenges to a hostile society.

The poised urbanity of her tone was made possible, in part,
by an intelligent circle of relatives and close friends who, sharing
her point of view and warmly appreciative of her novels, gave her
the sense that she was writing for a cultivated group of allies—
gave her, in fact, the emotional climate she needed to grow as a
satirist. The rest is her own creation, at the cost of great effort and
self-discipline. Such is the control Jane Austen achieves of herself

and of her tone as she progresses in the writing of fiction, that the delicate balance of her work is disturbed less and less by her deep personal involvement with the standards she applies. Emma Watson's reply to Lord Osborne reveals a good deal to us of Jane Austen's own thoughts and feelings, but *in the context of the passage as a whole* it simply imparts greater vitality and sparkle to a character who had so far seemed above reproach but somewhat passive and colourless.

So intense, at the same time, is the feeling with which personal concerns and problems are exposed and explored in the themes of the novels and the dilemmas of their heroines, that Jane Austen's work never becomes the mere theorem or didactic exercise into which, with her special gifts of precision, logic, and careful craftsmanship, it might so easily have hardened. In any passage from her maturer work, whether narrative, descriptive prose, or dialogue, the reader's mind is made to operate actively on at least two levels—first, the level of the obvious, where Jane Austen states what is, or seems to be, immediately apparent to everyone; and second, a level of implied criticism, even of denunciation, which uses *the very same words* to suggest that in a properly and justly ordered world this very same 'accepted' state of affairs would not be tolerated or allowed to go unchallenged.

Consider the opening sentence of *Pride and Prejudice*:

It is a truth universally acknowledged, that a single man in possession of a good fortune, must be in want of a wife.

In the first six words Jane Austen appears to state a fact that her use of the word *truth* implies to be a principle: a moral truth with which all mankind can be reasonably expected to agree. And what is this universally acknowledged principle? That a good income in the hands of a bachelor suffices in itself to make an attractive matrimonial proposition of him! The *tone*, which is dignified, oracular, elevated—as befits a person uttering edifying moral truths—has to keep uneasy company with *factual material* that savours of the cattle market rather than of religion or of philosophy. The crudeness of the idea expressed so simply in the second part of the sentence surprises the reader by its unexpectedness, after such a dignified beginning. It rouses, then amuses him.

At the same time, the opening phrase casts some of its own dignity over that crudity of sentiment, reminding the reader that this attitude to marriage has the influence of a religious maxim with a great many people: it is 'universally acknowledged'. Jane Austen holds up for examination in this way, society's tendency to place a price, quite blatantly and complacently, on an intimate human relationship such as marriage. With its implicit protest at a corrupt social morality, her opening sentence sets out one of the novel's major themes, and hints at Elizabeth Bennet's coming struggle to preserve her personality from socially countenanced attack and exploitation by her elders and social superiors.

Writing of this kind, whether in the comparatively simple form of Emma Watson's reply to Lord Osborne or in the complex narrative of *Pride and Prejudice*, is not within the range of a careless or a slovenly writer because it depends for its effects on exactness and precision. Irony becomes more than a sharp retort in dialogue, to be resorted to (as Emma Watson does) when politeness has failed: it becomes the stuff from which the novels are fashioned. Jane Austen's narration of incident and action, her portrayal of character, her management of dialogue—all these are conceived on two levels, how people present themselves to the world, and what they really are. As she matures, her characteristically ironic vision takes in landscape and environment as well, and an ever-widening range of human activity. The settings of the novels begin increasingly to participate in the action, to symbolise and comment upon it.

We have a late example of this aspect of Jane Austen's method among the minor works, in *Sanditon*, an unfinished novel written in 1817. Charlotte Heywood, on a visit to the local mansion, finds that the road to Sanditon House

was a broad, handsome, planted approach, between fields, & conducting at the end of a qr of a mile through second Gates into the Grounds, which though not extensive had all the Beauty and Respectability which an abundance of very fine Timber could give.—These Entrance Gates were so much in a corner of the Grounds or Paddock, so near one of its Boundaries, that an outside fence was at first almost pressing on the road...with clusters of fine Elms, or rows of old Thorns following its line almost everywhere.— *Almost* must be stipulated—for there were vacant spaces...

What, one might ask, is the point of such a passage of description, which must necessarily slow down the narrative's progress without seeming to add anything in the way of atmosphere or interest? There *is* a point, as we shall see, for it is through one of the 'vacant spaces' so carefully allowed for by Jane Austen that Charlotte accidentally glimpses two other characters, generally supposed to be fond of one another, in close and obviously private conversation. The relation between action and setting is immediately made clear:

Among other points of moralising reflection...Charlotte cd not but think of the extreme difficulty which secret Lovers must have in finding a proper spot for their stolen Interveiws.—Here perhaps they had thought themselves so perfectly secure from observation!—the whole field open before them—a steep bank & Pales never crossed by the foot of Man at their back... Yet here, she had seen them.

The setting has been visualised in great detail, as we can recognise from the care with which, even in this preliminary outline of a novel, the description has been set out and its peculiarities 'stipulated' for. Despite the 'Beauty & Respectability' of the scene, it has been chosen by supposed lovers for a secret meeting; although sympathetic, Charlotte cannot wholly approve. Her *moralising reflection* makes clear that she imagines the relationship existing between Miss Brereton and Sir Edward Denham to be a mixture of intimate freedom and furtive guilt—an impression created in her mind by the two principal features of the hiding-place they have chosen—the open field and the fence protected and reinforced by thorn trees, whose cover has proved inadequate. Charlotte instinctively feels that the landscape before her reveals the motives and feelings of the two people who have chosen to meet each other there—*but the description tells us something of Charlotte, too*. Jane Austen's treatment of landscape here recalls her earlier use, in *Mansfield Park*, of the grounds at Sotherton Court as a setting for Henry Crawford's flirtation with the engaged Maria Bertram, seen through the eyes of Fanny Price (see Chapter 7).

In another piece, *Lesley Castle*, are indicated very clearly indeed, at least two craftsmanlike qualities Jane Austen possessed: a reluctance to attempt effects of which she did not have detailed inside knowledge and experience (or which she knew to be cheap

and worthless), and a complete understanding of the varied possibilities of her chosen materials. Charlotte Lutterell writes to one
friend of her acquaintance with another:

'Perhaps you may flatter me so far as to be surprised that one of whom I
speak with so little affection should be my particular freind; but to tell you
the truth, our freindship arose rather from Caprice on her side than Esteem
on mine. We spent two or three days together with a Lady in Berkshire with
whom we both happened to be connected—. During our visit, the Weather
being remarkably bad, and our party particularly stupid, she was so good as to
conceive a violent partiality for me, which very soon settled into a downright
Freindship and ended in an established correspondence. She is probably by
this time as tired of me, as I am of her; but as she is too polite and I am too
civil to say so, our letters are still as frequent and affectionate as ever, and
our Attachment as firm and sincere as when it first commenced'.     (1792)

The relationship pictured here between Charlotte Lutterell and
Susan Fitzgerald is insincere, tedious and unsatisfactory to both
parties, yet etiquette indicates no acceptable way in which it can
be brought to an end, and the two ladies continue to correspond.
Their real feelings are indicated by the words *violent, downright*,
and *established*, which would have been more appropriate to a
description of dislike, hatred, and mutual avoidance than to the
portrayal of a supposedly tranquil friendship. We might notice,
too, that the relationship (such as it is) has been created in the
first place by the pattern of living that obtains within a particular
social group: the pattern of country house parties, occasional
dances, morning visits, and intimate correspondence between the
ladies of the families concerned. It was a pattern that Jane Austen
knew intimately from lifelong experience, and her technique of
'collecting' her people, exemplified in the Berkshire house-
party Charlotte Lutterell describes in *Lesley Castle*, is deftly
employed in novel after novel, as bored young people plan
expeditions of pleasure to castles and seaside resorts, a fashionable
gentleman rents a country house and takes his guests to a neighbourhood ball, and young ladies travel to London or to Bath for
the 'season', visit their friends in a neighbouring county, engage
in amateur theatricals, paint portraits of their friends, and sit
down together to their embroidery or basketwork.

While novels written by her contemporaries picture incredibly beautiful and accomplished young women fleeing from wicked villains through mountainous Alpine or Italian country, menaced by lunatics, frightened by ghosts, weakened physically by their own delicate sensibility, imprisoned in charnel houses and in lonely castles, Jane Austen quite deliberately sends *her* youthful heroines on a different type of journey, and in a completely different setting. Their progress is made in the social world of the country town, and their journeys are journeys in self-knowledge and social experience, some stages of which are painful and some comic, all essential to the creation and preservation of an individual's moral integrity. Her scheme totally omits sensational events or incidents, and affords no characters who are entirely without fault or virtue. The last sentence of the passage we have just read from *Lesley Castle*, with its subtle insight into feminine psychology, is possible because the setting can be taken for granted. In the novel as a whole, although some of the characters circulate in fashionable London society, enjoying 'the uncertain and unequal Amusements of this vaunted City' (and we can easily imagine what some of Jane Austen's contemporaries would have made of *that* material!) the reader's attention is concentrated on the various dissatisfactions and minor cruelties that mark the relationships between the women described, rather than on details of luxurious living, elegant interiors, and sensational incidents.

'I had some amusement at each,' Jane Austen wrote after visits to the Liverpool Museum and the British Gallery in 1811, 'tho' my preference for Men & Women, always inclines me to attend more to the company than to the sight'. We can, if we please, imagine her as she watched the passing crowd in preference to the exhibits on display. She seems to have felt her own taste to be somewhat unconventional; we cannot but be glad that it was, as we turn from the repetitive painted backcloths, the exaggerated incidents, and the unnatural characters of contemporary fiction, to the thoughts and actions of her 'Men & Women', perceived with such profound insight and set down with so much delicacy and truth.

# 4

# 'NORTHANGER ABBEY'

(*a*) 'You may find, perhaps, signor,' said Emily with mild dignity, 'that the strength of my mind is equal to the justice of my cause; and that I can endure with fortitude, when it is in resistance of oppression.'

'You speak like a heroine,' said Montoni contemptuously; 'we shall see whether you can suffer like one.'

Ann Radcliffe, The Mysteries of Udolpho (1794)

(*b*) 'Oh! My sweet Catherine, in *your* generous heart I know it would signify nothing; but we must not expect such disinterestedness in many. As for myself, I am sure I only wish our situations were reversed. Had I the command of millions, were I mistress of the whole world, your brother would be my only choice.'

This charming sentiment, recommended as much by sense as novelty, gave Catherine a most pleasing remembrance of all the heroines of her acquaintance; and she thought her friend never looked more lovely than in uttering the grand idea. Jane Austen, Northanger Abbey (1818)

Passages (*a*) and (*b*) above are taken from works that differ fundamentally in tone and spirit, but are nearly identical in structure, for the reason that Jane Austen modelled *Northanger Abbey* quite deliberately on Mrs Radcliffe's *The Mysteries of Udolpho*, a best-selling 'terror' novel of the late eighteenth-century. If we ignore for a moment Jane Austen's intention to ridicule her model (evident in her dry observation regarding the silliness and triteness of Isabella Thorpe's gushing extravagances), we can recognise in these extracts two stock situations of the sentimental novel and the 'Gothic' novel of terror—(*a*) the heroine as she defies the villain, and (*b*) the heroine in conversation with her confidante. We notice that the 'heroine' in each passage demonstrates a fearless independence of spirit and a well-developed sense of drama. Montoni, the dark, Satanic villain of *Udolpho*, sneers at Emily St. Aubin: he will discover that she is as brave as she claims to be. Catherine Morland, youthful and inexperienced in judging character, is impressed by Isabella Thorpe, respects and admires her: she will learn before very long that her friend is a liar and a vain coquette. This is the pivot upon which *Northanger Abbey* turns. Isabella treats Catherine as her confidante (and dupe), but it is *Catherine*, not Isabella, who is the real heroine of Jane Austen's novel.

Catherine Morland begins as a burlesque by Jane Austen of the heroines in Mrs Radcliffe's *Udolpho* and Charlotte Smith's *Emmeline*, two extremely popular novels of her youth. Catherine is presented from the first as being what they are not, a rigid method of determining character that derives from Jane Austen's early interest in satirising foolish and dangerous elements in popular literature. Like some of the juvenilia that we met with in Chapter 3, *Susan* (the first version of *Northanger Abbey*, written in 1803 when the terror novels were still popular, but allowed to remain unpublished and probably unrevised until 1816, when Jane Austen recovered her manuscript from the publisher and worked on it again) seems to have been written with the intention of satirising the materials and methods of the writers of sentimental and sensational novels. This original motive plays an important part in shaping the structure of the version we know as *Northanger Abbey*, which was published posthumously by Jane Austen's brother, together with *Persuasion*.

Catherine Morland makes her first appearance in adult society by visiting Bath during the fashionable spring season in the company of her kindly neighbours, Mr and Mrs Allen. There she makes the acquaintance of Isabella Thorpe, the eldest daughter of a school-friend of Mrs Allen. An attachment quickly springs up between the two girls, whose brothers have already met at Oxford and become close friends. Catherine is delighted to acquire a companion of her own age, and thinks Isabella beautiful, accomplished, and well-read. In actual fact Isabella *is* beautiful (her fairness, in the opinion of Henry Tilney, is 'an open attraction'), but she is accomplished only in the arts of flirtation, expert in duplicity, and well-read merely in the genres of sentimental and terror fiction, on the heroines of which she models her own behaviour, and to the pleasures of which she introduces Catherine:

'. . . my dearest Catherine, what have you been doing with yourself all this morning? Have you gone on with Udolpho?'

'Yes, I have been reading it ever since I woke; and I am got to the black veil.'

'Are you, indeed? How delightful! Oh! I would not tell you what is behind the black veil for the world! Are not you wild to know?'

'Oh! yes, quite; what can it be? But do not tell me—I would not be told upon any account. I know it must be a skeleton, I am sure it is Laurentina's skeleton. Oh! I am delighted with the book! I should like to spend my whole life reading it. I assure you, if it had not been to meet you, I would not have come away from it for all the world.'

'Dear creature! how much I am obliged to you; and when you have finished Udolpho, we will read the Italian together; and I have made out a list of ten or twelve more of the same kind for you.'

It is a conversation that reveals a great deal about the speakers, and about their subject. Catherine's excited reaction to *Udolpho* indicates that the terror novelists depend for their popularity on prolonging mysteries and heightening suspense, on macabre effects of various kinds, and on providing their readers with the same or similar ingredients, differently wrapped each time— Isabella finds no difficulty in making a list 'of ten or twelve more of the same kind' as *Udolpho*. Catherine is fascinated by Mrs Radcliffe's novel—'I have been reading it ever since I woke. . . I should like to spend my whole life reading it'—and dwells on its incidents continually in her imagination. We also learn something about Isabella from her style of talking. Her affection for Catherine, which is expressed in so exclamatory and emphatic a manner, seems insincere—to us, if not to Catherine herself, who is quite bewitched by her lovely friend. Isabella has appointed herself Catherine's mentor, and hopes to become her sister-in-law. She has privately cast Catherine for the role of confidante in a real-life sentimental drama of which she intends to be herself the heroine, but Catherine's ignorance of the right moment 'when a confidence should be forced' soon makes Isabella lose interest in her except as James Morland's sister:

'. . . Your brother and I were agreeing this morning that. . . we would not live here for millions. We soon found out that our tastes were exactly alike in preferring the country to every other place; really, our opinions were so exactly the same, it was quite ridiculous!. . . I would not have had you by for the world; you are such a sly thing, I am sure you would have made some droll remark or other about it.'

'No, indeed I should not.'

'Oh, yes you would indeed; I know you better than you know yourself. You would have told us that we seemed born for each other, or some nonsense of that kind, which would have distressed me beyond conception; my cheeks would have been as red as your roses; I would not have had you by for the world.'

'Indeed you do me injustice; I would not have made so improper a remark upon any account; and besides, I am sure it would never have entered my head.'

Isabella smiled incredulously, and talked the rest of the evening to James.

Catherine now meets Henry and Eleanor Tilney, young people of informed taste and education, very different from Isabella and her brother, John Thorpe (who has been annoying Catherine with his lies and loutish attentions). Henry Tilney, confounding any hopes that the hero, at least, of this anti-romantic novel will contrive to afford us a mystery, seeks a formal introduction to Catherine for the conventional purpose of dancing with her, and a friendship begins between them that bears every sign of soon turning into love. Catherine knows nothing of disguise or affectation, and her innocent frankness (which has so disappointed Isabella!) appeals directly to Tilney while it makes her comically endearing to the reader:

'...Oh! Mr Tilney, I have been quite wild to speak to you, and make my apologies. You must have thought me so rude; but indeed it was not my own fault, was it, Mrs Allen?...I had ten thousand times rather have been with you...and, if Mr Thorpe would only have stopped, I would have jumped out and run after you.'

Is there a Henry in this world who could be insensible to such a declaration? Henry Tilney at least was not.

It is evident that Catherine is, 'in finding him irresistible, becoming so herself'.

Catherine's friendship with Henry and his sister Eleanor is encouraged by their father, General Tilney, who treats Catherine with an exaggerated courtesy and deference that makes her uneasy and embarrasses his children. She is invited by him to stay at Northanger Abbey, the family's country house. Isabella Thorpe and Catherine's brother, James, whom she leaves behind her in Bath, have just become engaged to be married; Catherine has lately thought her friend somewhat unwise in allowing the attentions of Captain Frederick Tilney (Henry's elder brother), but she forgets her fears for James's happiness in her own joy at the prospect of several weeks spent

under the same roof with the person whose society she mostly prized, and in addition to all the rest, this roof was to be the roof of an abbey! Her passion for ancient edifices was next in degree to her passion for Henry Tilney.

Once at Northanger Abbey, Catherine is alternately disappointed by the up-to-date comfort of the house, delighted by Eleanor's company and Henry's interest in her, and perplexed to the point of dislike by the General's odd mixture of solicitude for her comfort and carelessness regarding his children's. She builds a fantasy in her own mind on the pattern of the terror novels that she has been reading, in which she assigns to her host the part of torturer and murderer:

Catherine's blood ran cold...Could it be possible? Could Henry's father? And yet how many were the examples to justify even the blackest suspicions! And, when she saw him in the evening, while she worked with her friend, slowly pacing the drawing-room for an hour together in silent thoughtfulness, with downcast eyes and contracted brow, she felt secure from all possibility of wronging him. It was the air and attitude of a Montoni! What could more plainly speak the gloomy workings of a mind not wholly dead to every sense of humanity, in its fearful review of past scenes of guilt? Unhappy man!

The General *is* actually guilty—but of greed, callousness, and cold selfishness, commoner sins than his guest suspects him of. He has been informed by John Thorpe that Catherine is an heiress, and his compliments to her are inspired by the respect due to her imaginary wealth and his own designs to make her his daughter-in-law. Catherine's visit to the Abbey continues with these suspicions and misunderstandings unresolved. Henry Tilney finds her one day, fearfully exploring the part of the house in which his mother had died, and assures her that Mrs Tilney (evidence of whose murder by her husband Catherine has been instinctively expecting and unconsciously hoping she will discover) had died a natural death:

'...Dear Miss Morland, consider the dreadful nature of the suspicions you have entertained. What have you been judging from? Remember the country and the age in which we live. Remember that we are English, that we are

Christians. Consult your own understanding, your own sense of the probable, your own observation of what is passing around you...'

But this is just what Catherine has *not* been doing, and Tilney's reproaches (despite his kindness afterwards) lead her to acknowledge her folly. 'The visions of romance were over.' Catherine has the honesty to admit her mistake, and the good sense to ascribe it to its proper cause:

She remembered with what feelings she had prepared for a knowledge of Northanger. She saw that the infatuation had been created, the mischief settled long before her quitting Bath, and it seemed as if the whole might be traced to the influence of that sort of reading which she had there indulged.

Catherine's 'Gothic' romancings having now been effectively exposed as illogical and untrue, the false ideas she has absorbed from her reading of 'sentimental' novels are similarly treated. Having learned, in fact, what life is *not* like, she now experiences its realities: her former idol, Isabella, proves herself faithless and deceitful, and a letter from James announces that their engagement is at an end. Sustaining this disillusionment with the tactful help of Henry and Eleanor, Catherine finds it bearable: Isabella's affection for her and her apparent good-nature have been, after all, merely illusory, and real life offers Catherine much superior alternatives to Isabella's friendship in Henry and his sister. She is temporarily saddened by the thought of James's disappointment, but reflection steadies Catherine, who had discovered a little earlier that real life is not as sensational as a Gothic novel, and now perceives that its joys and sorrows go deeper than anything she has met in romantic fiction.

Catherine is soon called upon to put her newfound good sense to a difficult test. General Tilney has her turned out of his house and sent home—apparently in disgrace, although Catherine cannot understand how she can have offended him. In this situation (at last she is experiencing something of the common trials of a heroine in a Gothic novel!) Catherine behaves with dignity and good feeling:

It was with pain that Catherine could speak at all; and it was only for Eleanor's sake that she attempted it. 'I am sure', said she, 'I am very sorry if I have offended him. It was the last thing I would willingly have done.

But do not be unhappy, Eleanor. An engagement you know must be kept. I am only sorry it was not recollected sooner, that I might have written home. But it is of no consequence.'

Her admirable selfcontrol, her instinctive reliance upon the forms of social etiquette for support and protection ('An engagement you know must be kept', says Catherine, knowing as well as Eleanor does that the General's pretext for sending her home is an impolite fiction), above all her generous sympathy for Eleanor's embarrassment in the midst of her own disappointment and distress—all these indicate that Catherine has entered the adult world.

Henry Tilney follows Catherine to her parents' home, and explains his father's behaviour although he cannot attempt to excuse it: John Thorpe's interest in the Morlands having been upset by the ending of his sister's engagement to James, he had informed the General that Catherine (previously described by him as the heiress to Mr Allen's fortune) is nothing but a pauper. The General, who could not know that one report is as false as the other, had vented his own disappointment in furious anger on the innocent Catherine. When Henry Tilney tells her of the General's performances, Catherine feels

that in suspecting General Tilney of either murdering or shutting up his wife, she had scarcely sinned against his character, or magnified his cruelty.

Here, too, Catherine has learned something—that real people are more complex, and real life situations more difficult to cope with, than those to be found in fiction.

Such a plot lends itself to Jane Austen's characteristic interest in the formation and development of character: the novel traces Catherine's progress from immaturity and social unease to an adult ability to discriminate between the valuable and the worthless, in literature and in life. For this reason, *Northanger Abbey* has a great deal in common with Jane Austen's other novels. Differences between them spring essentially from the structure and the light, satiric tone of *Northanger Abbey*, both of which derive from Jane Austen's early interest in literary satire. A later, maturer interest in psychological motivation is likely to have had a major part in carving *Northanger Abbey* from the block of her thirteen-year-old manuscript, for in her depiction of certain characters and situations Jane Austen takes up matters for which the Gothic and the sentimental genres offer no equivalent.

Henry Tilney, for instance, who indeed fulfils 'heroic' specifications by rescuing Catherine (although merely from the fate of being partnerless at a public dance) and by making sacrifices for her (he asks her to marry him in spite of his father's angry forbiddal of the match) is much more interesting than a Valancourt or a Delamere:

> 'What beautiful hyacinths! I have just learnt to love a hyacinth.'
>
> 'And how might you learn? By accident or argument?'
>
> 'Your sister taught me; I cannot tell how. Mrs Allen used to take pains, year after year, to make me like them; but I never could, till I saw them the other day in Milsom-street; I am naturally indifferent about flowers.'
>
> 'But now you love a hyacinth. So much the better. You have gained a new source of enjoyment, and it is well to have as many holds upon happiness as possible...And though the love of a hyacinth may be rather domestic, who can tell, the sentiment once raised, but you may in time come to love a rose?'

Catherine is uncertain how to take such teasing, for no heroine she has read of has had for a lover an amusing young man of wit and intelligence. Henry Tilney's light-hearted burlesque of *Udolpho* on the way to Northanger, engaged in to tease and delight Catherine and to amuse himself, indicates how he will become in time the tutor and guardian of her thoughts and emotions. Although its long-term effect is to stimulate her imagination to produce a fantasy still more outrageous than Mrs Radcliffe's or his own, it makes Catherine temporarily ashamed of her passion for *Udolpho*.

Henry Tilney prides himself a little on his own discriminating taste (his lecture to Catherine on the proper use of the overworked word *nice* brings him a sisterly rebuke from the tactful Eleanor: 'You are more nice than wise.') It is perfectly obvious, however sympathetic the reader may be to Catherine's virtues, that she is hardly his intellectual equal. He is won, we know, by that shining honesty, that innocence of any kind of affectation or duplicity, which Catherine brings to her new experiences; which answers, for instance, the half-mocking, half-serious cross-examination by which Tilney means to correct any pretensions she might have to 'heroic' sentiment:

You feel, I suppose, that, in losing Isabella, you lose half yourself: you feel a void in your heart which nothing else can occupy...You feel that you have no longer any friend to whom you can speak with unreserve; on whose regard you can place dependence; or whose counsel, in any difficulty, you could rely on. You feel all this?'

'No,' said Catherine, after a few moments' reflection, 'I do not—ought I? To say the truth, though I am hurt and grieved, that I cannot still love her, that I am never to hear from her, perhaps never to see her again, I do not feel so very, very much afflicted as one would have thought.'

'You feel, as you always do, what is most to the credit of human nature.'

Yet Tilney's interest in Catherine is first aroused by her obvious and passionate hero-worship of him, which, despite his intelligence, he finds more gratifying and interesting than clever conversation or a subtle, intricate nature. Catherine, meanwhile, striving vainly after sophistication in order to please him, is quite unaware how appealing she is to him in her lack of it. These are difficult effects, requiring far more complex treatment than the flat relationships of sentimental fiction, and they are brilliantly achieved.

The structure of the novel, too, with its suggestion that romantic fiction must give way to the demands of reality, helps to emphasise Jane Austen's view of life as too involved and interesting to be reduced to the formulae of the popular novelist. As Catherine grows out of her sentimental attachment to Isabella Thorpe, and completes her emotional education at Northanger by abandoning her immature taste for sensational fiction under Tilney's influence, the point is satisfactorily made.

The organisation of this novel is extremely neat—so neat that Jane Austen can mimic the Radcliffe manner of ascribing to each terrifying event a rational explanation: she arranges that Eleanor Tilney should, at the conclusion of the story, marry the very young man whose washing-bills, left behind in a drawer at the Abbey, cost novel-struck Catherine a night of terror and anxious speculation! The novel opens with a description of Catherine that establishes her from the start as the opposite of the lovely, accomplished heroines of Ann Radcliffe and Charlotte Smith:

No one who had ever seen Catherine Morland in her infancy, would have supposed her born to be an heroine. Her situation in life, the character of her father and mother, her own person and disposition, were all equally against her...

Catherine will prove a heroine, but she will do so in spite of origins too respectable and ordinary, and a family history too tranquil, to give her the background appropriate to a heroine of fiction. 'Any body might expect,' complains her creator, that a kind fate could at least have arranged for Catherine to be an orphan—but no, Mrs Morland has a stronger constitution than the mother of Emily St. Aubin in *The Mysteries of Udolpho*. We learn further that unlike the beautiful and talented heroine of Charlotte Smith's *Emmeline*, Catherine Morland's accomplishments are as ordinary as her looks. She 'never could learn or understand any thing before she was taught', she has no talent for music, she is delighted to be thought 'almost pretty'. By Charlotte Smith's standards she is a dismal failure, her only claims to notice being her good nature, her innocence, her anxiety to do the right thing, and her genuine humility:

> ...though there seemed no chance of her throwing a whole party into raptures by a prelude on the pianoforte, of her own composition, she could listen to other people's performance with very little fatigue.

Here, then, is Jane Austen's justification of her choice of a heroine: Catherine possesses—only!—the very rarest of virtues, true modesty. She does not, unlike Isabella Thorpe, know how to act a heroine's part, and any suggestion of public notice or admiration tends to alarm and embarrass her. But she takes the centre of the real-life story by reason of her unpretentious, instinctive adherence to standards of feeling and behaviour that set her above the social world she moves in, and very far above the false values of the romantic novel.

The standards put forward by the principal exponents of sentimental and terror fiction are thus placed beside Jane Austen's own conception of the sensible and the moral, and the novel constructed by the deft interweaving of typically sentimental and 'Gothic' elements with the story of Catherine's disillusionment and her progress towards maturity. Characters are introduced in the traditional roles of Heroine's Mother, Duenna, Principal Villain, and so on, who stubbornly act very differently from the way they would have acted in a romantic novel:

'I beg, Catherine, you will always wrap yourself up very warm about the throat, when you come from the Rooms at night'

is Mrs Morland's sensible and unromantic injunction to her daughter as Catherine prepares for her entrance into the great world. She never thinks of warning her to beware of the activities of villainous noblemen—from a parent or a guardian in a romantic novel, such a warning might have been the only one. Mrs Allen, in the role of Duenna, duly misleads Catherine and 'betrays' her; but never by intercepting her letters, ruining her character, or turning her out of the house, or by anything more positive than vanity, indolence, and affectionate indifference, which together translate every moral or social problem into the language of her own preoccupation with dress:

'Young men and women driving about the country in open carriages!...It is not right; and I wonder Mrs Thorpe should allow it...Mrs Allen, are not you of my way of thinking? Do not you think these kind of projects objectionable?'

'Yes, very much so indeed. Open carriages are nasty things. A clean gown is not five minutes wear in them. You are splashed getting in and getting out; and the wind takes your hair and your bonnet in every direction. I hate an open carriage myself.'

John Thorpe fills the role of Principal Villain, but he is no suave, attractive adventurer of the Montoni stamp, merely a conceited and illbred undergraduate whom Catherine's good sense constrains her (albeit unwillingly) to identify as a liar long before his lies affect her own standing with General Tilney. Even the Abbey falls short of the Gothic ideal of ruin and decay, Isabella deceives her, and Henry (who should, like Mrs Radcliffe's Valancourt, be worshipping her at a respectful distance) teases, lectures, and scolds her.

We have here, in fact, a work that contains no irrelevant details: Jane Austen's satire wastes no time in getting to its target, and her aim is precise. Irony plays constantly, although not perhaps with great profundity, over every person and situation in the novel, and it is not the less cleverly managed because it seldom leaves the level of the literary joke. In later writing we shall see Jane Austen attempting more difficult things, and not always achieving the complete success she wins here. The novel is a minor masterpiece, particularly fine in its presentation of Catherine Morland, who satisfies the requirements of anti-romance, but goes beyond it to become an embodiment of crystal-clear honesty, spontaneity, and moral fastidiousness that is convincing and attractive. Neither priggish nor unnaturally virtuous, her artlessness is so perfectly captured that beside her even such a satisfactory creation as Henry Tilney appears somewhat contrived, too much his author's mouthpiece. Similarly, Isabella Thorpe is so admirably caught in the vulgarity of her mind and her speech, her hypocrisy and shallow insincerity, that her opposite, Eleanor Tilney, dwindles to a shadow.

The failure of Eleanor Tilney to take on flesh and blood appears to be the result of Jane Austen's attempt to try something new and unrelated to her own temperament—the creation of a 'heroine' who is at once intelligent and above reproach. Catherine and Isabella are, each of them, successes along lines Jane Austen explored earlier, for the juvenilia afford many caricatures of girls who appeal by reason of their silliness or amuse through Jane Austen's satiric treatment of their faults. Eleanor, perfectly 'good' and full of good sense and sympathetic feeling, cannot interest in either of these ways, and consequently fails to come to life. Her inadequacy, since she is not the central character, does not weaken the novel as a whole; and just as much as the more successful creations of Catherine, Isabella, and Henry Tilney, it reveals Jane Austen's increasing interest in the development and psychological motivation of character. These are the features of *Northanger Abbey* that transcend the literary satire in which its beginnings lie, and they share aspects of Jane Austen's maturer achievement in *Pride and Prejudice* and *Emma*.

Within its unified whole, the novel contains a mixture of immature and of extremely skilled elements. The satiric interest behind its brisk take-off of popular novel genres quite evidently belongs with Jane Austen's juvenile satires on various kinds of contemporary literature. But while her satire there was often an end in itself, it contributes here to a larger pattern, providing a structural framework and a basis for characterisation in a novel whose chief interest is psychological rather than satiric, centring upon Catherine Morland's metamorphosis from immature child to responsible adult:

> ...soon were all her thinking powers swallowed up in the reflection of her own change of feelings and spirits since last she had trodden that well-known road. It was not three months ago since, wild with joyful expectation, she had there run backwards and forwards some ten times a-day, with an heart light, gay, and independent; looking forward to pleasures untasted and unalloyed, and free from the apprehension of evil as from the knowledge of it. Three months ago had seen her all this; and now, how altered a being did she return!

It is this 'alteration' in Catherine, part of the natural process of growing up, that the novel is about, and the subordination of satiric elements to the psychological in *Northanger Abbey* seems to suggest that the process of rewriting and revision, undertaken many years after the writing of the original version, built up the development of Catherine's character through the course of her disillusionment around what had been a literary joke in *Susan*. The texture of the novel suggests this too, for although literary satire was one of Jane Austen's early interests, her method of using it in this novel has a sureness and poise that seems to belong to her most mature work:

> The anxiety, which in this state of their attachment must be the portion of Henry and Catherine, and of all who loved either, as to its final event, can hardly extend, I fear, to the bosom of my readers, who will see in the tell-tale compression of the pages before them, that we are all hastening together to perfect felicity.

This is the voice of an experienced writer, and one, very probably, who had seen more than one of her own novels in print. It is the tone most often used in the presentation of Catherine, warming then to an affectionate amusement that indicates an author very much older than the heroine herself.

It is possible, of course, that Jane Austen may have worked on this novel at various times during her life, for it is known that she kept a copy of *Susan* when she sent her manuscript to her publisher. But Mrs Radcliffe went quickly out of fashion, and there would have been little point in publishing a satire on her novels when popular taste had already fastened on a new enthusiasm. Besides, we know that while *Susan* was out of Jane Austen's power to publish she had been experimenting in other directions, and in *Pride and Prejudice*, *Mansfield Park*, and *Emma* she left literary satire far behind her. It is more likely that the chance by which Jane Austen got back her manuscript tempted her to work upon it, and that she revised and rewrote drastically in 1816. If we compare *Northanger Abbey* with *Persuasion*, another novel whose mixture of mature and apparently immature elements puzzles the reader, we are reminded that revision, for Jane Austen, was in itself an artistic process. *Northanger Abbey*, which we know to have been thoroughly revised, has the lustre of a polished jewel; *Persuasion*, which does not have a history of an early version, and of which the only evidence of revision we have is a cancelled version of Chapters 10 and 11 in the second volume that we know, appears patchy and unequal beside it and beside the artistic perfection of *Emma*.

Despite the technical mastery Jane Austen displays in her writing of *Northanger Abbey*, which obviously relates to a point in her literary career later than (at least) the publication of *Sense and Sensibility*, this discussion of it has been placed at a point in our study of Jane Austen's work where its element of literary satire can establish its connection with the juvenilia we considered in the last chapter, and with Jane Austen's treatment of the character of Marianne Dashwood in *Sense and Sensibility*, the novel we will take up in the next. One disadvantage of such a position is that *Sense and Sensibility*, with its many real immaturities, may seem grossly clumsy when we come to it fresh from *Northanger Abbey*'s graceful dexterity. What we should have here is, of course, *Susan*. But this early version of Catherine's story is, unluckily, no longer in existence, and we must content ourselves with remembering as we read *Northanger Abbey*, that its very remarkable artistic skill probably belongs to a much later stage in Jane Austen's development as a writer.

# 5

## 'SENSE AND SENSIBILITY'

(*a*) 'No, no,' cried Marianne, 'misery such as mine has no pride. I care not who knows that I am wretched. The triumph of seeing me so may be open to all the world. Elinor, Elinor, they who suffer little may be proud and independent as they like—may resist insult, or return mortification—but I cannot. I must feel—I must be wretched—and they are welcome to enjoy the consciousness of it that can.'

(*b*) Elinor saw that it *was* his hand, and she could doubt no longer...for a few moments, she was almost overcome—her heart sunk within her, and she could hardly stand; but exertion was indispensably necessary, and she struggled so resolutely against the oppression of her feelings, that her success was speedy, and for the time complete.

The two passages above, taken from Jane Austen's first published novel, *Sense and Sensibility*, picture the emotions of Marianne and Elinor Dashwood, two sisters of rather different temperaments and habits of thinking, in the moment of a major disillusionment and disappointment. Each has just discovered that her trust in a lover's affection and sincerity has been misplaced, perhaps betrayed. Each has made that discovery in the presence of a watchful adversary: Marianne meets her former lover, Willoughby, in the company of his future wife at an evening party, Elinor is forced into the role of confidante by her rival for the affections of Edward Ferrars, Lucy Steele. 'I must feel—I must be wretched,' cries Marianne, and the passionate urgency of her words prepares the reader for emotions that will be allowed to run unchecked, a determined and proud individuality that has no thought for any one or any thing outside its own immediate concerns. On Marianne's sister Elinor, on the other hand, the world outside exercises so compelling an influence that she finds 'exertion...indispensably necessary' even in the moment of her surprise and sorrow. Not, we are informed later, until she is left alone by her tormentor has Elinor 'liberty to think and be wretched', but Marianne does not resort to any such self-imposed

63

discipline; she begins—in the presence of her fellow-guests—'to give way in a low voice to the misery of her feelings, by exclamations of wretchedness'. We perceive another point of difference between these two sisters. In passage (*b*) Elinor's sources of strength are seen to lie within herself, and her struggle for self-control is won without the help or the suffering of any other person. But passage (*a*) is Marianne's retort to Elinor's request that she should try to control her feelings; in her 'they who suffer little may be proud and independent', we find Marianne turning upon her sister in her misery, reproaching Elinor for the calmness she mistakes for insensitivity, comparing, with bitter self-pity, her own unhappy situation with her sister's presumed prosperity. So effectively has Elinor concealed and controlled her own feelings that nobody, not even her sister, guesses the tortures to which Lucy Steele has delivered her.

Elinor is as sensitive as Marianne, and feels quite as deeply, but it is clear that a system of checks and controls works for her that is scorned and ridiculed by Marianne, who will have no recourse to it:

'But I thought it was right, Elinor,' said Marianne, 'to be guided wholly by the opinion of other people. I thought our judgments were given us merely to be subservient to those of our neighbours. This has always been your doctrine I am sure.'

'No, Marianne, never. My doctrine has never aimed at the subjection of the understanding. All I have ever attempted to influence has been the behaviour. You must not confound my meaning.'

Marianne's actions are guided by rules too, but those rules are very different from Elinor's. Obedience to them, Jane Austen suggests, is irrational, unwise, and dangerous:

'Her systems have all the unfortunate tendency of setting propriety at nought.'

She would not wound the feelings of her sister on any account, and yet to say what she did not believe was impossible.

...it was impossible for her to say what she did not feel, however trivial the occasion.

*Impossible, doctrine, system.* To explore the values that guide Marianne, to turn upon her code of behaviour the rays of reason and sound good sense, is the purpose of the novel. Its title is itself an indication of the writer's concern with the impulses that move people to think and behave in certain ways.

*Sensibility*, the capacity for deep, intense feeling that was praised as a heroic virtue by several of Jane Austen's fellow-novelists, is adopted as a doctrine by Marianne Dashwood; despite her intelligence, Marianne's youthful idealism inclines her to artistic enthusiasm, rather than to sober judgment, and a system that licenses the free indulgence of arrogance and individualism has obvious attraction for a character such as hers. *Sense* is the guiding principle of her sister Elinor, who possesses

strength of understanding, and coolness of judgment...an excellent heart; her disposition was affectionate, and her feelings were strong; but she knew how to govern them.

Elinor's *sense* sharpens her intelligence, arms her in caution when managing her own affairs, and helps her to promote, prudently and sympathetically, the happiness of her friends and her family. Marianne's *sensibility* violates her intelligence, exposes her defenceless heart to betrayal and to transports of sorrow, and plunges her family into perpetual concern for her health, at one point even for her very life. Jane Austen's interest in exposing the danger of the doctrine of sensibility may (like her satire of Gothic romance and sentimental heroines in *Northanger Abbey*) have had roots in impatience with the accepted values of contemporary literature. The tone of both novels is that of satiric comedy, playing over a steady moral seriousness that decides the issues. Elinor and Marianne progress to a better understanding and a firmer control of their own feelings, to a keener perception of other people's motives and points of view. Experience makes adults of them, strips them of sentimentality and arrogance, confirms them in their natural intelligence and generosity of heart. Elinor, like Marianne, has much to learn:

'...The composure of mind with which I have brought myself at present to consider the matter, the consolation that I have been unwilling to admit, have been the effect of constant and painful exertion; they did not spring up of themselves.'

Her sense equips Elinor to face life's realities, while sensibility robs Marianne of the power even to defend herself. In the exercise of her judgment and selfcontrol, Elinor develops a resolution of spirit that makes her almost invincible to attack, and gives her the strength to comfort and support her weaker sister.

The successful exposition of such a theme must depend on the effective contrast of the two central characters, and on their involvement in a course of events that at once exercises their respective temperaments and develops their characters. The plot is, briefly, as follows: on the death of Mr Henry Dashwood, his estate at Norland in Sussex passes to his son by his first wife, Mr John Dashwood. His widow and her three daughters accept the tenancy of Barton Cottage in Devonshire at the invitation of Sir John Middleton, a landowner and a distant relation of Mrs Dashwood. At Barton Marianne meets in romantic circumstances, and falls in love with, John Willoughby, an attractive young man who satisfies the yearnings of her sentimental imagination by appearing to share enthusiastically her every thought, opinion, and artistic taste. Their affection for each other is openly displayed but not, to Elinor's dissatisfaction, as openly acknowledged; and when Willoughby is called suddenly away from Devonshire an engagement between him and the mourning Marianne is presumed to have been formed, but does not in fact exist. Marianne nurses her sorrow:

In books too, as well as in music, she courted the misery which a contrast between the past and the present was certain of giving. She read nothing but what they had been used to read together.

Such violence of affliction indeed could not be supported for ever; it sunk within a few days into a calmer melancholy; but these employments, to which she daily recurred, her solitary walks and silent meditations, still produced occasional effusions of sorrow as lively as ever.

Elinor, meanwhile, has her own troubles. While at Norland she had become attached to Edward Ferrars, a brother of her sister-in-law Fanny Dashwood, and she believes her affection to be returned. Nothing has been said on the subject by the two young people themselves, but Mrs John Dashwood has made *her* opinion clear: their mother expects Edward to marry well, and any young woman should beware 'who attempted to *draw him in*'. At Barton Elinor meets Lucy Steele, a poor and pretty cousin of Lady Middleton, who is paying her relations a visit with her elder sister Anne. Noticing that Sir John and his mother-in-law, Mrs Jennings, enjoy teasing Elinor about Edward Ferrars, Lucy takes care to inform Elinor that *she* has a prior claim on Edward:

'...I only wonder that I am alive after what I have suffered for Edward's sake these last four years. Every thing in such suspense and uncertainty; and seeing him so seldom—we can hardly meet above twice a-year. I am sure I wonder my heart is not quite broke.'

Here she took out her handkerchief; but Elinor did not feel very compassionate.

'Sometimes,' continued Lucy, after wiping her eyes, 'I think whether it would not be better for us both, to break off the matter entirely.' As she said this, she looked directly at her companion.

Although Lucy's motives are obvious in making Elinor her confidante, and although Elinor bitterly resents having to feign sympathy for a woman she considers crafty and altogether unworthy of Edward, she resolves to get the better of her own affection for him. Elinor knows that such a step is essential to the preservation of her own peace of mind, for while Edward seems tired of his early entanglement with Lucy, she believes he will not be allowed to escape from it. Elinor decides to keep Lucy's story and her own regrets to herself, believing silence on the subject a duty she owes to her family (who would be distressed on her account) and also to Lucy, whose revelations have been made in strict confidence.

Elinor and Marianne go to London, as the guests of Mrs Jennings. Colonel Brandon, a friend met originally at Barton, continues to admire Marianne, but must do so at a distance for Marianne is wholly preoccupied with thoughts of Willoughby. She writes to him, and finally meets him, only to find that he is on the point of marriage with another woman, an heiress. Elinor supports Marianne through the agony of this disappointment and, unhappy as she is herself, must bear without defence or explanation Marianne's bitter accusations of insensitivity and coldheartedness. When the secret of Lucy's engagement to Edward is accidentally disclosed by Anne Steele to Mrs John Dashwood and her enraged mother, and freely discussed by everyone else, the sisters come to a better understanding, and

Marianne perceives for the first time the full extent of her sister's heroism:

Marianne was quite subdued.

'Oh! Elinor,' she cried, 'you have made me hate myself for ever. How barbarous have I been to you! you, who have been my only comfort, who have borne with me in all my misery, who have seemed to be only suffering for me! Is this my gratitude!...Because your merit cries out upon myself, I have been trying to do it away.'

Elinor and Marianne leave London for Cleveland in Somersetshire, the home of Mrs Jennings's younger daughter, Mrs Palmer. There Marianne, careless and neglectful of her own health, contracts pneumonia and very nearly dies. Hearing that she is in danger of death, Willoughby rides to Cleveland and interviews Elinor, to whom he speaks of his unhappy marriage and explains his cruel treatment of Marianne, which had been necessitated by his own extravagance and selfishness:

'The struggle was great—but it ended too soon. My affection for Marianne, my thorough conviction of her attachment to me—it was all insufficient to outweigh that dread of poverty, or get the better of those false ideas of the necessity of riches, which I was naturally inclined to feel, and expensive society had increased. I had reason to believe myself secure of my present wife, if I chose to address her, and I persuaded myself to think that nothing else in common prudence remained for me to do.'

Marianne recovers her health, and the sisters return to Barton. Told by Elinor of Willoughby's confession, Marianne has the good sense to ascribe her sorrows to their true cause: 'I have nothing to regret—nothing but my own folly.' Elinor, through whom Colonel Brandon has presented Edward Ferrars with a living on his estate that will presumably enable Edward to take orders and marry Lucy in spite of Mrs Ferrars's disinheritance of him, now daily expects news of Edward's marriage. It comes at last, reported by a servant, and it would seem that Elinor and Marianne are now to be equally unhappy, and will need all the sense they can muster to help them through a future of spinsterhood. But the last three chapters of the novel bring Edward himself to Barton to declare that Lucy has broken their engagement and married his younger brother Robert (now the owner of the property Edward has lost); explain the true nature

of Edward's unhappy relationship with Lucy Steele; and by
means of Mrs Ferrars's worthless forgiveness but useful financial
assistance, establish Elinor and Edward at Delaford Parsonage, as
a consequence of which Marianne eventually becomes the wife of
Colonel Brandon.

Even such a brief retelling of the novel's plot as this (for many
details have been omitted, including the history of Willoughby's
seduction of Eliza Williams, Colonel Brandon's ward) creates an
impression of a crowded canvas. Jane Austen's growing skill in
handling large groups of people appears in her sketches of the
Middletons' parties at Barton, which spring from their fear of
being left to each other's company:

Sir John was a sportsman, Lady Middleton a mother. He hunted and shot,
and she humoured her children; and these were their only resources.

From the Middletons' dislike of solitude arise many opportunities for Willoughby and Marianne to progress rapidly in their
acquaintance; besides an unforgettable scene in which Elinor,
wishing to show Lucy that she is unaffected by the news of
Edward's engagement, deliberately and unwisely invites a
repetition of the revelations that tear her inwardly—and which
Lucy embellishes with feline delight. 'Seated side by side at the
same table, and with the utmost harmony engaged in forwarding
the same work'—a filigree basket for Lady Middleton's spoilt
child—Elinor and Lucy engage in verbal combat while the other
ladies play cards, and Marianne's piano-playing fills the room
with sound:

Elinor blushed for the insincerity of Edward's future wife, and replied, 'This
compliment...raises my influence much too high; the power of dividing two
people so tenderly attached is too much for an indifferent person.'

''Tis because you are an indifferent person', said Lucy, with some pique,
and laying a particular stress on those words, 'that your judgment might
justly have such weight with me. If you could be supposed to be biassed in
any respect by your own feelings, your opinion would not be worth having.'

Their duel ends only when Elinor is called to the card-table by
the beginning of a second rubber. She has taken the measure of
her adversary, and knows better than to engage her in battle again,
for while *she* has suffered, Lucy has enjoyed herself:

she felt such conversations to be an indulgence which Lucy did not deserve, and...dangerous to herself.

Elinor and Lucy meet again, however, when the scene shifts to London, where the circles of their relations and acquaintances widen and interlock. Jane Austen's talent for 'collecting... People delightfully' is demonstrated in her hint that Lady Middleton and Mrs Dashwood are certain to get on—

There was a kind of cold hearted selfishness on both sides, which mutually attracted them; and they sympathised with each other in an insipid propriety of demeanour, and a general want of understanding.

The Steeles' fawning, flattering ways charm Fanny Dashwood as they have pleased Lady Middleton, and from the meetings prompted by such flocking together as this among some of the characters, and the social intermingling required of them all, spring a series of exchanges rich in ironic comedy. Elinor is slighted and Lucy Steele distinguished by their future mother-in-law, Mrs Ferrars, at the John Dashwoods' dinner-party, on which occasion 'no poverty of any kind, except of conversation, appeared—but there, the deficiency was considerable'. There is a comic, yet distressing scene in which an embarrassed Edward interrupts an interview between Elinor and Lucy; and a very lively description, by Mrs Jennings, of Fanny Dashwood's reaction to the news of Edward's engagement to Lucy—

'She fell into violent hysterics immediately, with such screams as reached your brother's ears, as he was sitting in his own dressing-room down stairs, thinking about writing a letter to his steward in the country. So up he flew directly, and a terrible scene took place...'

Through these meetings Jane Austen exposes the meanness of society's motives and the emptiness of its pretensions, its substitution of commercial for humane values, and especially its unjust valuation of superior characters and personalities. Society's special victim in *Sense and Sensibility* is Marianne Dashwood, and Jane Austen's rendering of her character is one of the high points in the novel.

Marianne's personality begins in satire, for the structure of the novel, pitting Sense against Sensibility, demands that her romantic enthusiasms should be criticised through laughter.

Accordingly Marianne is upset by Edward's temperate reading of Cowper's poetry, her regret at leaving Norland finds expression in a soliloquy addressed to the trees along the avenue, and like her mother, she can admit no sentiment inferior to love—'Esteem him! Like him! Cold-hearted Elinor!' All this is amusing enough. But when Marianne goes to Barton, and mingles more in society than she has done at Norland, Jane Austen's satire acquires a second dimension:

'And what sort of a young man is he?'

'As good a kind of fellow as ever lived, I assure you. A very decent shot, and there is not a bolder rider in England.'

'And is *that* all you can say for him?' cried Marianne, indignantly. 'But what are his manners on more intimate acquaintance? What his pursuits, his talents and genius?'

Sir John was rather puzzled.

'Upon my soul,' said he, 'I do not know much about him as to all *that*. But he is a pleasant, good humoured fellow, and has got the nicest little black bitch of a pointer I ever saw. Was she out with him today?'

But Marianne could no more satisfy him as to the colour of Mr Willoughby's pointer, than he could describe to her the shades of his mind.

Marianne's idealism and artistic enthusiasms, although dangerously exaggerated, serve to show up many shortcomings in her neighbours—in this case Sir John Middleton's tendency to judge men as sportsmen rather than as human beings. We see at the same time how insensitive Marianne is to everything outside her own interests; Sir John finds her powers of observation as poor as she would rate his insight into character! Yet she is, despite her faults, of far finer quality than most of the people in her circle who laugh at her, and, later, pity her. Her statements sometimes have an inner truth that wins our agreement:

'It is not time or opportunity that is to determine intimacy; it is disposition alone. Seven years would be insufficient to make some people acquainted with each other'.

'The rent of this cottage is said to be low; but we have it on very hard terms, if we are to dine at the park whenever any one is staying either with them, or with us.'

Jane Austen has undertaken a very difficult task, in attempting to convey a sympathetic impression of Marianne's character, while exposing the exaggerated sensibility that leads her astray. Unlike Catherine Morland in *Northanger Abbey*, Marianne does not seek to please other people; she remains, on the contrary, arrogantly aloof, and refuses to conform. It is an attitude that says a great deal for her discriminating taste, and nothing at all for her tact, good manners, or good sense. On her way to London with her hostess, Mrs Jennings, Marianne

sat in silence almost all the way, wrapt in her own meditations, and scarcely ever voluntarily speaking, except when any object of picturesque beauty within their view drew from her an exclamation of delight exclusively addressed to her sister. To atone for this conduct therefore, Elinor took immediate possession of the post of civility which she had assigned herself, behaved with the greatest attention to Mrs Jennings, talked with her, laughed with her, and listened to her whenever she could.

Marianne's high standards and uncompromising frankness force upon her sister the unpleasant task of 'telling lies when politeness required it', and provide Marianne herself with a carapace that nothing, seemingly, can penetrate—until, on her desertion by Willoughby, romantic passion turns to painful and very real sorrow. She finds herself helpless to withstand the pricks of the very society she has despised:

'I cannot stay here long, I cannot stay to endure the questions and remarks of all these people. The Middletons and Palmers—how am I to bear their pity? The pity of such a woman as Lady Middleton! Oh! what would *he* say to that!'

Marianne's agony is entirely convincing. It is hard for *her* to accept because she has neglected to build the defences about her heart and mind that have served Elinor well in similar distress. The problems of portraying Marianne's complex character are many and Jane Austen's success in this part of her undertaking can be measured by her failure in another part of it; for when, at the end of the novel she fufils her satiric intention by marrying Marianne to Colonel Brandon, the reader is left with a sense of dissatisfaction. Logically, mathematically 'right' though the marriage is, completing the scheme according to which the novel has been planned, Marianne Dashwood has become too real in the evocation of her troubled, passionate nature, to be fitted arbitrarily into a pattern or provided with a destiny that her spirit, however chastened it might have become through experience, must naturally rebel against.

The companion portrait of Elinor Dashwood suffers similarly from the rigidity of the novel's structure—in this case, from the strictness of the antithesis upon which the story rests. Elinor, one might feel justified in thinking, is almost too selfcontrolled, too unselfish for a girl of nineteen. Her affection for Edward Ferrars makes her unwilling to settle as far from Sussex as Devonshire, yet she makes no demur to her mother's plan. It is difficult, too, to imagine a nineteen-year-old girl discussing a sister of seventeen in the folllowing terms:

'...a better acquaintance with the world is what I look forward to as her greatest possible advantage.'

What experience of 'the world' has Elinor had, that Marianne has not? This conversation (with Colonel Brandon) takes place at Barton, before Elinor has met Lucy Steele or Marianne been disappointed by Willoughby. A more mature experience than Elinor at nineteen can possibly claim to have shows itself in her analysis of Willoughby's temperament and state of mind:

'At present,' continued Elinor, 'he regrets what he has done. And why does he regret it? Because he finds it has not answered towards himself. It has not made him happy. His circumstances are now unembarrassed—he suffers from no evil of that kind; and he thinks only that he has married a woman of a less amiable temper than yourself. But does it thence follow that had he married you, he would have been happy? The inconveniences would have been different...He would have had a wife of whose temper he could make no complaint, but he would have been always necessitous—always poor; and probably would soon have learnt to rank the innumerable comforts of a clear estate and good income as of far more importance, even to domestic happiness, than the mere temper of a wife.'

These words might have more appropriately been spoken by Mrs Dashwood, rather than by Elinor; but by giving her mother a romantic delicacy as fine as Marianne's, Jane Austen forces on Elinor a seriousness beyond her years. Such weaknesses apart, the portrait of Elinor Dashwood makes its point effectively: that the complete human personality needs certain qualities in balanced proportion. Sense and sensibility, reason and passion, mind and heart, complement each other in her. Jane Austen explores in this novel the weakening tendencies of excessive emotionalism, and in Elinor she establishes a positive alternative, for through her disciplined, voluntary efforts to control her emotions and regulate her behaviour Elinor achieves true strength and balance of character.

While the novel presents a number of characters whom we think of as 'minor' beside the principals, there are few whose presence is not necessary to the plot of the novel and illustrative, in some way, of its themes. Miss Anne Steele, for example, is as carefully drawn as her sister Lucy, a clear differentiation being made between Anne's well-meaning foolishness and Lucy's calculating slyness. Poorer than the Dashwood sisters, the Steeles' obsequiousness to Mrs Ferrars, Fanny Dashwood, and Lady Middleton encourages the haughty pride that considers itself affronted by the independence of Elinor and Marianne. Lucy's speech betrays her lack of education ('I am sure I should have seen it in a moment, if Mrs Ferrars had took a dislike to me'). So does Anne's, with the addition of an element of vulgar silliness that has been so well established in our early encounters with her, that her revelation of Lucy's secret to Mrs Ferrars and Fanny Dashwood is entirely credible, as another characteristic example of it. The climax of the novel arises in this way through Jane Austen's careful characterisation of Anne Steele, and not merely by chance.

A certain immaturity in the author betrays itself, however, in the presence of some characters who have not, like Anne Steele, been satisfactorily woven into the fabric of the novel. The Palmers are perhaps necessary to the plot—it is in their house that Marianne falls ill, and Elinor hears Willoughby's confession— but they are little more than clever caricatures:

'You may believe how glad we all were to see them,' added Mrs Jennings...
'but...it was wrong in her situation. I wanted her to stay at home and rest this morning, but she would come with us; she longed so much to see you all!'
   Mrs Palmer laughed, and said it would not do her any harm.
   'She expects to be confined in February', continued Mrs Jennings.
   Lady Middleton could no longer endure such a conversation, and therefore exerted herself to ask Mr Palmer if there was any news in the paper.
   'No, none at all', he replied, and read on.

Mrs Palmer exists in order to laugh and speak foolishly, Mr Palmer to treat his acquaintances casually and his own relations with contempt. The latter affords a certain amount of light relief in a novel whose most amusing moments are shadowed by present or imminent sorrow, but it is hard to believe that the fastidious Elinor later 'found him very capable of being a pleasant companion, and...liked him...much better than she had expected'. Such an alteration as this in a previously formed opinion is perfectly acceptable in the case of Mrs Jennings. Unabashedly vulgar as she is, the Dashwood sisters change their opinion of her in the course of closer association, as we often have to do in real life on coming to know someone better whom we had rather disliked on first acquaintance. In her tactless and misguided attempts to help them, a human, generous sympathy shines through each comic thought and ridiculous action:

Their good friend saw that Marianne was unhappy, and felt that every thing was due to her which might make her at all less so. She treated her therefore, with all the indulgent fondness of a parent towards a favourite child on the last day of its holidays. Marianne was to have the best place by the fire, was to be tempted to eat by every delicacy in the house, and to be amused by the relation of all the news of the day...Elinor...could have been entertained by Mrs Jennings's endeavours to cure a disappointment in love, by a variety of sweetmeats and olives, and a good fire.

*Absurdity* and *impertinence*, the words first used by Marianne to describe Mrs Jennings's usual conversational drift, give way to earnest gratitude, *respect*, and *kind wishes* when she bids her hostess goodbye. Yet Mrs Jennings has not altered—it is Marianne who has changed.

Mrs Jennings, Colonel Brandon, Edward Ferrars, his mother and his younger brother, Robert, and Mr and Mrs John Dashwood are all characters whose presentation is affected by Jane Austen's preoccupation, in *Sense and Sensibility*, with money—its effect on those who have an abundance of it, and on those who must do without very much of it. The reduction of Mrs Dashwood and her daughters from wealth and ease to comparative poverty provides an opportunity to interpret aright the true characters of their relatives and friends. Mrs Ferrars, fearful that Edward means to marry Elinor, bullies and slights her. We hear of her spectacular reception of the news of Edward's engagement to Lucy Steele through John Dashwood, her son-in-law. She has, 'with the truest affection' been planning to marry Edward to an heiress with thirty thousand pounds; she is 'quite in agony' at the news of his engagement to Lucy; she has 'liberal designs' to settle an estate worth a thousand pounds a year on Edward if he will give up Lucy and marry Miss Morton; she is prepared 'even, when matters grew desperate, to make it twelve hundred'; she plans to disinherit him if he disobeys her wishes, and to hinder him in any attempt to enter a profession; her conduct throughout, according to the awed and equally mercenary John Dashwood,

'has been such as every conscientious, good mother, in like circumstances, would adopt.'

All this, in its strong outline and bitter satire, deftly contrasted with Mrs Henry Dashwood's unworldliness and Mrs Jennings's outspoken and generous humanity to Edward, is caricature. Her daughter Fanny, who, as John Dashwood's wife has a better opportunity than any one else to comfort her mother-in-law and show kindness to Elinor and Marianne in their bereavement, directs all her influence to keeping them all as poor as possible, and humiliating them on that account as much as she can. Her delineation is one of the finest things in the novel. Chapter 2 of the first volume presents Mrs John Dashwood in conversation with her husband, approving at last his decision to give his sisters 'a present of fifty pounds, now and then', a sum to which her arguments have whittled down the present originally planned, of three thousand pounds:

'To be sure it will. Indeed, to say the truth, I am convinced within myself that your father had no idea of your giving them any money at all. The assistance he thought of, I dare say, was only such as might be reasonably expected of you; for instance, such as looking out for a comfortable small house for them, helping them to move their things, and sending them presents of fish and game, and so forth, whenever they are in season. I'll lay my life that he meant nothing farther; indeed, it would be very strange and unreasonable if he did. Do but consider, Mr Dashwood, how excessively comfortable your mother-in-law and her daughters may live on the interest of seven thousand pounds...They will live so cheap! Their housekeeping will be nothing at all. They will have no carriage, no horses, and hardly any servants; they will keep no company, and can have no expenses of any kind! Only conceive how comfortable they will be! Five hundred a-year! I am sure I cannot imagine how they will spend half of it; and as to your giving them more, it is quite absurd to think of it. They will be much more able to give *you* something.'

Here, with a satiric undertone of concentrated savagery, is Fanny Dashwood's authentic voice. We hear it in a chapter of dialogue, of which this passage is the climax. Jane Austen does not tell us what the Dashwoods look like; there is no need, for as we read we become familiar with the topography of their minds and seem to catch the tones of their voices. We know that he is grave throughout, while she is sweetly reasonable: they are in perfect agreement in seeking a passable excuse to avoid their obligations. Every speech begins with a *Certainly*, a *To be sure*, an *Undoubtedly*, an *I believe you are right*, or a *That is very true*, and each such phrase ushers in a fresh modification of John Dashwood's original intention. He needs to be convinced, she knows how to convince him. For she is the cleverer of the two, although, as in the case of Lucy Steele, her grammar betrays ('how excessively *comfortable* your mother-in-law may live!') her poorer education. Her arguments are infinitely varied and beautifully timed: she reminds him of the need to provide for their son's future, suggests that her father-in-law was delirious when he asked his son to assist his family, reminds him that money once given cannot be recalled, exclaims at the luxurious life she professes to imagine Mrs Dashwood and her daughters will lead, warns him of the dangers attending annuities, and complains peevishly of the inferiority of their own set of china—arguments that could not succeed with a truly determined or a generous man, but more than sufficient to convince a man who looks only for a justifiable pretext.

And what of John Dashwood himself? Is he merely a weakling, putty in the hands of a selfish wife? As the nearest relation of his father's daughters and the occupant of their former home, it is reasonable, surely, that in their distress they should look to him for help. But he so frequently talked of the increasing expenses of housekeeping, and of the perpetual demands upon his purse, which a man of any consequence in the word was beyond calculation exposed to, that he seemed rather to stand in need of more money himself than to have any design of giving money away.

We have only to look once again at his words, quoted on page 41, lamenting Marianne's loss of marketable 'bloom', or at the passage below, in which he urges Elinor to set about capturing Colonel Brandon, to recognise that natural feeling has been replaced in his mind by insensitivity, moral coarseness, and love of money:

'Two thousand a-year;' and then working himself up to a pitch of enthusiastic generosity, he added, 'Elinor, I wish, with all my heart, it were *twice* as much, for your sake.'

'Indeed, I believe you,' replied Elinor; 'but I am very sure that Colonel Brandon has not the smallest wish of marrying *me*.'

'You are mistaken, Elinor; you are very much mistaken. A very little trouble on your side secures him. Perhaps just at present he may be undecided; the smallness of your fortune may make him hang back; his friends may all advise him against it. But some of those little attentions and encouragements which ladies can so easily give, will fix him, in spite of himself...'

Marriage, implies John Dashwood (who is something of a spaniel himself, in his own marriage relationship), is a blood-sport in which women are the hunters, and the game men of rank and fortune. It is for Elinor to *secure* a husband, with true aim and cunning to *fix* him. If her quarry refuses to be lured, it is because she has not taken the trouble to make the bait attractive enough. It is, we feel, with the utmost patience and selfcontrol that Elinor bears with his conversation and his advice. Congratulating her on her friendship with Mrs Jennings, John Dashwood reveals a mind that runs on money:

'She seems a most valuable woman indeed. Her house, her style of living, all bespeak an exceeding good income; and it is an acquaintance that has not only been of great use to you hitherto, but in the end may prove materially advantageous...She must have a great deal to leave.'

As his interpretation of the word *valuable* shows, he is incapable of witnessing a kind action or hearing of a generous one, without imputing to it a motive connected with money. He is genuinely astonished to hear of Colonel Brandon's gift of Delaford living to

Edward Ferrars; he assures Elinor that Mrs Jennings's affection for Marianne and herself must be a sign of legacies to come. His constant application of material values to human relationships is more than comic—it becomes disgusting. Is the picture exaggerated? Does Jane Austen's satiric poise waver slightly, allowing hatred to enter and objective impartiality to leave her writing at moments such as this? It may have been that the portraits of John and Fanny Dashwood derive their strength from Jane Austen's dislike of persons she knew in real life, even, perhaps, members of her own family. Most of us have met people of outlook as squalid as the Dashwoods at some time in our lives, even if we have not been left to their mercies as Elinor and her family have been left by her father's death. Jane Austen's characterisation of John and Fanny Dashwood gains power from a sense of bitter exasperation, that finer, more sensitive people should have to defer to people of their type, and be forced to choose between the indignity of accepting or expecting their charities and the hardship of doing without them. *Sense and Sensibility* voices her resentment on this point most clearly, providing her at the same time with an opportunity to externalise her feelings and expose them to a process of artistic self-discipline.

Other characters, not all of them minor, reflect aspects of the theme of wealth and its uses. Robert Ferrars, his mother's favourite child, gives Elinor who meets him by chance at a jeweller's shop

the remembrance of a person and face, of strong natural, sterling insignificance, though adorned in the first style of fashion.

Willoughby, owner of a 'person of uncommon attraction, that open, affectionate, and lively manner which it was no merit to possess', is betrayed by habits of selfish extravagance. Edward Ferrars, 'a gentlemanlike and pleasing young man', is doomed by his dependence on his mother to low-spirits and dejection for years, until Lucy's marriage to his brother and Elinor's acceptance of him create in him 'such a genuine, flowing, grateful cheerfulness, as his friends had never witnessed in him before.' Plagued by his mother and sister to choose a profession or a wife that will enable him to make some display in society,

Edward remains loyally attached to Elinor and to her mother, a woman now poor, but still generous, improvident, and warmly sympathetic:

> He valued their kindness beyond any thing, and his greatest happiness was in being with them.

Jane Austen's attitude to money in marriage, which we considered in Chapter 2, is explicit in her comparison of Elinor's unspectacular but real contentment as Edward's wife with the material rewards that crown Lucy Steele's career of fawning and self-seeking:

> ...perseverance in humility of conduct and messages, in self-condemnation for Robert's offence, and gratitude for the unkindness she was treated with, procured her in time the haughty notice which overcame her by its graciousness, and led soon afterwards, by rapid degrees, to the highest state of affection and influence.

The deepening moral seriousness that underlies such satire as this, the growing conviction that true worth must learn to go unrecognised in society, are inseparable from Jane Austen's mature artistic achievement. Despite its unwieldy plot and its uneven surface—weaknesses due in each case to Jane Austen's immaturity at the time she published *Sense and Sensibility*—the novel is supported by the same moral convictions that will provide a framework for the livelier and seemingly lighthearted perfection of *Pride and Prejudice*.

# 6

## 'PRIDE AND PREJUDICE'

We have already, on pages 44–5, considered the ironic implications of the provocative sentence with which *Pride and Prejudice* begins:

It is a truth universally acknowledged, that a single man in possession of a good fortune, must be in want of a wife.

The atmosphere it generates, the warning it gives that highly explosive material may lie hidden beneath a decorous, polite mode of expression, are justified by the story that follows, and by Jane Austen's method of telling it. We will come to identify its serious, yet playful tone particularly with the character and behaviour of the heroine, Elizabeth Bennet.

Until Mrs Bennet and her five daughters gather to discuss the Meryton assembly ball at which Jane Bennet has been distinguished by the attentions of Mr Bingley and his sisters, wealthy newcomers to nearby Netherfield Park, Jane's younger sister Elizabeth has played but a minor part in the unfolding pattern of the story. We have learned from the preceding pages only that she has a lively sense of humour, for although Mr Bingley's aristocratic friend, Fitzwilliam Darcy, has pronounced Elizabeth not pretty enough to dance with, the ungracious remark has been retold and ridiculed by Elizabeth herself among her friends, as reflecting much more to Mr Darcy's disadvantage than to her own. But now, as her mother overflows with premature and exaggerated hopes regarding Jane's chances of marrying Bingley, as her younger sisters exult over their own triumphs at the ball, as even Jane shows herself to be 'gratified...though in a quieter way' by Bingley's admiration of her, Elizabeth alone 'felt Jane's pleasure'. An affectionate heart and true generosity of mind set Elizabeth Bennet apart from and above the rest of her family; her concerns will provide the central interest of the novel.

Elizabeth has a high opinion of her own ability to read the

characters and motives of other people; she confidently declares, when questioned on the subject, 'Yes; but intricate characters are the *most* amusing.' The comedy of errors in which she is soon involved proves her weakness and fallibility, and teaches her that real life does not permit a stance of detached observation. For Elizabeth, unlike her father, is no disillusioned cynic. On all important matters she thinks and feels deeply, to a few chosen people she is closely and affectionately bound. In spite of herself, Elizabeth will be drawn into conflicts in which she cannot remain an observer, and will find herself fighting to defend the right to self-respect and high principles that, in the world of Jane Austen's novels, constitute the moral basis of a heroine's life.

'His pride', said Miss Lucas, 'does not offend *me* so much as pride often does, because there is an excuse for it. One cannot wonder that so very fine a young man, with family, fortune, every thing in his favour, should think highly of himself. If I may so express it, he has a *right* to be proud.'

'That is very true,' replied Elizabeth, 'and I could easily forgive *his* pride if he had not mortified *mine*.'

Despite her apparently lighthearted dismissal of the incident, Darcy's slight has hurt Elizabeth's vanity and initiated the prejudice she will nourish against him. She now meets George Wickham, the orphan son of the steward who had formerly managed Darcy's family property at Pemberley in Kent. According to Wickham, now an army officer stationed at Meryton, his early hopes of a future as a clergyman have been maliciously and dishonestly destroyed by Darcy. Elizabeth, prejudiced against Darcy by the earlier incident, believes every word of these accusations, and her dislike of Darcy is increased when she discovers that he has actively intervened to separate Bingley from her sister Jane. These circumstances combine with her early pique to pitch Elizabeth into a state of active hostility towards Darcy. The balance of her judgment seems permanently lost—for she does not *wish* to think well of him—and it is at this inauspicious period in their acquaintance that Darcy unexpectedly proposes marriage to her, and is, predictably, refused.

While Elizabeth has been moving from dislike to hatred in her feelings towards Darcy, he has found his original indifference to her beauty changing to admiration. Her wit and her liveliness attract him, and he learns to respect her individuality and finally to love her, in spite of his disgust at the vulgarity of her mother and her younger sisters, and at her father's irresponsibility. He is unaware that her polite manners mask deep dislike and resentment, and believes that Elizabeth, like every other woman of his acquaintance, would be glad to accept his affection, and the wealth and rank that must accompany it. Darcy does not expect a refusal:

He spoke well, but there were feelings besides those of the heart to be detailed, and he was not more eloquent on the subject of tenderness than of pride. His sense of her inferiority—of its being a degradation—of the family obstacles which judgment had always opposed to inclination, were dwelt on with a warmth which seemed due to the consequence he was wounding, but was very unlikely to recommend his suit...

She could easily see that he had no doubt of a favourable answer. He *spoke* of apprehension and anxiety, but his countenance expressed real security.

Darcy's proposal and Elizabeth's refusal of it provide the climax towards which the pride and the prejudice they have in common has been leading. The rest of the novel pieces together the stages by which Darcy comes to a humbler way of thinking and Elizabeth, stripped of her prejudices by a better knowledge of his character and her own, grants him her respect, her gratitude, and finally, her affection. Darcy's progress towards good sense is not detailed, like Elizabeth's, from within; until the novel's end, as Elizabeth tours Derbyshire with her relations, the Gardiners, and meets Darcy again while visiting Pemberley, as Lydia Bennet elopes with Wickham and the money is mysteriously found to marry them and establish him in a new profession, as Lady Catherine de Bourgh undertakes a journey from Hunsford to Longbourn in order to scotch a rumour that her nephew Darcy is to marry Elizabeth, and as Bingley returns to Netherfield and renews his attentions to Jane, the reader guesses and speculates with Elizabeth until it is revealed that Darcy has been responsible for arranging Lydia's marriage, buying Wickham his army commission, and bringing his friend back to Netherfield.

Although the tension in Elizabeth's mind is never allowed to relax entirely, the role she plays in the novel after her refusal of Darcy's proposal of marriage is a passive one. She, who has been an active antagonist in fighting for her own and Jane's cause, must now accept her share (with the rest of her family) in the social disgrace of Lydia's elopement. She learns at second-hand, as the result of a chance slip of Lydia's, that Darcy had been present at the wedding. She is even uncertain and doubtful regarding Darcy's intentions in returning to Hertfordshire. Comedy is still present, as in the scenes of Lydia's return to Longbourn, and in Lady Catherine's interview with Elizabeth; but the author's concern in this part of the novel is to engage Elizabeth in reflection and a thoughtful reconstruction of the past. Her mood has changed from lighthearted gaiety to a philosophic resignation:

...she found, what has been sometimes found before, that an event to which she had looked forward with impatient desire, did not in taking place, bring all the satisfaction she had promised herself. It was consequently necessary to name some other period for the commencement of actual felicity; to have some other point on which her wishes and hopes might be fixed, and by again enjoying the pleasure of anticipation, console herself for the present, and prepare for another disappointment.

*Prepare for another disappointment*: Elizabeth is disillusioned and unhappy. Until the penultimate chapter of the novel has her 'spirits soon rising to playfulness again' on the happy conclusion of her errors and misunderstandings, *Pride and Prejudice* moves slowly, each incident accompanied by deep reflection and re-arrangement of earlier conclusions.

Besides providing the novel's plot with its climax, Elizabeth's rejection of Darcy's proposal of marriage substantiates her claim to selfrespect, proves the sincerity of her passionately held personal code, and illustrates that independence of spirit we have seen asserted on previous occasions, in her indifference to the sneers of Bingley's sisters and in her refusal of Mr Collins's proposal of marriage. It has been Charlotte Collins's opinion, when considering the possibility of Darcy's being in love with Elizabeth, 'that all her friend's dislike would vanish, if she could suppose him to be in her power'. Elizabeth's refusal emphasises the gap between Charlotte's attitude to marriage and her own, and demonstrates her spiritual independence on this point of the social attitudes and opinions that bind Charlotte. Elizabeth's personality generates the special atmosphere of *Pride and Prejudice*, a novel tense with hidden, unspoken conflicts. It is she who is in perpetual opposition to such universally 'acknowledged' facts of life as the view that 'a single man in possession of a good fortune must be in need of a wife'; her views on marriage, on society, and on her own position in society reflect her independent spirit and her critical intelligence, and they are masked (for her own safety) behind the external surface of good manners, polite acquiescence to her superiors in age and status, and of feminine diffidence that society expects to see—and that she presents for its inspection. Occasionally, when her judgment deems it right, the mask is put aside and mere propriety gives way to what is sympathetic, human, and necessary: Jane is ill at Netherfield, having been sent there on horseback during a downpour by her mother, in the hope that she will have to delay her return home, and thereby improve her chances of snaring Bingley. Elizabeth walks to Netherfield, in order to see her:

'How can you be so silly', cried her mother, 'as to think of such a thing, in all this dirt! You will not be fit to be seen when you get there.'

'I shall be very fit to see Jane—which is all I want.'

To Caroline Bingley, Elizabeth's affectionate action seems to show only 'an abominable sort of conceited independence, a most country town indifference to decorum'. Darcy doubts whether she has been right to venture so far, unaccompanied. Bingley alone recognises in her coming 'an affection for her sister that is very pleasing'. His view of the matter is the right one, and his the attitude that Darcy himself adopts when his uncertain opinion of Elizabeth begins to incline towards love.

We see, in this way, that Elizabeth can deliberately set decorum aside when her good sense and affections tell her that she should, and that a few discriminating people admire and love her for doing so. But we perceive at the same time that the majority do not think in this way; they are only too ready to condemn affection when it defies decorum and convention, and so—like Elinor Dashwood in *Sense and Sensibility*—Elizabeth is often forced to deceive. Disappointed by Charlotte Lucas's recent marriage to Mr Collins, and disillusioned by Wickham's defection to Miss

King, Elizabeth hides her sense of isolation and betrayal beneath a cynicism that resembles her father's, but that she does not feel:

'Pray, my dear aunt, what is the difference in matrimonial affairs, between the mercenary and the prudent motive? Where does discretion end, and avarice begin?'

Invited by Mr Bennet to share his amusement at a rumour that she is to marry Darcy, Elizabeth finds that 'it was necessary to laugh, when she would rather have cried'. The great difference between Elinor and Elizabeth—a difference that affects the temper and tone of the entire novel—is, that Elizabeth occasionally deceives by choice; she loves to tease, to mimic, and to laugh, and her conversation is often (especially when she dislikes or despises her opponent) as full of hidden traps and dangers as a mine-field. She takes mischievous delight in playing a part, as when she informs Darcy that she has

'always seen a great similarity in the turn of our minds. We are each of an unsocial, taciturn disposition, unwilling to speak, unless we expect to say something that will amaze the whole room',

a deliberately provocative, obviously false statement that Darcy immediately takes note of—and remembers, as his remark, made much later on at Hunsford ('I have had the pleasure of your acquaintance long enough to know, that you find great enjoyment in occasionally professing opinions which in fact are not your own') reveals quite clearly. Elizabeth's playful, obvious deceptions represent a means of venting irritation or administering a rebuke without transgressing the rules of decorum and convention; they pass as lively repartee with the hearers, and fasten themselves only in the memories of those people they are intended to arouse or provoke. Her wit has a sharpness, a scintillating edge that makes her seem a graceful duellist, daring often to take the initiative in a battle of wills, where Elinor Dashwood was merely on the defensive, and too often wounded and discouraged. Elizabeth's opponents are many, and their authority over her is socially 'accepted'—there is, for example, no permissible weapon she can use to fend off her mother's attacks, not even her wit, nothing but silence (interpreted as stubborn obstinacy) and the lucky chance by which a usually indifferent father supports her refusal to marry Mr Collins. The portrayal of such an isolated heroine could constitute a direct invitation to both author and reader to indulge in self-identification and sentimentality. This does not happen, for Elizabeth Bennet is treated throughout the novel with a sympathetic, but unfaltering irony.

Like Catherine Morland and Marianne Dashwood, Elizabeth makes mistakes and corrects them, as part of the emotional education that prepares Jane Austen's heroines for adult responsibilities. Conscious of her intelligence, proud of her penetrating eye, Elizabeth thinks too well of her own judgment, which is warped and rendered useless by the first blow her vanity receives. She never asks herself why Wickham's revelations regarding Darcy's character win her ready acceptance. Wickham hints the worst, and Elizabeth finds 'the interest of the subject increase'. By habit a critic of society, she does not pause to examine the feelings that place her for once in agreement with it on the question of Darcy's character:

'Upon my word I say no more *here* than I might say in any house in the neighbourhood, except Netherfield. He is not at all liked in Hertfordshire. Every body is disgusted with his pride. You will not find him more favourably spoken of by any one.'

Jane urges caution, but Elizabeth is confident that her own conclusions regarding Darcy are correct:

'It is difficult indeed—it is distressing. One does not know what to think.'
    'I beg your pardon; one knows exactly what to think.'

Elizabeth is 'determined to hate' him. Her faults are faults of judgment, however, not of character, so that even as her errors provide the comic stages by which the plot progresses, her ideas of right thinking and behaviour place Elizabeth on a moral plane very far above that occupied by most of the inhabitants of Longbourn, Meryton, Netherfield, and Hunsford. Jane Austen points out where Elizabeth goes wrong, as in her reminder that she is 'less clear-sighted perhaps' in Wickham's case than in Charlotte Lucas's, on the question of marriage for the sake of financial security. But Elizabeth, despite her errors of judgment, is morally superior to her society, and we will see her resist all attempts to make her accept that society's valuation of her as a saleable article, available to the first comer at a certain fixed price.

The structure of the novel accommodates itself exactly to Jane Austen's intention. Elizabeth's independent spirit, which inspires her solitary walk to Netherfield as it does her ill-judged championship of Wickham, manifests itself most importantly in her rejection of Darcy's proposal of marriage, which is in effect a challenge to the selfish meanness of the motives that govern marriage in their society. It teaches Darcy that she is unaffected by considerations of rank or wealth, and he learns with surprise that (despite the flattery he is accustomed to receive from those around him) he does not satisfy *her* standards of right—as distinct from fashionable—behaviour. He is led to reconsider his attitude to Elizabeth, and to value her even more highly than he had done before she refused him. As he becomes involved with her in a relationship that matures them both, and is later to be confirmed by marriage, they are surrounded by other couples whose experience and example illustrate in various ways the difficulties and dangers attending the choice of a marriage-partner. Each, when they come to marry, has rejected the opinions of society, which had attempted to guide or force them towards other choices.

Elizabeth's caution and extreme fastidiousness on the question of marriage originates from her acute sense of the inequalities, perpetually before her eyes, of her parents' marriage. She resembles her father in her lively wit and her appreciation of the ridiculous: Mr Bennet found Mr Collins

as absurd as he had hoped, and he listened to him with the keenest enjoyment...except in an occasional glance at Elizabeth, requiring no partner in his pleasure.

They are good friends, almost confederates, as Mrs Bennet has occasion to complain. But for all his wit, Mr Bennet's view of life is empty and cynical:

'For what do we live, but to make sport for our neighbours, and laugh at them in our turn?'

He can contribute nothing to Elizabeth's moral education beyond the example of an experience to be avoided. Life having cheated him of married happiness and selfrespect, he derives a malicious delight from seeing other people similarly hurt and humiliated. He is a foil for his idealistic, high-principled daughter, providing in his casual dismissal of the responsibilities of marriage and parental duty an unconscious spur to her determination to act and think differently. Unlike Elizabeth, who revolts inwardly against her mother's free display of weak judgment and low standards of behaviour, Mr Bennet can observe his wife with amused detachment. His cynical indifference is shaken, but not destroyed, by Lydia's elopement with Wickham; although he realises that his daughter's weakness is the direct result of his wife's indulgence and his own irresponsibility, Mr Bennet's impulse towards regret and self-blame will, as he says himself, 'pass away soon enough'. It is worth noting that the most deeply moving moment in the novel occurs, not between Elizabeth and Darcy nor between Jane and Bingley, but between Elizabeth and her father. Roused from his selfish lethargy for the first time by genuine concern for another person, Mr Bennet urges his favourite daughter to refuse Darcy's proposal:

'...let me advise you to think better of it. I know your disposition, Lizzy. I know that you could be neither happy nor respectable, unless you truly esteemed your husband; unless you looked up to him as a superior. Your lively talents would place you in the greatest danger in an unequal marriage. You could scarcely escape discredit and misery. My child, let me not have the grief of seeing *you* unable to respect your partner in life. You know not what you are about.'

Elizabeth has often been allowed access to her father's thoughts, understands his prejudices and his habits of mind, even enjoys his confidence—up to a point. Here, at last, the barriers between parent and child are down, and Elizabeth is permitted to see, in all its desolate waste, the barrenness of her father's life.

Elizabeth learns another important lesson when her friend and special confidante, Charlotte Lucas, marries Mr Collins, a clergyman and vicar of Hunsford in Kent. Mr Collins treats his patroness, Lady Catherine de Bourgh, with the awed adoration that others reserve for a deity. Discussing her with Elizabeth, he is on one occasion so moved that words fail him and he is 'obliged to walk about the room' in an effort to regain selfcontrol;

he arranges for Lady Catherine's pleasure 'such little elegant compliments as may be adapted to ordinary occasions' much as a devout cleric might compose prayers for use in chapel or church—we cannot miss the flavour in that last phrase, *adapted to ordinary occasions*, so reminiscent of the wording of the Book of Common Prayer. His plans to marry have been blessed by Lady Catherine's approval, and her refusal to 'sanction' any proceeding (such as, for instance, a marriage between Elizabeth and her nephew, Darcy) would in his opinion render it immoral. And yet, despite his comic mixture of self-importance and cringing humility, Mr Collins is socially respectable. Patronised by Lady Catherine, deferred to by Mrs Philips, Elizabeth's aunt, approved of by Mrs Bennet as a suitable husband for Elizabeth herself, regarded by the (admittedly easy-going) society of Meryton as a clever and intelligent man, Mr Collins even assumes the responsibility of voicing general social opinion: he enlarges on the importance of his own vocation, reminds Elizabeth with great tactlessness and crudity—and in the middle of his own proposal of marriage—that her fortune is 'unhappily so small that it will in all likelihood undo the effects of your loveliness and amiable qualifications' (a sentiment reminiscent of John Dashwoods' speeches to Elinor in *Sense and Sensibility*), and proffers 'respectable' opinions and advice on the subject of Lydia's elopement. When Elizabeth endures without comment her mother's reproaches for having refused him, she is asserting her right to reject society's valuation of her.

Believing Charlotte Lucas's ideas on all important matters to coincide exactly with her own, and inclined to playful deception herself, Elizabeth has hitherto interpreted her friend's 'practical' philosophy of life as merely characteristic of a lively wit:

'In nine cases out of ten, a woman had better shew *more* affection than she feels...Happiness in marriage is entirely a matter of chance...it is better to know as little as possible of the defects of the person with whom you are to pass your life.'

'You make me laugh, Charlotte; but it is not sound. You know it is not sound, and that you would never act in this way yourself.' ·

But Charlotte does *not* know, and when opportunity offers in the person of Mr Collins, she acts precisely according to her philosophy in accepting him. She defends her action to Elizabeth—'I am not romantic you know. I never was'—but in her own eyes it needs no justification. She has done the prudent, sensible thing in providing for her own future, and although Elizabeth is shocked and revolted and Mrs Bennet annoyed, there is no doubt that Charlotte's decision has the approbation of her own family and of society in general.

The match attracts comment from people of all ages, diverse interests, and different status. Charlotte's parents, Sir William and Lady Lucas, give their consent 'with a most joyful alacrity'. Mr Collins is comfortably off, respectably connected, and will inherit Longbourn estate on Mr Bennet's death. They are relieved to have Charlotte off their hands. Their 'joy' is quickly shown to spring from mercenary considerations, and from Sir William's love of ceremony and display. 'The whole family...were properly overjoyed on the occasion.' Again, on examination, we find that 'joy' has its roots in selfishness; Charlotte's brothers and sisters rejoice at the imminent removal of their plain elder sister, the boys because her marriage will free them from the irksome duty of providing for her single old age, the girls because it improves their chances of an earlier entrance into society. These motives are matched in their selfish crudity only by the reflections of the two people most concerned. Mr Collins is 'longing to publish his prosperous love' at Longbourn, so that Elizabeth may regret her own rejection of him. Charlotte, who values Mr Collins only as the means to financial security and an independent establishment, congratulates herself on securing both without 'having ever been handsome', that is, without possessing the beauty that women in her society are forced to display and trade on to gain these essentials. We would not be wrong to recall here the calculating tones of John Dashwood as he assesses his sister Marianne's fallen market value, and we realise that the intelligent, sensible Charlotte has assessed *herself* according to similar values, and in doing so has identified herself with the standards of the marketplace. If Mr Collins broods more on revenge than on love, Charlotte in her turn sees him as a prize in a lottery rather than as a husband, or even, indeed, as a man.

As the news spreads by degrees beyond the family circle, favourable reactions to the marriage range from Lady Catherine's condescending approval to Jane Bennet's characteristically optimistic belief and sincere desire that Charlotte will be happy. Criticism of the match comes mainly from Longbourn. Mrs Bennet seeks relief in an orgy of selfpity and an unwearying persecution of Elizabeth, who should (she says peevishly) have accepted Collins. Mr Bennet forgets compassion in the pleasure of indulging his malicious wit at Charlotte's expense. True respect for Charlotte and real concern for her integrity and her future happiness is evident in the reaction of Elizabeth alone: 'Engaged to Mr Collins! my dear Charlotte, impossible!' That is Elizabeth's instinctive, unstudied response. Her 'sensible', practical friend has, incredibly, 'sacrificed every better feeling to worldly advantage'. Elizabeth insists on setting out the facts clearly, unequivocally. To Jane, who contends that the marriage is perfectly in keeping with Charlotte's prudence and Collins's respectability, she retorts:

'My dear Jane, Mr Collins is a conceited, pompous, narrow-minded, silly man; you know he is, as well as I do; and you must feel, as well as I do, that the woman who marries him, cannot have a proper way of thinking. You shall not defend her, though it is Charlotte Lucas. You shall not, for the sake of one individual, change the meaning of principle and integrity, nor endeavour to persuade yourself or me, that selfishness is prudence, and insensibility of danger, security for happiness.'

When Elizabeth later visits Charlotte and Mr Collins at Hunsford Parsonage, she is forced to admit that her friend, despite her own gloomy forebodings, appears contented with her lot:

When Mr Collins said any thing of which his wife might reasonably be ashamed, which certainly was not unseldom, she involuntarily turned her eye on Charlotte. Once or twice she could discern a faint blush; but in general Charlotte wisely did not hear...Elizabeth in the solitude of her chamber had to meditate upon Charlotte's degree of contentment, to understand her address in guiding, and composure in bearing with her husband, and to acknowledge that it was all done very well.

Jane Austen's picture of Elizabeth's distress at the idea of Charlotte's marriage to Collins is an excellent instance of her habit of gazing through the social interminglings of the community to the moral standards they fulfil, or deny and betray. When her friend surrenders to the temptations of 'worldly advantage', Elizabeth experiences a sense of betrayal; Charlotte has never had the moral fastidiousness Elizabeth has believed her to possess, never in reality been the ally she had thought her against the pressures exerted upon them by society to lower their standards and abandon their selfrespect. Charlotte's complacency shows, on the contrary, an *acceptance* of the inferior rating she has been granted by a money-minded society incapable of appreciating her intelligence. Disillusioned, Elizabeth turns for support to the familiar virtues of her relations, the Gardiners, and to Jane who shares them:

Her disappointment in Charlotte made her turn with fonder regard to her sister, of whose rectitude and delicacy she was sure her opinion could never be shaken.

Her surprise at Charlotte's engagement and her later acknow-ledgment that Charlotte seems perfectly content as the wife of Mr Collins do not alter Elizabeth's own attitude to marriage, nor make it approximate more to Charlotte's. She has learned that her own ability to judge character and predict the actions and feelings of her acquaintances is far from perfect; and this is an important step on the way to self-knowledge, to her meditation on the contents of Darcy's explanatory letter, her recognition at last of the extent of her own misjudging, and her penitent admission: 'Till this moment, I never knew myself.'

Elizabeth's career can be seen as a continuous refusal to accept such a valuation of herself as Charlotte has accepted. Miss Bingley and Mrs Hurst, representatives of the world of wealth and fashion, agree heartily with Darcy's dictum that the vulgarity of Mrs Bennet's relations 'must very materially lessen' her daughters' chances of 'marrying men of any consideration in the world'. Caroline Bingley, whose jealousy of Elizabeth prompts her to play on Darcy's greatest weakness, his pride of rank, accuses her to him of 'conceited independence' and of 'self-sufficiency without fashion'; she feels that Elizabeth has no right to think well of herself, an independent spirit such as hers being appropriate only to a woman of higher rank and greater fortune. Ironically, her remarks on the inappropriateness of Elizabeth's behaviour to her social sphere merely serve to direct Darcy's thoughts towards its appropriateness to his! Elizabeth, on her side, treats Bingley's sisters and Darcy himself with the same cool indifference. When she goes to Rosings, she is 'quite equal to the scene', and is not to be bullied by Lady Catherine nor overwhelmed by the grandeur of the house. Lady Catherine has perception enough to miss in Elizabeth the alarm and the flattering obsequiousness she is used to inspiring in her social inferiors. Elizabeth's refusal to conform and to defer unquestioningly to her will spells danger to the values that hold Lady Catherine's world of rank and wealth together, danger, that is, if she is allowed to go on in this shocking way and to succeed in it. Lady Catherine's journey to Longbourn is undertaken to eliminate a nuisance; Elizabeth's triumph lies in forcing her to accept defeat at the hands of an equal.

Elizabeth's refusal of Darcy's proposal of marriage can thus be recognised as the culmination of her struggle to assert her right to selfrespect. In his pride and his arrogance—carried to extremes in his aunt, and in her rightly derided by Elizabeth—Darcy represents the values that oppose her. There is no affection on her side—yet—to shield him from her irony or her anger; we have had occasion to see, during her conversations with Jane and with Mr Bennet, that Elizabeth does not hurt where she loves. She is unimpressed by the rumours of Darcy's wealth, by his property, least of all by his rank. Her polite indifference, which is maintained outwardly even when she has begun actively to dislike him, makes her intriguing to a man accustomed to the flattery of every woman he meets.

The point is made sufficiently clear on several occasions during Elizabeth's enforced stay at Netherfield. Consider the scene in Vol. 1, Chapter 10, for instance, when none of Miss Bingley's relentlessly flattering interruptions on the subject of his family, his house, his library, even his handwriting, can distract Darcy from the letter he is writing to his sister, but a single observation from Elizabeth—a warm, amused sentence addressed to Bingley that reveals her liking for *him*—draws Darcy into an argument on the nature of actual and feigned humility; it is Elizabeth who must remind him that his letter is unfinished. Perpetually in unspoken opposition, they are in fact very much alike in their critical attitude to society. 'We neither of us perform to strangers', says Darcy, and this is true. Both are frank and out-spoken. Darcy cannot simulate emotions he does not feel—'disguise of every sort is my abhorrence'; Elizabeth would echo this, but as we have already seen, she is forced by her femininity and her dependent status in society, to take occasional refuge in polite disguise. While social distinctions and their own prejudices appear to hold them apart in apparently unalterable opposition to each other, the very patterning of the novel establishes a series of links between them. Darcy's conversations with Bingley, balanced by Elizabeth's with Jane, establish them as a more interesting pair, and harder to please; a similar sense of their responsibilities makes Elizabeth urge that Lydia's proposed holiday in Brighton should be given up, and sends Darcy to London to seek out Wickham and arrange his marriage with Lydia; each is disci-plined and matures through a better knowledge of the other's character; and having once met the Gardiners, Elizabeth's relations, and seen Darcy's embarrassment at Lady Catherine's ill breeding match Elizabeth's shudders over her mother's behaviour, the reader is far more conscious of their natural affinity for one another than of the social considerations that keep them apart.

The qualities she has in common with Darcy strike Elizabeth herself, however, only after she has refused him and has come to learn his true character. There is, perhaps, an element of triumph, of wish-fulfilment, in Jane Austen's presentation of Elizabeth as conqueror and Darcy as her victim in their interview at Hunsford Parsonage: Mr Darcy, who once slighted her on the grounds of her personal appearance, has proposed marriage and been spurned! But Elizabeth's moment of triumph is shortlived (she receives Darcy's letter the following day, and from that time onward is thinking more of her own errors and weaknesses than of his), and extends besides, in its repudiation of Darcy's wealth and its recollection of Jane's unhappiness, beyond purely selfish or personal limits.

When Elizabeth, on her visit to Pemberley, sees the reality she has spurned in abstract, she is awakened in a new way to the compliment of Darcy's affection and respect. The beauty of the house and its grounds lies in a natural excellence developed, without distortion or artificial elaboration, by the wealth and the cultivated taste of the Darcy family; and this associates itself in Elizabeth's mind with what she now knows to be the real disposition of its owner. She realises that in preferring her to all others, a generous affection has triumphed in Darcy over considerations of status and of empty decorum; and *we* perceive that Darcy possesses, besides a capacity for affection, his family's good sense and discriminating taste. His affection and respect for Elizabeth are extended later to the Gardiners who, like her, defeat the expectations of society, persisting in being cultured, well-bred, and a credit to their friends in spite of their trading connections. In Darcy, finally, Elizabeth finds her best and truest ally, who brings to her cause all the zeal and devotion of a convert:

'By you, I was properly humbled. I came to you without a doubt of my reception. You shewed me how insufficient were all my pretensions to please a woman worthy of being pleased.'

We have seen, in this way, how the progress of Elizabeth's acquaintance with Darcy, as developed by Jane Austen, illustrates and explores several important themes: that vanity, equally with pride, distorts a balanced judgment; that mutual respect and affection constitute the best and safest basis for marriage; and that the individual has a right to self-respect and self-expression within the rules of convention and social decorum.

The second of these is fully and satisfactorily explored through vivid characterisation that makes the fullest possible use of dialogue, and a brilliant satiric exposure of marriage in the society of the age. Mr and Mrs Bennet, Charlotte Lucas and Mr Collins, Bingley and Jane Bennet, Lydia and Wickham, Mr and Mrs Gardiner, are all brought under the critical gaze of Elizabeth, who in any case relishes her role as a 'studier of character', but to whom they represent useful signposts to the sloughs of despond and the delectable mountains she may meet in her own progress towards the ideal marriage relationship. At the same time, these characters help to define Elizabeth's personality. Contrasted with her sister, for example, Elizabeth proves to be the more intelligent and discriminating of the two; to Jane's uncritical, enthusiastic praise of Caroline Bingley, Elizabeth 'listened in silence, but was not convinced'. She thinks well of Bingley, who has the sense to appreciate Jane, but she is not blind to his weak irresolution. Bingley's marriage to Jane, although a happy one, will unite less intelligent minds and much less interesting personalities than Elizabeth's to Darcy.

Similarly, Elizabeth's conversations with Charlotte Lucas on the subject of marriage reveal her finer moral fibre. Despite Charlotte's good sense, and the fact that the reader sympathises with her situation, her action in accepting Mr Collins reveals the coarse insensitivity that lay unperceived all the while beneath her practical, wittily non-'romantic' approach to life. For Mr Collins is a joke, comic in his claims to respectability, and in his filial devotion to his quarrelsome father's disputes, comic in his unique blend of servility and pompous self-consequence. It is only Charlotte's blunted sensibility that permits her to contemplate marriage with him, and to find contentment as his wife.

Lydia Bennet presents an interesting example of Jane Austen's developing skill in drawing character. Lydia's elopement with Wickham typifies the marriage relationship wherein physical desire has outrun reason and good sense, repeats her parents' folly in the second generation, and contrasts with the gradual recognition by Elizabeth and Darcy of each other's true worth through a reappraisal of their own weaknesses. But besides her part in the larger pattern of the novel, Lydia is vividly realised in speech and action, as an exuberant, vigorous girl with a mature body and an undeveloped mind, selfcentred, inconsiderate, wishing only to be noticed and admired:

'And in the first place, let us hear what has happened to you all, since you went away. Have you seen any pleasant men? Have you had any flirting? I was in great hopes that one of you would have got a husband before you came back. Jane will be quite an old maid soon, I declare. She is almost three and twenty! Lord, how ashamed I should be of not being married before three and twenty!...'

Lydia's youth and her animal spirits form her chief attraction, and her judgment is too immature for her to be expected to make moral decisions. Jane Austen convicts Lydia of silliness, rather than of sin; her neglect of such practical matters as Wickham's lack of funds indicates ignorance and inexperience, not a fine moral nature. The moral responsibility for the whole episode of her elopement rests squarely on the shoulders of Mr Bennet, who knew his daughter's weakness perfectly well, and should have had her properly controlled. Elizabeth's thoughtful conversation with her father about Lydia's plans to visit Brighton, the intervention of the Gardiners in the arrangements for her wedding, the patience with which her father and sisters treat her after it are all indications of a tacit recognition of her immaturity. Lydia exerts that kind of claim on the good nature of those around her that any child in trouble exerts on any responsible adult. Elizabeth and Jane, who make their decisions independently and responsibly, are treated quite differently by their creator; indeed Elizabeth, in her readiness to believe ill of those against whom she is already prejudiced, is more severely censured than Lydia in her elopement. A *moral* contrast is drawn between Elizabeth and Charlotte Lucas, far more pointed and deeply defined than the inequality (in age and intelligence) between Elizabeth and Lydia.

Lydia plays an important part in the structure of the novel—her elopement, disastrous as it seems at the time to any hope that the reader might have entertained of Elizabeth's eventually marrying Darcy, provides him with the means of winning Elizabeth's gratitude and, with it, her love. He realises that an act performed in Elizabeth's service would be worth performing for that reason alone, even at the cost of associating himself with Wickham and the least admirable member of her despised family. Lydia's careless chatter gives Elizabeth the first hint that Darcy was present at her wedding in London, and sets in motion the reflections that lead to Elizabeth's acceptance of Darcy's second proposal:

'Lizzy, I never gave *you* an account of my wedding, I believe. You were not by, when I told mamma, and the others, all about it—'

Although Lydia has impressed us already as a thoughtless and foolish chatterer in earlier appearances in the novel, her slip betrays an element of contrivance. It is one of the very few points in *Pride and Prejudice* at which the underlying framework of the artist's plan has been insufficiently concealed. In the novel as a whole, we are overwhelmed by the wealth and liveliness of the dialogue; conversations carry the story smoothly and swiftly along, illuminating character and incident, bringing Elizabeth, especially, to vivid life. So naturally does the story develop that we only perceive on very close examination (or when a 'slip' like Lydia's reminds us to watch for it) how tightly the novel has been organised and with what mathematical precision events and personalities have been worked together to serve the author's intention.

Lady Catherine de Bourgh and Mrs Bennet, for example, are two ladies whom birth and fortune have placed socially far apart. Yet they have much in common, being equally illbred, mercenary and overbearing, equally fond of getting their own way in everything and of bullying those who oppose their right to do so. It is a fine ironic touch that when, for a brief moment, fate brings them together, they communicate at first through an interpreter, and that interpreter is Elizabeth:

> Mrs Bennet all amazement, though flattered by having a guest of such high importance, received her with the utmost politeness. After sitting for a moment in silence, she said very stiffly to Elizabeth,
> 'I hope you are well, Miss Bennet. That lady I suppose is your mother.'
> Elizabeth replied very concisely that she was.
> 'And *that* I suppose is one of your sisters.'
> 'Yes, madam,' said Mrs Bennet, delighted to speak to Lady Catherine.

Elizabeth is the very person that each would have liked to have made a victim of her will, Mrs Bennet in forcing her to marry Mr Collins, Lady Catherine to give up Mr Darcy. Yet it is Elizabeth who must act as each lady's advocate with the other, defending her mother's family to Lady Catherine during their conversation in the garden, and later inventing politenesses on their visitor's behalf for her mother's satisfaction.

Another character, indisputably minor but interesting in a very special way, is Elizabeth's sister, Mary Bennet. Plain, pedantic, Mary has little reason to be vain. Yet she is *vain*, of the accomplishments she has laboriously acquired; her eagerness to display them at Netherfield contributes to Elizabeth's sense of shame at her family's behaviour on that evening, besides helping to confirm the contempt in which they are all held by Mr Darcy. Her affectation of learning makes her conversation a source of entertainment to the reader, though it bores all her sisters, even Jane and Elizabeth; and yet, what Mary has to say is sometimes very much to the point. Her addition to Elizabeth's conversation with Charlotte Lucas on the subject of Darcy's pride (which we quoted on page 82) is an illustration of her function in the novel—

'That is very true', replied Elizabeth, 'and I could easily forgive *his* pride, if he had not mortified *mine*.'

'Pride', observed Mary, who piqued herself upon the solidity of her reflections, 'is a very common failing I believe. By all that I have ever read, I am convinced that it is very common indeed, that human nature is particularly prone to it, and that there are very few of us who do not cherish a feeling of self-complacency on the score of some quality or other, real or imaginary. Vanity and pride are different things, though the words are often used synonimously.'

Elizabeth would not, perhaps, have been quite so ready to condemn Darcy for his pride if she had taken Mary's timely observation to heart and reflected a little on her own vanity. It is only when she has been brought to recognise that her prejudice has had its beginnings in vanity that she regains peace of mind and her judgment steadies at last. Jane Austen's handling of Mary Bennet represents a significant advance on her introduction of an amusing but unnecessary character such as Charlotte Palmer in *Sense and Sensibility*. It is not that *Pride and Prejudice* derives any moral strength from Mary's opinions, which are quotations of extracts she has made from books and learned by heart. In situations that call for spontaneous affection and compassion (look, for instance, at her remarks to Elizabeth on the subject of Lydia's elopement) Mary's morality is empty and cold. She is remembered as a comic character, the only one among the five Bennet girls who might have been persuaded to accept Mr Collins —a reflection that immediately does away with any claims she might have had to seriousness or to good sense. But, although her appearances are but few in the course of the novel, she never does appear without contributing in a positive way to its pattern. Her remarks on vanity pedantically state a theme and utter a warning, her own vanity helps the plot along, and her personality defines by contrast the characters of her livelier, more attractive sisters. She is, in her own way, as much a bore as her mother and her sister Lydia—they all weary the listener. Such a family resemblance, like the more obvious one between Elizabeth and her father, recalls Marianne Dashwood's similarity to her mother in *Sense and Sensibility*, and will recur between the Crawfords in *Mansfield Park*, Isabella Knightley and Mr Woodhouse in *Emma*, and Sir Walter and Elizabeth Elliot in *Persuasion*. It reflects Jane Austen's interest in character, not only in the intricacies of individual personalities, but as a means of holding together and managing increasingly large groups of people.

We see this interest displayed in *Pride and Prejudice* itself, for Meryton seems full of people of whose general level of intelligence and breeding Mrs Bennet (the solace of whose life 'was visiting and news') is a typical example. Her undiscriminating mind—new clothes, in her eyes, confer greater validity on Lydia's marriage than the church's ceremonies, a well-dressed dinner and the beauty of her eldest daughter do her equal credit!—responds only to flattery or an opinion that chimes in with hers. Her vigorous enjoyment of Meryton's social life creates an atmosphere about her of bustling activity—in fact, creates Meryton itself; for besides the personalities of whom her conversation sketches brief pictures for the reader, we actually meet only the Lucas family, Elizabeth's aunt Philips and her husband, and the officers of Wickham's regiment. Some of these are 'mentioned only to be delineated', as in the case of 'broad-faced, stuffy uncle Philips, breathing port wine'; in the process they serve their purpose by creating an atmosphere of bustling, small town life. One character, however, is vividly realised as a personality in her own right. Mrs Philips is a tiny sketch, but important, and brilliantly executed. She is Mrs Bennet's chief source of gossip and news, being on the best possible terms with such retailers of it as the doctor's shop-assistant and Mr Bingley's housekeeper. Her easy manners and inelegant hospitality ('Mrs Philips protested that they would have a nice comfortable noisy game of lottery tickets, and a little bit of hot supper afterwards') are important in advancing Wickham's acquaintance with Elizabeth and Lydia, and her vulgarity and delight in gossip make her an appropriate sister for Mrs Bennet. Like Mrs Bennet, she is awed and impressed by the formality of Collins's manners, and she shares her sister's anxiety to see the girls married ('My aunt Philips wants you so to get husbands, you can't think,' says Lydia affectionately). The family resemblance helps to extend Mrs Bennet's way of thinking to Meryton, and Mrs Philips's circle, together with those of Lady Lucas and of Mrs Long (other intimates of Mrs Bennet) represent the society which comments, chorus-like, on the fortunes of the Bennet girls, the society which is so little discriminating as to prefer Bingley to the more reserved Mr Darcy, to make much of Wickham, and to welcome Mr Collins as a well-bred man.

In contrast to the unevenness that we noticed in *Sense and Sensibility*, the surface of *Pride and Prejudice* has been polished until it shines. Jane Austen herself commented that the novel seemed to her 'too light and bright and sparkling', a remark that suggests a deepening concern with moral issues and the inner workings of human personality, pointing forward, perhaps, to *Mansfield Park*, a novel to whose special features it seems to have contributed much. The portrait of George Wickham lends something to the more intricate character of Henry Crawford. Mrs Norris derives, with Lady Catherine de Bourgh, from Jane Austen's caricature of Lady Greville in her early writing, but no doubt the experience gained with the characters in *Pride and Prejudice* adds much to the skill with which Mrs Norris is drawn. In Fanny Price we discern an attempt to capture a gentle personality at the level of a heroine, after the encouraging success Jane Austen has had with Jane Bennet. But *Pride and Prejudice* is far from being a mere signpost on the way to somewhere else. Skilfully organised, convincing in every detail of character and incident, its serious intention appropriately and feelingly expressed through the ironic tone that illuminates both narrative and dialogue, *Pride and Prejudice* is a major work of art in its own right. It represents Jane Austen's first complete success along a certain line of experiment, the tracing of a young woman's progress from immaturity and inexperience to a better understanding of herself and her world.

# 7

## 'MANSFIELD PARK'

...the advantages of early hardship and discipline, and the consciousness of being born to struggle and endure. *Mansfield Park*, Vol. 3, Chapter 17

The world of *Mansfield Park* comprehends a greater variety of character and setting than any other novel Jane Austen had yet written or was to write. Much longer than *Pride and Prejudice*, its extra length could have resulted in tedium or diffuseness, but this does not happen. 'Major' characters are no longer drawn exclusively from among the young, but old and young alike are involved instead in an experience that puts their personalities and moral standards to a severe test; the difference in length goes into an extended and detailed exploration of character in action.

Fanny Price is not a 'heroine' in the sense that Elizabeth Bennet was at the centre of *Pride and Prejudice*; for although Jane Austen's ideals and values seem more nearly identified with Fanny's than with those of any other character in the novel, her interest as an artist dwells in turn on Fanny and on the two young women who flank and contrast with her—Maria Bertram and Mary Crawford. Sir Thomas Bertram and Mrs Norris, although directly responsible for the scheme of education that brings about Fanny's acute sense of insecurity, Maria's downfall, and Julia Bertram's rash elopement, are further from caricature than were Mr and Mrs Bennet in *Pride and Prejudice*, characters equally guilty of selfishness and irresponsibility that endanger younger and more helpless people. Sir Thomas's character develops in a manner that calls for a complex response from the reader of *Mansfield Park*, Mrs Norris is a psychological study of depth and insight; both contribute a great deal to our impression of a more detailed and subtly shaded canvas that any other Jane Austen has so far presented to our view.

There is space on a canvas such as this for an accumulation

of small but significant details, which diversify the subject without sacrificing the pattern that orders and unifies the picture as a whole. Thus, although *Mansfield Park* progresses at a leisurely pace that allows us to view its characters from many angles and examine incidents and events from many different points of view—although 'action' as far as the plot is concerned, must be delayed until our close analysis of each separate development is over—the general impression that this method creates, of slow and deliberate movement, is perfectly in keeping with the ceremonious rhythms of life at Mansfield Park, the country home of Sir Thomas and Lady Bertram. In a novel that extends, as this one does, not only in space but in time (it covers the period between Maria Ward's marriage to Sir Thomas and the marriages of their children—some thirty years—and takes in parallel incidents in the family life of Mr and Mrs Norris at Mansfield Parsonage, of the Prices at Portsmouth, and of Henry and Mary Crawford), a unifying principle is essential if the variously interesting characters and incidents of the novel are to coalesce; it would be only too easy for elements so rich in themselves to exist as independent units within the framework of the story, destroying in the process the total effect of the work of which they are the parts.

The principle upon which *Mansfield Park* is constructed—for it is, of course, *constructed*, despite the lifelike naturalness with which personalities meet and mingle, and incidents lead to other incidents—is neatly summed up in the words we quoted at the head of this chapter; the Bertram family at the Park, the Crawfords of London, and the Price family in Portsmouth illustrate through their several experiences and mental attitudes, 'the advantages of early hardship and discipline, and the consciousness of being born to struggle and endure'. The pessimistic realism of such a theme reminds us that Jane Austen's connection with the moralists of the eighteenth century—and especially with Dr Johnson—extended much further than a related choice of diction and common features of style. It may also, perhaps, reflect some period of depression and despondency in the novelist's experience that the writing of *Mansfield Park* helped her to sustain, the causes of which may possibly have lain in experiences similar to the special 'hardship' and privations that Fanny Price is called upon to endure in the novel.

For Fanny and her brother William, life is a struggle to be bravely met and patiently endured: Fanny strives to act according to a high moral code and a lively sense of duty despite neglect, persecution, and the temptations of selfpity and worldliness, William to follow the profession of a sailor honestly and independently, grateful for any stroke of good fortune but resigned and unresentful when a bad one comes his way. At ten years old, Fanny leaves her parents' poor home in Portsmouth to live at Mansfield Park, as the dependent niece of its owners, Sir Thomas and Lady Bertram. While her uncle launches William on his career, Fanny is brought up and educated by his good will and charity among her young cousins: Tom (the eldest son and Sir Thomas's heir), Edmund, Maria, and Julia, all but one of whom ignore her, patronise her, ridicule her ignorance, or exploit her gentle nature. The exception is Edmund, who has been kind to Fanny in the early days of her life at Mansfield, sympathises with her affection for her brother William, and knows her well enough to understand the strength of her sense and her intelligence. His encouragement and his steady affection help to protect Fanny from their aunt, Mrs Norris, to whom Lady Bertram has delegated the duty (eagerly seized upon by her sister) of supervising the girls' education. Mrs Norris believes it her duty to subject Fanny to ceaseless, petty tyranny, and continually reminds her of her poverty, her dependent status, and her supposed personal, intellectual, and social inferiority to Maria and Julia Bertram: as in the matter of the provision of a horse for Fanny's use, when her old grey pony dies—

Mrs Norris could not help thinking that some steady old thing might be found among the numbers belonging to the Park, that would do vastly well, or that one might be borrowed of the steward, or that perhaps Dr Grant might now and then lend them the poney he sent to the post. She could not but consider it as absolutely unnecessary, and even improper, that Fanny should have a regular lady's horse of her own in the style of her cousins. She was sure Sir Thomas had never intended it... 'Fanny must have a horse', was Edmund's only reply.

Edmund's championship of his defenceless and unhappy cousin earns him Fanny's special affection, a combination of 'all that was respectful, grateful, confiding, and tender', which gradually turns—unsuspected by him, and most carefully concealed by her—into love. At seventeen, Fanny Price is sensitive, shy, and retiring. She has discovered that patience under injustice is a mental habit worth cultivating, a discipline essential to her peace of mind if she is not to be perpetually provoked and made unbearably unhappy by the irritations of her daily life at Mansfield Park. She is convinced, too, that she cannot expect to be valued or loved by any one. A pitiful insecurity betrays itself when Fanny discusses with Edmund a proposal that she should leave the Park to live with her widowed Aunt Norris:

'...I cannot like it. I love this house and every thing in it. I shall love nothing there. You know how uncomfortable I feel with her.'

'I can say nothing for her manner to you as a child; but...you are now of an age to be treated better; I think she *is* behaving better already; and when you are her only companion, you *must* be important to her.'

'I can never be important to any one.'

'And what is to prevent you?'

'Every thing—my situation—my foolishness and awkwardness...Oh! cousin, if I am to go away, I shall remember your goodness, to the last moment of my life.'

'Why, indeed, Fanny, I should hope to be remembered at such a distance as the White house. You speak as if you were going two hundred miles off, instead of only across the park. But you will belong to us almost as much as ever...'

Edmund is quick to comfort and reassure Fanny, but he does not hide his amusement. He cannot appreciate, having never known anything similar, Fanny's acute sense of *not* belonging, either to the Portsmouth family who seem to have almost forgotten her existence, or to the Bertrams among whom she is of no account. He does not guess at her lonely struggles against selfpity and depression.

The education of Fanny and her Bertram cousins has been just completed, and the latter are beginning to display their accomplishments in the society of Northampton, when Sir Thomas leaves England for the West Indies where matters connected with his estates in Antigua detain him ten months. During his absence from Mansfield Park, two fashionable and

wealthy young people enter the neighbourhood—Henry Crawford and his sister Mary, relations and guests of Mrs Grant, the
wife of Mansfield's vicar. The social meetings that bring the
Crawfords and Bertrams together culminate, first, in an expedition to Sotherton Court, the country residence of Mr Rushworth,
a young man of fortune to whom Maria Bertram has just become
engaged; and afterwards centre upon the staging of a play, *Lovers'*
*Vows*. Fanny, whose part in these activities is chiefly that of a
spectator, involuntarily witnesses Crawford's unscrupulous seduction of Maria at Sotherton, and during the preparations for the
play becomes the unwilling confidante of Mary Crawford and of her
cousin Edmund, who are attracted to each other and do not suspect
that Fanny's own affection for Edmund has been turning into love.

The unexpected return of Sir Thomas prevents the play being
staged, and restores superficial order among his children, whom
the influence of the Crawfords had thrown into jealous rivalry
and selfish disunion. Maria Bertram, who had secretly expected
Crawford to apply to her father on his return to England for her
hand in marriage, is disappointed, and fulfils her engagement to
marry Rushworth. Her departure from Mansfield Park, taking
Julia with her as a companion, forces Fanny to venture more into
social life than she has been so far used to do. She is now seen,
as if for the first time, by Crawford, to whose epicurean palate
Fanny's innocence promises a new and intriguing pleasure, and
whose vanity is piqued by her polite indifference:

'And how do you think I mean to amuse myself, Mary, on the days that I do
not hunt?...I do not like to eat the bread of idleness. No, my plan is to make
Fanny Price in love with me...I cannot be satisfied without Fanny Price,
without making a small hole in Fanny Price's heart. You do not seem properly
aware of her claims to notice...I do not understand her...What is her
character? Is she solemn? Is she queer? Is she prudish? Why did she draw
back and look so grave at me? I could hardly get her to speak. I never was
so long in company with a girl in my life—trying to entertain her—and
succeed so ill!...Her looks say, "I will not like you, I am determined not
to like you," and I say, she shall.'

Unaware that Fanny's love for Edmund Bertram guards her
heart against attack from any other quarter, unaware too that
Fanny's ideas of happiness centre in a continued residence in the

familiar setting of Mansfield Park and that she cannot bear to contemplate a second removal, Crawford sets about a flirtation that turns, as he comes to know more of her, into serious thoughts of love and marriage. Fanny's convictions regarding her own lack of 'importance' to anyone are severely shaken by Crawford's open and ardent pursuit of her. Her difficulties increase when Crawford secures a promotion for her brother William, and Edmund—in the intervals of pouring out to Fanny his doubts and confidences regarding Mary Crawford—becomes Crawford's advocate with her. From these tests Fanny emerges exhausted, but with a clear conscience. She had steadfastly refused to admit Crawford's attentions, basing her opinion of him on his behaviour during the expedition to Sotherton and the 'Mansfield theatricals'. She is proved to have been justified in her caution, for Crawford eventually elopes with Maria Rushworth, whom vanity has tempted him to try once again to subdue. Fanny has also refrained from doing anything to influence Edmund against Mary Crawford; she believes Mary to be almost as corrupt as her brother Henry, but she is convinced, too, that Edmund's recognition of Mary's worthlessness, if it ever comes, must come from within himself. In the course of time, Edmund marries Fanny.

It is clear, then, that Fanny's long practised self-discipline, her humility and her patience, have guaranteed her eventual happiness. They have limited the demands she might have made on life to provide for her comfort, and *in consequence*, they have protected her: Edmund's confidence and the right of permanent residence at Mansfield Park being all that Fanny needs to make her content, neither Crawford's admiration nor a new-found independence as his wife are essential to her happiness. Fanny's ultimate contentment is great, being infinitely more than she ever hoped or expected to have.

Her career contrasts at every point with that of her cousin, Maria Bertram, whose selfish irresponsibility attracts our notice early in the novel:

Being now in her twentyfirst year, Maria Bertram was beginning to think matrimony a duty; and as a marriage with Mr Rushworth would give her the enjoyment of a larger income than her father's, as well as ensure her the house in town, which was now a prime object, it became, by the same rule of moral obligation, her evident duty to marry Mr Rushworth if she could.

The opening phrases, regarding Maria's meditations on her duty to society as an adult member of it, appear quite straightforward: there is nothing obviously objectionable in a young woman who has been well educated and equipped with the accomplishments regarded as necessary to her position in life, considering that the time has come to serve society through a suitable marriage. But what of the rest of the sentence? ...'*and as a marriage with Mr Rushworth would give her the enjoyment of a larger income than her father's...*'. We discover that the adult responsibilities Maria contemplates are responsibilities *to herself*, and relate to the increase of *her own* wealth and enjoyment! The dangerous logic and the selfish crudeness of her reasoning are exposed by the use Jane Austen makes of the perfectly placed phrase *by the same rule of moral obligation*, which connects the particulars of her ambitions regarding her future status—the 'larger income' and the 'house in town'—with the final, bald statement of her determination to see her 'duty' in marrying Mr Rushworth if she could.

Like Charlotte Lucas in *Pride and Prejudice*, Maria has placed a price on herself, although her beauty, wealth, and superior social status as a baronet's daughter allot to her a far grander 'establishment' than Charlotte could expect. Between Mr Collins and Mr Rushworth, however, we shall find little to choose, Mr Rushworth being a silent fool while Mr Collins was a talkative one. Maria, equally with Charlotte, has tried to act as if 'selfishness is prudence, and insensibility of danger, security for happiness'. The cold determination with which she advances her own interests initiates an analytic exposure of selfishness in its many different aspects that provides the novel's second great theme.

Selfishness and its opposite, generous affection, can make everything or nothing of 'the ties of blood', a point established early in the novel, when Lady Bertram and Mrs Norris disown their younger sister, Mrs Price:

Miss Frances married, in the common phrase, to disoblige her family, and by fixing on a Lieutenant of Marines, without education, fortune, or connections, did it very thoroughly...To save herself from useless remonstrance,

Mrs Price never wrote to her family on the subject till actually married. Lady Bertram, who was a woman of very tranquil feelings, and a temper remarkably easy and indolent, would have contented herself with merely giving up her sister, and thinking no more of the matter: but Mrs Norris had a spirit of activity, which could not be satisfied till she had written a long and angry letter to Fanny, to point out the folly of her conduct, and threaten her with all its possible ill consequences. Mrs Price in her turn was injured and angry; and an answer which comprehended each sister in its bitterness, and bestowed such very disrespectful reflections on the pride of Sir Thomas, as Mrs Norris could not possibly keep to herself, put an end to all intercourse between them for a considerable period.

Lady Bertram's casual abandonment of her younger sister is matched, towards the end of the novel, by that sister's perfect unconcern at the news of Tom Bertram's illness. For them both, 'so long divided, and so differently situated...an attachment, originally as tranquil as their tempers, was now become a mere name'. Lady Bertram's indifference, although less provoking than Mrs Norris's malicious activity, is merely the other side of the same coin of selfishness and callous neglect. Selfishness as the source of family disunion and disgrace reappears in the second generation, as Maria and Julia Bertram become jealous rivals for Crawford's attention, and a rift opens between the sisters:

With no material fault of temper, or difference of opinion, to prevent their being very good friends while their interests were the same, the sisters, under such a trial as this, had not affection or principle enough to make them merciful or just, to give them honour or compassion. Maria felt her triumph, and pursued her purpose careless of Julia; and Julia could never see Maria distinguished by Henry Crawford without trusting that it would create jealousy, and bring a public disturbance at last.

Selfish jealousy of Edmund's moral superiority is at the root of Tom and Maria Bertram's squalid triumph over their brother's reluctant decision to take a part in the play, as

they congratulated each other in private on the jealous weakness to which they attributed the change, with all the glee of feelings gratified in every way. Edmund...was to act, and he was driven to it by the force of selfish inclinations only. Edmund had descended from that moral elevation which he had maintained before, and they were both as much the better as the happier for the descent.

A selfish desire to gratify her idle 'curiosity' makes Mary Crawford bring her brother and Maria Rushworth together again in

London—and thus bring about the elopement that will disgrace and cheat them both: Henry of Fanny Price, and Mary of her own hopes of Edmund Bertram. In clear contrast with these several disloyalties is Fanny's generous affection for her brother William and her cousin Edmund, 'the two most beloved of her heart'.

The novel develops as a masterly study of selfishness, as it works to destroy the peace of talented and trained minds. The Bertrams are intelligent, well-educated people; Sir Thomas is a thoughtful, deliberate, sensible man, and guided by him, Lady Bertram thinks 'justly on all important points'. And yet a lack of human sympathy is apparent in their attitude to the world outside, even in their very generosity—for instance, to Fanny's family. Sir Thomas, we learn, would have been glad to assist Mrs Price at the time of her marriage

from principle as well as pride, from a general wish of doing right, and a desire of seeing all that were connected with him in situations of respectability.

His charitable decision to take charge of Fanny herself, to educate and provide for her, is as much prompted by theory and equally lacking in real warmth. Although a just and well-intentioned man, his attitude to Fanny until his return from Antigua is coldly critical; and his characteristically 'grave' manner, together with his apparent sanction of the methods Mrs Norris employs to maintain 'the distinction proper to be made between the girls as they grow up', does away much of the real value of his generosity to his niece. Sir Thomas's personality changes during his absence from England and his long separation from his family. He returns altered in his manner, 'all that had been awful in his dignity... lost in tenderness'. He becomes warmly appreciative of Fanny, affectionate to his children, and as sympathetic as it is in his nature to be, to them all: 'I come home to be happy and indulgent.' But it is too late. Maria, asked by Sir Thomas whether she would like to withdraw from her engagement to marry Rushworth, cannot confide in a father who has hitherto shown her such reserve. Disappointed in the brilliant children that he had believed to be 'in person, manner, and accomplishments, every thing that could satisfy his anxiety', Sir Thomas must turn at last for consolation and support to the more real and permanent comfort to be found

in Fanny's excellence, in William's continued good conduct, and rising fame, and in the general well-doing and success of the other members of the family, all assisting to advance each other, and doing credit to his countenance and aid.

Lady Bertram, whose relationship with Fanny begins in a thoughtless exploitation of her niece as cruel (in its own way) as Mrs Norris's malicious attacks upon her—'she saw no harm in the poor little thing—and always found her very handy and quick in carrying messages, and fetching what she wanted'—is forced at last, like Sir Thomas, to admit real feeling into her easy and indolent life. Her selfishness, unlike his, had been extended to their daughters; to the education of Maria and Julia she had 'paid not the smallest attention. She had not time for such cares'. When Sir Thomas leaves Mansfield Park on his journey, she is undisturbed 'by any alarm for his safety, or solicitude for his comfort'; when her eldest son is ill at Newmarket, Lady Bertram continues to write 'very comfortably about agitation and anxiety'. It is only when Tom is brought home to Mansfield Park, and his mother sees him in his sickness that her expression becomes at last 'the language of real feeling and alarm'; and it is only when fate deprives her of the daughters she had never really troubled herself much about that she begins to appreciate and value Fanny.

The companion portrait of her sister, Mrs Norris, often regarded as providing comic relief in an otherwise sombre novel, is no simple caricature but a complex and interesting psychological study that bears the marks of close and accurate observation. Mrs Norris is no amusing 'extra' in a crowded cast of characters, but the person directly responsible for the principal developments in the novel: she has supervised her nieces' upbringing, encouraged two of them in the selfish pride that causes their ultimate downfall, and bullied the third into the spirit of humble resignation that ensures *her* ultimate happiness. It is difficult to think of Mrs Norris as 'comic' in such circumstances, except in such minor traits as her complaints of Mrs Grant's extravagance (which recall, surely, Lady Catherine de Bourgh's interest in Charlotte Collins's over-large joints of meat in *Pride and Prejudice*?) and her talent for saving her own money while advising other people to spend theirs as freely as possible. Her major faults spring, like those of her nieces, from selfishness; her restless, ill-advised meddling, that blinds her to everything but the value of the part *she* has played:

> She took to herself all the credit of bringing Mr Rushworth's admiration of Maria to any effect. 'If I had not been active,' said she, 'and made a point of being introduced to his mother, and then prevailed on my sister to pay the first visit, I am as certain as I sit here, that nothing would have come of it... I was ready to move heaven and earth to persuade my sister, and at last I did persuade her. You know the distance to Sotherton; it was in the middle of winter, and the roads almost impassable, but I did persuade her.'

Mrs Norris's ill-natured victimisation of Fanny is a form of emotional relief and selfish gratification perpetually resorted to, without mercy or restraint. While Fanny has reason to think herself unfortunate, her aunt's grievances are largely imaginary, and spring from her swollen sense of her own importance.

Mrs Norris enters the novel on its very first page, as 'Miss Ward', lucky Lady Bertram's older and less fortunate sister, who is obliged to wait six years before discovering a timely affection for a clerical friend of Sir Thomas Bertram. Although her position at Mansfield Park is, in effect, a dependent one—her husband has occupied the living of Mansfield Parsonage, which is in Sir Thomas's gift—Mrs Norris acquires, as a result of Lady Bertram's lethargy and the courtesy of Sir Thomas, a great measure of control over duties which would ordinarily have been her sister's: the supervision of her nieces' education and the direction of the servants are almost entirely in her charge. Mrs Norris enjoys her power; but deputising for a younger sister is a constant reminder of her own inferior status. Her discontent manifests itself in a spirit of angry activity, aimed at securing, at second-hand if necessary, the satisfactions of which she considers herself to have been cheated. It is this selfish turbulence that leads her continually to call Sir Thomas's attention to her own good management of his wife's proper duties; to her officious tyranny over the Park servants and their families. The break with Mrs

Price, Fanny's mother, is made by Sir Thomas at her instigation, and it is she who originates the proposal that Fanny should be brought to Mansfield Park:

Mrs Norris was often observing to the others, that she could not get her poor sister and her family out of her head, and that much as they had all done for her, she seemed to be wanting to do more: and at length she could not but own it to be her wish, that poor Mrs Price should be relieved from the charge and expense of one child entirely out of her great number.

Mrs Norris is always ready, as we have seen, to exercise any power that properly belongs to her sister. But Sir Thomas can be excused for presuming that this latest charitable notion, seeming to outdo everything so far done for the Prices—even by himself—is prompted by his sister-in-law's natural desire for a child. He expects that she will be eager to take over entirely, or at least claim a share in, the care of Fanny. Sir Thomas is mistaken. Mrs Norris has no intention whatever of claiming 'more than the credit of projecting and arranging so expensive a charity'. She has at last procured, at no expense to herself, that best of satisfactions, a victim more dependent and helpless than herself, whom she can exploit, humiliate, and bully without fear of reprisal, and with the moral justification for such treatment that it is prescribed by Sir Thomas for Fanny's own good. Luckily for Fanny, her future is to be in her uncle's responsible and careful hands; although cold and critical towards her, Sir Thomas is never unjust. But it is her Aunt Norris who has the practical direction of the activities of every day.

Mrs Norris is presented in an ironic rather than a comic spirit; her nature is shot through with such venomous and authentic malice that the reader can be amused by nothing connected with her except her discomfiture. It is an indication of Jane Austen's artistic maturity in *Mansfield Park* that such setbacks as Mrs Norris receives are not contrived for our entertainment, but seem to arise out of the realities of her character and situation. One person of consequence at Mansfield Park (besides Edmund, for Fanny's opinion would not matter to any body) wields real power over her, controls and exploits her! Sir Thomas might be flattered and hoodwinked by his sister-in-law, but Lady Bertram (although her indolent good temper, her perfect indifference to every consideration but her own comfort, and the many uses she has for the employment of her sister's time and energy prevent any actual or open humiliation of Mrs Norris) occasionally reminds her that *she* is not deceived:

'Then you will not mind living by yourself quite alone?'

'Dear Lady Bertram! what am I fit for but solitude?...If I can but make both ends meet, that's all I ask for.'

'I hope, sister, things are not so very bad with you neither—considering. Sir Thomas says you will have six hundred a year.'

'Lady Bertram, I do not complain. I know I cannot live as I have done, but I must retrench where I can...I own it would give me great satisfaction to be able to do rather more—to lay by a little at the end of the year.'

'I dare say you will. You always do, don't you?'

Mrs Norris has, after all, witnessed the tranquil ease with which Lady Bertram once severed all connections with their sister Frances Price. Against her benefactress, and against reminders administered so idly—even (it might almost appear) unconsciously—Mrs Norris cannot afford to show resentment. Her sufferings, as Fanny begins to rise in the estimation of those around her, and to attract the attentions formerly paid to her cousins, are another and more obvious source of bitter comedy. Her end is yet another; but although the rest of Mrs Norris's life, devoted to the thankless care of an errant niece, is no doubt a fair retribution for her torture of her virtuous one, it is a punishment that we cannot *laugh* at. Maria's disgrace makes her aunt 'an altered creature, quieted, stupified, indifferent to every thing that passed'. Her love for Maria introduces the selfish and embittered Mrs Norris to the discipline of real suffering; but her punishment, like Maria's, has been delayed until it can make no appreciable difference to her, nor do any one else any real good.

Fanny's Bertram cousins, an attractive group, popular and admired among their neighbours, securely confident of their own perfections, do not *appear* to be selfish. The girls combine with 'beauty and brilliant acquirements, a manner naturally easy, and carefully formed to general civility and obligingness'; Maria, particularly, is thought to possess extraordinary merit—she is 'indeed the pride and delight of them all'. Tom Bertram, less intelligent and less serious than his younger brother Edmund, is still 'the sort of young man to be generally liked', possessing 'easy manners, excellent spirits, a large acquaintance, and a great deal to say'. Their presents to Fanny are as frequently, generously, and carelessly given as their contempt, and although Tom occasionally makes fun of her, she receives from her cousins 'no positive ill-nature'. It is clear, however, that the Bertrams' acceptable manners mask real selfishness. Maria and Julia will not inconvenience themselves for Fanny's benefit, even for the benefit of her health; they are willing to consider Mary Crawford 'most allowably a sweet pretty girl, while they were the finest young women in the country'. Despite Sir Thomas's careful plans for their education, the fundamentals have been neglected, for they are

with all their promising talents and early information...entirely deficient in the less common acquirements of self-knowledge, generosity, and humility. In every thing but disposition, they were admirably taught.

These deficiencies become apparent and threaten ominous results when the Crawfords come to Mansfield. Henry Crawford's admiration of the engaged elder sister flatters Maria's vanity, and makes Julia jealous; for although when the acting of a play was first proposed Julia was 'quite as determined in the cause of pleasure' as Maria or Tom could be, their bitter conflict over Crawford creates a situation in which 'the sister with whom she was used to be on easy terms, was now become her greatest enemy'. Relations between them are apparently restored to their former state when, on their father's return, Crawford's withdrawal disappoints Maria and pacifies Julia. They go off harmoniously together after Maria's wedding to Brighton, and later to 'the wider range of London'. But the reports that filter through to Fanny suggest that her cousins are still unchanged in outlook. Informed of their brother Tom's dangerous illness, they show no desire to give up London pleasures in order to comfort their parents or help to nurse Tom at Mansfield. Selfish vanity is the cause of Maria's downfall, for the passion to which it made her vulnerable earlier is rekindled when she sees Crawford again in London, and she has not developed the selfcontrol or the good sense that can help her to resist it.

The placing of the young Bertrams, with the treacherous attractions of the Crawfords on one hand and the unprized virtues of their Price cousins on the other, suggests the grouping of characters in a morality play, an impression heightened by Jane Austen's presentation of Mary Crawford and Fanny as the Bad and Good Angels that alternately confuse and counsel the wavering, sorely tempted Edmund. It is a patterning that emphasises the novel's moral seriousness, yet such is Jane Austen's mature skill that her careful scheme imposes no rigidity on the characters. Maria Bertram, although ruled by selfish vanity, does not lack feeling—of a kind. She knows vexation and anger, and her good manners are severely taxed to conceal these emotions when Edmund and Julia are invited to dine at the Parsonage and herself excluded on account of Rushworth's expected visit. She discovers the 'irritation' of jealousy, 'which her own sense of propriety could but just smooth over', when Julia mounts the barouche-box and sits laughing with Crawford all the way to Sotherton. The kind and the intensity of the feeling Maria is capable of are well concealed by her 'carefully formed' manners. Her future mother-in-law, Mrs Rushworth—later to be her outraged accuser—is misled by Maria's 'amiable qualities and accomplishments' into supposing her an ideal wife for her son. Edmund himself believes, on the grounds of his sister's acceptance of Rushworth, that 'her feelings are not strong'; Sir Thomas 'had never supposed them to be so'. They are mistaken, for Maria's love of Henry Crawford, beginning in vanity, is so deeply felt that it verges—almost—on unselfishness. She is secretly prepared to sacrifice Sotherton, Rushworth's great fortune, even the long-desired house in town, in order to become Crawford's wife. Her marriage with Rushworth is unwisely undertaken to 'console' and compensate herself for her disappointment, and her real feelings remain unsuspected by her family and their force unknown even to Crawford himself, until he is trapped by them:

...in triumphing over the discretion, which, though beginning in anger, might have saved them both, he had put himself in the power of feelings on her side, more strong than he had supposed. She loved him; there was no withdrawing attentions, avowedly dear to her. He was entangled by his own vanity, with as little excuse of love as possible, and without the smallest inconstancy of mind towards her cousin.

Maria Bertram is a complex, disturbing character, 'guilty' in the eyes of the social world she has been accustomed to lead, yet a victim of the corrupt and mercenary values of that world and of the deficiencies in her education and upbringing. In the final account, Maria's 'guilt' is much more than a social error, something has been wanting 'within', and her father's sorrowful meditations identify the missing element—

He feared that principle, active principle, had been wanting, that they had never been properly taught to govern their inclinations and tempers, by that sense of duty which can alone suffice.

Maria's is a moral fault, for which she is publicly punished according to the ideas of an earlier age, exiled to a separate establishment that she shares with Mrs Norris, where

on one side no affection, on the other, no judgment, it may be reasonably supposed that their tempers became their mutual punishment.

Maria's end helps to create a sense of fatalism in *Mansfield Park*, a sense of cause and effect being irrevocably linked together; Lady Bertram's successful and happy 'captivation' of Sir Thomas on the first page (see Chapter 1) prepares the way for her elder daughter's irresponsible essay for the less worthy Mr Rushworth. We witness, for the first time in our reading of Jane Austen's novels, the preparations, the event, the course, *and the end* of a marriage. Maria's nature, undisciplined by her faulty education, seems to doom her and her marriage from the start:

To such feelings, delay, even the delay of much preparation, would have been an evil, and Mr Rushworth could hardly be more impatient for the marriage than herself. In all the important preparations of the mind she was complete; being prepared for matrimony by an hatred of home, restraint, and tranquillity; by the misery of disappointed affection, and contempt of the man she was to marry. The rest might wait. The preparations of new carriages and furniture might wait for London and spring, when her own taste could have fairer play.

Jane Austen's irony is serious and effective. Maria might *seem* to have done right in giving the proper spiritual and mental preparation for marriage priority over non-essentials such as carriages and new furniture, but *The rest might wait* is an ominous phrase. It prophesies what, with such dangerous preparations as these, *must* happen when Maria finds herself freed at last from the restraints of Mansfield Park, and at liberty in 'the wider range of London'.

London, the fashionable world in which Henry Crawford and his sophisticated sister move with enjoyment and ease, is regarded with pleasurable anticipation by Maria and Julia Bertram who are soon to go there, and with grave doubt by Fanny and Edmund who perceive its frivolous emptiness and appreciate the tranquil peace of Mansfield Park. The standards and values of 'the world' are brought to Mansfield when the Crawfords visit Dr and Mrs Grant at Mansfield Parsonage. Mary Crawford is relieved to find that her sister's husband—a clergyman—'looked the gentleman', and as she and Crawford are of very prepossessing appearance and manner themselves, Mrs Grant 'immediately gave them credit for every thing else.' Mary, having seen Tom Bertram in town, thinks his appearance unobjectionable, and is prepared to consider marrying him. There is a superficiality about the Crawfords' values, a tendency to base judgment upon appearance and display, that emerges clearly in Mary's cynical remarks on marriage:

'Oh! dear—Let him stand his chance and be taken in. It will do just as well. Every body is taken in at some period or other.'

'Not always in marriage, dear Mary.'

'In marriage especially...there is not one in a hundred of either sex, who is not taken in when they marry. Look where I will, I see that it *is* so; and I feel that it *must* be so, when I consider that it is, of all transactions, the one in which people expect most from others, and are least honest themselves.'

Deception, according to Mary Crawford, is the rule rather than the exception in social exchanges, and 'in marriage especially'. It is her tacit consent to this rule, and her acceptance of it as a guiding principle that makes her a symbol of danger. Her 'principle' is supported by her brother Henry, an adept in the arts of flattery and passionless flirtation:

'An engaged woman is always more agreeable than a disengaged. She is satisfied with herself. Her cares are over, and she feels that she may exert all her powers of pleasing without suspicion. All is safe with a lady engaged; no harm can be done.'

The Crawfords' standards are those of fashionable London, where Mary's impressions of marriage have been formed; as she says to Edmund, while discussing the social position of clergymen, 'The metropolis, I imagine, is a pretty fair sample of the rest.' Her standards turn out to be inadequate and false, and in applying them to life at Mansfield Park, Mary is led into error after error. Acknowledging that two such young men as Tom and Edmund Bertram are 'not often seen together even in London', she believes Tom at first to be the more presentable of the two, he having been 'much in London'. She imagines that in the country, as in the town, 'every thing is to be got with money'. Her most serious mistake is made when she applies her familiar standards to Fanny:

'I begin now to understand you all, except Miss Price', said Miss Crawford, as she was walking with the Mr Bertrams. 'Pray, is she out, or is she not? I am puzzled. She dined at the parsonage, with the rest of you, which seemed like being *out*; and yet she says so little, that I can hardly suppose she *is*.'

Fanny does not fit the rule of fashionable practice, and Edmund, who knows her best, gives a more realistic estimate in his blunt reply:

'I believe I know what you mean—but I will not undertake to answer the question. My cousin is grown up. She has the age and sense of a woman, but the outs and not outs are beyond me.'

'The outs and not outs' are, in Edmund's opinion, absurdly complicated, and in any case irrelevant and inadequate when brought to the judgment of a human personality. But Miss Crawford perseveres; and not all her talents and her wit can compensate for the poor judgment she displays in her estimate of Fanny, her own most observant critic: 'Oh! then the point is clear. Miss Price is *not* out.' Mary's errors, although not all are equally serious, occur frequently and consistently enough to disturb Edmund, who has begun to fall in love with her. They irritate and perplex him, and he fears that her flippancy is the sign of a corrupted mind. Fanny is quite convinced that it is, and her distrust turns to fear as Mary's influence over Edmund grows.

He is soon to be a clergyman, and Mary's determined attempts to shake his intention by a combination of charm and raillery make her a source of moral danger to Edmund. Her beauty becomes a trap, her gaiety a snare, her free and vivacious conversation an invitation to indulgence and error. Edmund, in spite of himself, is fascinated by her, and Fanny is quick to see this:

he was deceived in her; he gave her merits which she had not; her faults were what they had ever been, but he saw them no longer—

yet she can do nothing to save him, because her own love for him imputes a selfish motive to any act of hers against Mary Crawford.

To Fanny, the Crawfords seem to be agents of a depraved and evil world, ready to lure the weak and unsteady to certain destruction. When Julia enters that world, her brother notes that she 'seems to enjoy London exceedingly'. Maria goes to London and is destroyed. Mary Crawford is a child of the fashionable world, and it is to her love of London and its false values that Edmund must at last leave her:

'I have no jealousy of any individual. It is the influence of the fashionable world altogether that I am jealous of.'

Portsmouth, where Fanny is sent on a visit to her family by Sir Thomas in the hope that a view of her original home might mend her unwillingness to accept Henry Crawford, receives ten chapters in a three-volume novel. Jane Austen's description of the Prices' home has no counterpart in her published work. Noisy, graceless, glaring, life cannot follow ordered patterns there. Our picture of the delicately nurtured Fanny in her parents' home is minutely and realistically detailed:

There was neither health nor gaiety in sun-shine in a town. She sat in a blaze of oppressive heat, in a cloud of moving dust; and her eyes could only wander from the walls marked by her father's head, to the table cut and knotched by her brothers, where stood the tea-board never thoroughly cleaned, the cups and saucers wiped in streaks, the milk a mixture of motes floating in thin blue, and the bread and butter growing every minute more greasy than even Rebecca's hands had first produced it...

This sensuous description of a sordid interior creates a close, stifling atmosphere very different from the spacious grandeur of Mansfield Park, where similar occasions began ceremoniously as 'the solemn procession, headed by Baddeley, of tea-board, urn, and cake-bearers, made its appearance'. Indeed, we discover what Mansfield Park is really like from Fanny's comparisons of its remembered graces with her Portsmouth home and her Portsmouth relations:

The elegance, propriety, regularity, harmony—and perhaps, above all, the peace and tranquillity of Mansfield

are recalled by her in every moment of her exile. Mrs Price is recognised by her daughter to be

a partial, ill-judging parent, a dawdle, a slattern, who neither taught nor restrained her children, whose house was the scene of mismanagement and discomfort from beginning to end

and Lady Bertram, in spite of her indolent selfishness, rises in the reader's estimation as well as in Fanny's affections. Mr Price's loud brutality compels comparison with Sir Thomas Bertram's composed and civilised manners. Fanny has no doubts now as to where her heart lies: 'Portsmouth was Portsmouth; Mansfield was home.' But Portsmouth, although a trial to Fanny's sensitive nerves, is a source of positive and lively virtue as London is a source of moral danger and unsteady principles. Mr Price may be rough in his speech and hasty in delivering judgment, but his morality will countenance no equivocation:

'I don't know what Sir Thomas may think of such matters; he may be too much of the courtier and fine gentleman to like his daughter the less. But by G—— if she belonged to me, I'd give her the rope's end as long as I could stand over her. A little flogging for man and woman too, would be the best way of preventing such things.'

Portsmouth yields a new recruit to Mansfield Park's sadly depleted forces in Susan Price, Fanny's sister. Love and loyalty are positives in the Prices' upbringing as they have not been in the experience of their Bertram cousins. Until Fanny went to Mansfield she had had little formal education (her cousins think her stupid and ignorant), but she remembered her brother William with loyal affection, and thought sadly of the beloved home she had left. When she returns to Portsmouth and finds that the old life completely disgusts her, she can still begin a relationship with her younger sister, Susan, that is based on affection and mutual respect. Portsmouth, then, is Mansfield Park's auxiliary in its struggle to defend itself against the encroaching, destructive influences of the fashionable world. Life at the Park moves slowly, according to long-established, orderly patterns; so much is taken for granted that its inmates do not recognise the presence of danger until they are overwhelmed by it. The arrival of the Crawfords, fresh from a background of domestic discord in their uncle's home, spells danger to the harmony of life at Mansfield, and betrays the young Bertrams into selfish rivalry, from the wreckage created by which only Fanny and Edmund emerge safe and comparatively unscarred.

In its perfect wedding of theme, characters, and an actual, physical situation and setting, *Mansfield Park* displays a technical mastery unmatched by anything in Jane Austen's earlier work. Let us turn, in order to see this mastery in action, together with a development of that skill in handling large groups of people that we first saw demonstrated in *Sense and Sensibility*, to Chapters 9 and 10 of the first volume. Maria, Julia, and Edmund Bertram, Henry and Mary Crawford, Fanny Price, and Mrs Norris (in the role of chaperon) have assembled at Sotherton Court for the purpose of considering certain 'improvements' that Mr Rushworth plans to carry out at his country house. He does not quite know what these improvements are to be, and they are invited in order to assist his judgment with their invention, taste, and opinions. The expedition has been embarked on as a pleasurable outing, but by the time the party return to Mansfield, a number of unexpected things have happened. Maria Bertram, who had approached Sotherton with 'Rushworth-feelings and Crawford-feelings', leaves it very much in love with Henry Crawford. Julia has become her rival for Crawford's notice and attention. Mary Crawford has learned with surprise of Edmund's intention to be ordained, and their exchanges have left Edmund aware of her potent attraction for him and also of the chasm that seems to separate their respective attitudes to life. It is, in fact, a shared experience in which lie buried the roots of many later developments. A close reading of an extract from this part of the novel may help us to examine, more satisfactorily than a general description could do, the subtlety with which Jane Austen works out her intention.

Fanny has been left to rest herself on a bench in a wood at Sotherton while Edmund and Mary walk a little further—it is clear that they enjoy each other's company, and that Edmund's usual concern for Fanny's comfort is here strengthened by a certain self-interest. While she sits there alone, Maria Bertram, Mr Rushworth, and Henry Crawford come upon her:

'Miss Price all alone!' and 'My dear Fanny, how comes this?' were the first salutations. She told her story. 'Poor dear Fanny,' cried her cousin, 'how ill you have been used by them! You had better have staid with us.'

Then seating herself with a gentleman on each side, she resumed the conversation which had engaged them before, and discussed the possibility of improvements with animation. Nothing was fixed on—but Henry Crawford was full of ideas and projects, and generally speaking, whatever he proposed was immediately approved, first by her, and then by Mr Rushworth, whose principal business seemed to be to hear the others, and who scarcely risked an original thought of his own beyond a wish that they had seen his friend Smith's place.

After some minutes spent in this way, Miss Bertram observing the iron gate, expressed a wish of passing through it into the park, that their views and their plans might be more comprehensive. It was the very thing of all others to be wished, it was the best, it was the only way of proceeding with any advantage, in Henry Crawford's opinion; and he directly saw a knoll not half a mile off, which would give them exactly the requisite command of the house. Go therefore they must to that knoll, and through that gate; but the gate was locked. Mr Rushworth wished he had brought the key; he had been very near thinking whether he should not bring the key; he was determined he would never come without the key again; but still this did not remove the present evil. They could not get through; and as Miss Bertram's inclination for so doing did by no means lessen, it ended in Mr Rushworth's declaring outright that he would go and fetch the key. He set off accordingly.

'It is undoubtedly the best thing we can do now, as we are so far from the house already', said Mr Crawford, when he was gone.

'Yes, there is nothing else to be done. But now, seriously, do not you find the place altogether worse than you expected?'

'No, indeed, far otherwise. I find it better, grander, more complete in its style, though that style may not be the best. And to tell you the truth,' speaking rather lower, 'I do not think that *I* shall ever see Sotherton again with so much pleasure as I do now. Another summer will hardly improve it to me.'

After a moment's embarrassment the lady replied, 'You are too much a man of the world not to see with the eyes of the world. If other people think Sotherton improved, I have no doubt that you will.'

'I am afraid I am not quite so much the man of the world as might be good for me in some points. My feelings are not quite so evanescent, nor my memory of the past under such easy dominion as one finds to be the case with men of the world.'

This was followed by a short silence. Miss Bertram began again. 'You seemed to enjoy your drive here very much this morning. I was glad to see you so well entertained. You and Julia were laughing the whole way.'

'Were we? Yes, I believe we were; but I have not the least recollection at what. Oh! I believe I was relating to her some ridiculous stories of an old Irish groom of my uncle's. Your sister loves to laugh.'

'You think her more light-hearted than I am.'

'More easily amused,' he replied, 'consequently you know,' smiling, 'better company. I could not have hoped to entertain *you* with Irish anecdotes during a ten miles' drive.'

'Naturally, I believe, I am as lively as Julia, but I have more to think of now.'

'You have undoubtedly—and there are situations in which very high spirits would denote insensibility. Your prospects, however, are too fair, to justify want of spirits. You have a very smiling scene before you.'

'Do you mean literally or figuratively? Literally I conclude. Yes, certainly, the sun shines and the park looks very cheerful. But unluckily that iron gate, that ha-ha, give me a feeling of restraint and hardship. I cannot get out, as the starling said.' As she spoke, and it was with expression, she walked to the gate; he followed her. 'Mr Rushworth is so long fetching this key!'

'And for the world you would not get out without the key and without Mr Rushworth's authority and protection, or I think you might with little difficulty pass round the edge of the gate, here, with my assistance; I think it might be done, if you really wished to be more at large, and could allow yourself to think it not prohibited.'

'Prohibited! nonsense! I certainly can get out that way, and I will. Mr Rushworth will be here in a moment you know—we shall not be out of sight.'

'Or if we are, Miss Price will be so good as to tell him, that he will find us near that knoll, the grove of oak on the knoll.'

Fanny, feeling all this to be wrong, could not help making an effort to prevent it. 'You will hurt yourself, Miss Bertram,' she cried, 'you will certainly hurt yourself against those spikes—you will tear your gown—you will be in danger of slipping into the ha-ha. You had better not go.'

Her cousin was safe on the other side, while these words were spoken, and smiling with all the good-humour of success, she said, 'Thank you, my dear Fanny, but I and my gown are alive and well, and so good bye.'

Crawford and Maria Bertram, like Edmund and Mary, wish to be alone, and Crawford's demand to be allowed to view Sotherton

Court from the knoll, eagerly supported by Maria, is a pretext to get rid of Mr Rushworth. Fanny, of course, does not count for much with either of them, and the conversation that follows, with its succession of veiled ambiguities (the kind of sophisticated game that Crawford excels at playing, and Maria is trying to play herself) takes place as if she were not within sight and hearing. Crawford, having first skilfully turned affront into compliment, suggests that Maria's imminent marriage with Rushworth will blight Sotherton's beauty for him; and having got the reaction he was after, reminds her of her pleasant 'prospects' as Rushworth's wife and the mistress of Sotherton. At once the landscape before them becomes symbolic of Maria's situation. The sight of the spiked iron gate and the deep ditch (or ha-ha) that prevent her walking in the park beyond is an irritating reminder of her engagement to their owner, which must prevent Maria in the future from enjoying Crawford's admiration and companionship except under such a pretext as had just been contrived. The 'smiling scene' and the 'cheerful park' symbolise for Maria all the pleasures of freedom that she must lose on marrying Rushworth. Her feelings are deeper than Crawford's, and show themselves in her language, which is more direct and forceful, less subtly ambiguous than his. Maria Bertram is no match for the experienced, amoral Crawford, her feelings involve her deeply in a situation which *he* can manipulate with detachment. In urging her to 'pass round the edge of the gate, here, with my assistance', if she really wished for greater freedom and could allow herself to 'think it not prohibited', Crawford is tempting Maria to enter, voluntarily, into more intimate association with him. He is guided by her self-confessed jealousy of Julia, and works deliberately on the weaknesses she has been unguarded enough to reveal: her arrogant impatience with any form of restraint, and her feeling that she has been trapped. Maria's triumphant farewell to Fanny (we notice that despite her concern at Fanny's desertion by the others, she issues no invitation to her cousin to attempt the gate herself!) spells the end of any serious relationship with Mr Rushworth.

Julia now appears, and her jealousy of Maria kindles as she

learns from Fanny that the two have evaded Mr Rushworth and gone into the park. Following them across the fence enacts in microcosm her own future action in eloping with Mr Yates as soon as she learns of their flight, just as Fanny's agitated warning to Maria has foretold the damage that intimacy with Crawford will do to *her* personality and reputation. Reading such a passage, and relating it to the section of the novel from which it has been extracted, we become aware of its rich symbolism, of a complex whole in which no detail is irrelevant or extraneous to the writer's intention. Landscape and setting are so closely woven into the texture of the scene that they are inseparable from the action and the dialogue; the words spoken by Crawford, Maria, and Fanny could not have been the same nor symbolised so much, their actions could not have taken a similar course—nor had quite the same artistically satisfactory, psychologically 'natural' effect —in any other setting. In the detailed observation upon which it is based, in the closeness of its organisation, and its entirely satisfying communication of a human situation, this passage is representative of the novel as a whole.

Landscape and setting seem more important in *Mansfield Park* than in any other of the six novels except, possibly, *Persuasion*. We recall Marianne Dashwood's soliloquies to the trees at Norland, and Catherine Morland learning to admire the picturesque aspects of landscape under Henry Tilney's guidance, but never yet has the setting seemed to participate so much in the action, at once influencing and informed by the consciousness of the character through whose eyes we see it, as it does here. Close observation, carefully selected detail, and a mature skill in the communication of atmosphere, whether ceremonious and quiet or noisy and sordid, equally characterise Jane Austen's presentations of landscapes and interior settings in *Mansfield Park*; never allowed to serve as mere background for the characters, they integrate with the action of the novel in such a way as to illustrate and comment upon it.

Incidents, too, are no mere stages to help the plot along, but become living parts of the novel's organic development. Consider, for example, that part of *Mansfield Park* that concerns the production of a play by Tom Bertram's company of amateur actors. The idea of acting a play to pass the time is brought to Mansfield Park by Mr Yates, a frivolous friend of Tom Bertram's, and is eagerly taken up by all the young people except Edmund and Fanny. The determination of the others carries the day. Despite Edmund's objections and resistance, Mansfield Park—whose quiet harmony had hitherto exposed by contrast the glittering emptiness of London life as described in the conversation of Mary Crawford—becomes a scene of noise and bustle, of petty rivalries and practised deceptions. The question of acting, the considerations of those who can act well and those who cannot (or will not) become subtly inter-related with the larger problem, amounting to a third theme, of real and pretended worth.

Henry Crawford, as Lady Bertram rouses herself to exclaim, has 'a great turn for acting'; like many of her comments, this one probes deeper than it is intended to, for Crawford's practised charm is intended to deceive and mislead. Mary Crawford and Tom Bertram prefer comedy to a serious play, an indication of their superficiality, and their flippant disregard of serious considerations. Maria and Julia Bertram sink their intellectual pretensions to admire tragic drama when they decide on the poor quality play, *Lover's Vows*, and scramble without dignity for the role of Agatha which will give the actress greater opportunity for private rehearsals and public freedom with Crawford, who is to play Frederick. Maria acts well: 'too well,' thinks Fanny fearfully, having herself refused to take part on the grounds that she cannot act. Fanny cannot deceive; as Crawford himself realises later on, it is not in her nature to 'speak or write a falsehood'. The relation of their elders to the acting of the play is characteristic of their respective roles in the greater drama of the novel; Sir Thomas, far away in the West Indies, knows as little of the play as he knows of his children's real characters and dispositions, so perfectly exposed in the course of the theatricals. Lady Bertram remains as indolently remote from the excitement around her as she has contrived to keep herself from the supervision of her daughters' education. Mrs Norris involves herself so deeply in selfish, self-congratulatory bustle about inessentials (such as the making of the green baize curtain that is to set off the stage) that she perceives neither Maria's danger nor Julia's jealousy; we know that a similarly ill-judged enthusiasm has led her to promote Maria's engagement to Rushworth, and that she has never reflected on the real (as distinct from the social and material) advisability of the match.

The action of the play itself comments on the actors. It provides license and opportunity for Maria to speak, act, and feed the passion she is forbidden to express in the ordinary way; it is not surprising that the theatre is continually engaged, as Mary Crawford remarks with careless amusement, 'by those indefatigable rehearsers, Agatha and Frederick'. Mary herself is committed, with Edmund, to a scene the whole subject of which is love—'a marriage of love was to be described by the gentleman, and very little short of a declaration of love be made by the lady'. Mr Rushworth finds consolation and distraction in the splendid costumes he is to wear, and his mental powers are taxed to the utmost by his two and forty speeches. Mr Yates loves to rant, and the part of Baron Wildenhaim gives him as much melodrama as he desires. The play itself, its shoddy quality and its false values, becomes (through the Bertrams' dedication to its presentation, and the sacrifice of so much time and labour) symbolic of the misguided ideals of worth, supported by wrong and false standards, that they are ready to adopt. In the opportunities it provides for selfishness to thrive and flourish, the play contributes significantly to the novel's main theme:

Fanny looked on and listened, not unamused to observe the selfishness which, more or less disguised, seemed to govern them all, and wondering how it would end.

The play is the chief instrument by which a glittering outer surface, the Crawfords' pleasant manners and the impressive array of talents and accomplishments mustered by Maria and Julia Bertram, is stripped away to expose the selfish vanity 'within'.

Beside the Bertrams and the Crawfords, Fanny Price appears occasionally colourless. She has a tendency to ill health and low spirits, which is understandable in the face of her aunts' merciless exploitation of her gentle nature and her dependent status. Yet the reader notices that fatigue and headaches seem to trouble Fanny particularly when Edmund Bertram has been showing Mary Crawford some marked attention. Fanny is not unaware that the dangers of selfish irresponsibility threaten her as well as her cousins, and that the temptation to advance her own interests approaches *her* in the deceptive guise of selfpity. To Fanny at Portsmouth, as much as to Maria at Sotherton, Crawford comes in the role of tempter:

'I know Mansfield, I know its way, I know its faults towards *you*. I know the danger of your being so far forgotten, as to have your comforts give way to the imaginary convenience of any single being in the family...This will not do.'

Fanny thanks him, 'but tried to laugh it off.' He has touched her defences at their weakest point, but she has been alarmed (and ignored) by him too often in their acquaintance to welcome or credit his belated championship of her—and against Mansfield Park, too, to whose owner she owes so much and whose peace he has done so much to destroy! The temptation to selfpity has, in any case, been fought and conquered during Fanny's lonely exile from Mansfield, and she is not to be tempted again. Her gentle manners conceal 'the sternness of her purpose'; and Crawford mistakes her determination for shy reserve.

'I *should* have thought...that every woman must have felt the possibility of a man's not being approved, not being loved by some one of her sex, at least, let him be ever so generally agreeable. Let him have all the perfections in the world, I think it ought not to be set down as certain, that a man must be acceptable to every woman he may happen to like himself. But even sup-posing it is so...He took me wholly by surprise. I had not an idea that his behaviour to me before had any meaning...How then was I to be—to be in love with him the moment he said he was with me? How was I to have an attachment at his service, as soon as it was asked for? His sisters should consider me as well as him...And, and—we think very differently of the nature of women, if they can imagine a woman so very soon capable of return-ing an affection as this seems to imply.'

Fanny here defends her refusal of Crawford to Edmund, who has retailed to her the reproaches and ridicule of Mrs Grant and Mary. Uttered in Fanny's characteristically diffident manner, this is nevertheless recognisably the same refusal to surrender her selfrespect that we have met already in Elinor Dashwood and Elizabeth Bennet. Fanny's wish to have her claim to an independent choice respected is not less passionately felt because it is expressed in tones of sorrowful reflection rather than of firm resolve or angry indignation. This kind of strength goes often unnoticed by the reader who is 'disappointed' by Fanny's showing beside the more vivid portraits of Mary Crawford and Maria Bertram. A heroine, it has been felt, should be allowed a few more personal advantages than Jane Austen allows Fanny; she should not be so constantly overshadowed by other characters livelier and more attractive than herself.

This weakness—if it *is* a weakness, and not every reader would accept it as one—does not affect the central purposes of the novel. Fanny is not at the centre of *Mansfield Park* as, for instance, Catherine Morland and Elizabeth Bennet are at the centre of *Northanger Abbey* and *Pride and Prejudice*. She is but one of a number of people, young and old, involved in experiences that test their emotional and spiritual resources. Her growth into greater assertiveness and attractiveness is pictured with tact and delicacy, the responsibility of even a gentle and timid character to assert moral values plainly and firmly when occasion calls for it being taken up at the same time and explored; but never as more than a minor theme. A heroine's progress to maturity is not a major concern of *Mansfield Park*, as it is of *Northanger Abbey*, *Sense and Sensibility*, and *Pride and Prejudice*. Fanny needs no disciplining, for her customary relegation to an inferior position among the Bertrams has formed her character, by giving her plenty of opportunity to practise humility and selfrestraint.

Fanny's hidden and unpublicised strength of character, far from being a fault in *Mansfield Park*, is in fact essential to the novelist's purpose and consonant with the novel's major themes. Selfishness and vanity lead Maria and Julia Bertram to think themselves entitled to public admiration, and encourage them to compete for Crawford's notice; their cousin's diffidence, which is rooted in real humility, guards her peace of mind and renders it safe from the attacks of worldliness. The Bertrams appear to be—and think themselves—perfect in every way; Fanny at sixteen seems almost 'entirely without improvement'. Her appearance is (and must be, for Jane Austen's purposes) as deceptive as that of her cousins, for the moral strength of her character is exposed to public view—like the weakness of theirs— at the end of the novel. It is a reproach to the inhabitants of Mansfield Park (always excluding Edmund, of course) that Fanny's virtues have to be 'discovered' by them instead of being as wellknown and familiar as they deserve to be; and it is characteristic of most of them that their 'discoveries' gratify their own selfish needs and vanities. Lady Bertram, a successful beauty all her life, is pleased to discover in the niece she has hitherto neglected—now soon, perhaps, to become the mistress of Crawford's country residence of Everingham—a family likeness unperceived before Crawford took notice of Fanny. Mary Crawford, who had neglected Fanny while her cousins were at Mansfield, finds visits from her 'in the gloom and dirt of a November day, most acceptable.' Crawford discovers, in the absence of Maria, that Fanny has 'claims to notice'. It is he, when selfish gallantry turns unexpectedly into love, who identifies the special quality exclusive to Fanny that interests and intrigues him: she has 'feeling, genuine feeling'. His sister confesses a similar awareness (that includes Edmund) when, on leaving Mansfield Park, she tells Fanny:

'You have all so much more *heart* among you, than one finds in the world at large. You all give me a feeling of being able to trust and confide in you; which, in common intercourse, one knows nothing of.'

A developing clarity of vision such as these remarks imply in the Crawfords, on the important question of Fanny's character (undervalued by nearly everybody else), indicates *Mansfield Park*'s striking advances on earlier work as regards judgment of character and skill in presentation. Mary and Henry Crawford arouse fear and repulsion in Fanny, but Edmund's view of them is more just and true. When Fanny cries out at Mary's 'cruelty', she has allowed herself to forget Mary's kind attempts to soothe away the injuries of Mrs Norris's insulting behaviour during the casting of the play. Edmund gravely corrects Fanny. Mary is not corrupt in herself, but has been corrupted by the world to an extent that will soon set her beyond hope of reclaim. Henry Crawford must be more severely judged than his sister, being farther abandoned to selfish worldiness than she is, but even he cannot with justice be condemned outright. Crawford's character is an artistic triumph for Jane Austen, with its mixture of good intentions and weak-principled practice, polished manners and crudity of mind, witty speech and insensitive heart. His response to William Price's stories of naval life crystallizes the contradictions of his personality:

He longed to have been at sea, and seen and done and suffered as much. His heart was warmed, his fancy fired... The glory of heroism, of usefulness, of exertion, of endurance, made his own habits of selfish indulgence appear in shameful contrast; and he wished he had been a William Price, distinguishing himself and working his way to fortune and consequence with so much self-respect and happy ardour, instead of what he was!

The wish was rather eager than lasting. He was roused from the reverie of retrospection and regret produced by it, by some inquiry from Edmund as to his plans for the next day's hunting; and he found it as well to be a man of fortune at once with horses and grooms at his command...

*Rather eager than lasting.* Crawford and Mary are, both of them, too much creatures of 'the world' to relinquish their established habits. The period spent by them at Mansfield and their contact with Fanny and with Edmund Bertram brings them nearer than they have ever been to altering their attitudes and their way of life; but the moment of decision passes. Crawford slips back into vanity and easy pleasure, Mary cannot clear a judgment that has been clouded too long by worldly influences. Her readiness, acknowledged without attempt at concealment to the appalled Edmund, to suggest that Crawford must be artfully distracted into the paths of virtue, her inability to see, from the standpoint of a future Mrs Crawford, the 'regular standing flirtation' between her brother and Maria Rushworth that she advocates as the surest guarantee of their future good behaviour—all these, like the tactless flippancy that has continually disturbed Edmund, are characteristic symptoms of an incurably blunted sensitivity. It is not in the nature of Crawford or of Mary to change; but there has been a time when they, and we, believed that they might.

Looking back on the novel, and comparing it with *Pride and*

*Prejudice*, we recognise the effects of a steadier, profounder moral vision, and a more mature technique. They can be seen in the confidence with which a large number of complex characters are introduced, and the skill with which they are kept in motion; in the replacement of purely comic or satiric interests by an accurately observed psychological motivation of character; in the symbolic use of a wide range of interior and outdoor settings; and in the way each of these contributes to the exploration of serious themes and interests, uniting with the others to enrich and diversify what seems eventually to us a living organism rather than a work of art.

Placed between *Pride and Prejudice* and *Emma* on the scale of Jane Austen's developing artistic skill, *Mansfield Park* may be thought to lack the finish of these two technical masterpieces. It expresses, however, a deeper human sympathy and wider interests, and tries to achieve more complex and difficult effects than she attempted in either of them. It remains, in some ways, the greatest novel she ever wrote.

# 8

## 'EMMA'

'A young farmer, whether on horseback or on foot, is the very last sort of person to raise my curiosity. The yeomanry are precisely the order of people with whom I feel I can have nothing to do. A degree or two lower, and a creditable appearance might interest me; I might hope to be useful to their families in some way or other. But a farmer can need none of my help, and is therefore in one sense as much above my notice as in every other he is below it.'
*Emma*, Vol. 1, Chapter 4

This is a speech that is characteristic, with its emphasis on the words *order* and *degree*, of Emma Woodhouse, a young woman with an acute sense of the divisions of social rank in the country town of Highbury, where her own family is the first in 'consequence and large fortune'. In expressing, too, Emma's willingness to be *useful* to her social inferiors, it captures the mixture of arrogance and generosity in her nature, characteristically emerging in a determination to 'superintend the happiness' of those around her.

Emma Woodhouse, 'handsome, clever, and rich', the indulged daughter of a kindly hypochondriac, resembles Maria Bertram in being beautiful, intelligent, wealthy, and the centre of an admiring world. Like Maria, Emma is ruled by vanity: but there the resemblance ends, for while Maria's vanity was lent entirely to advancing her own pleasures and interests, Emma's—directed by principle!—'lies another way', becoming benevolent interference in the private lives of other people. And while the history of Maria Bertram begins ominously and ends in disaster and disgrace, an illustration of the damage that can be done to talent and worth by a lack of moral principle and an unconsciousness of having been born 'to struggle and endure', Emma is presented with a lighter touch:

The real evils indeed of Emma's situation were the power of having rather too much her own way, and a disposition to think a little too well of herself.

It is as if Jane Austen, turning from her serious examination of the theme of selfish irresponsibility in *Mansfield Park*, has set

herself in *Emma* to the artistic exercise of treating the same theme
—though no less seriously—in a spirit of pure comedy. For
*Emma* is a work of comic art, indeed, as well as an exploration of
moral standards and of social behaviour. The events of a year
educate and discipline its heroine, but *her* vanity (unlike Maria
Bertram's) is checked at its very source and partially redeemed
by her own uneasy conscience. Mr Knightley, Emma's brother-
in-law and childhood friend, perceives the conflict in her nature:

'I shall not scold you. I leave you to your own reflections.'
  'Can you trust me with such flatterers? Does my vain spirit ever tell me
I am wrong?'
  'Not your vain spirit, but your serious spirit. If one leads you wrong, I am
sure the other tells you of it.'

Emma's 'serious spirit' is not powerful enough to halt her in her
headstrong career of wilful interference, but it does make her
pause from time to time in order to reconsider, regret, even to
repent; and her repentance always leads Emma to penance or
reparation of some kind. Being Emma, her very impulse to reform
sometimes leads her to comic extremes as when, disgusted by the
results of her own actions, she elevates her ignorant friend
Harriet Smith's simple-mindedness to the level of a desirable
virtue; and sometimes to near-disaster, as when her decision to
cease meddling in the affairs of others prevents Emma discovering
that it is Mr Knightley whom Harriet admires and not Frank
Churchill. But Emma, unlike Maria Bertram, has 'qualities that
may be trusted'. She leads her friend into error and disappointment, but the liveliness of her conscience and the depth and
sincerity of her sympathy open a path to better judgment and
future good sense from within her own character; and so Emma
escapes Maria's grim experience in which vanity brings, not
regret and unhappiness alone, but permanent disgrace and social
isolation.

There are many such features that seem to connect *Emma* with
*Mansfield Park*. Its structural framework is built on elements that
might have been deliberately selected from the earlier novel
according to the prompting of a very different artistic intention,
although some of them may well (as has been convincingly

suggested) owe their origin to Jane Austen's unfinished piece, *The Watsons*. Miss Taylor's influence over her pupil, like Mrs Norris's decisive influence over Maria Bertram, is prompted by 'such an affection for her as could never find fault'. Emma's love for Mr Knightley is founded, like Fanny's for Edmund Bertram, on sisterly affection and a friendship of many years' standing; and like Fanny, Emma discovers her own true feelings for him when she is almost certain that he is bound in affection to another woman, having been herself treated by that other woman as a sympathetic confidante. Like Frances Ward in *Mansfield Park*, a young woman of rank is disowned 'with due decorum' by her family on her marriage, and her child—like Fanny Price—is brought up and educated by wealthy and proud relations. Like Mrs Norris, Emma Woodhouse prides herself on her successful matchmaking, and in very similar words to hers declares that, but for her own intervention, the attachment between her governess and their pleasant neighbour, Mr Weston, 'might not have come to any thing after all'; like Mrs Norris, Emma is punished for her meddlesome irresponsibility.

That irresponsibility, captured perfectly in her own words to Harriet Smith that appear at the head of this chapter, emerges in Emma's determination to see only what she wants to see in the complex and many-sided world around her, which hinders a proper understanding of the society she wishes to control. Her anxiety to detach Harriet from the 'yeomanry' as represented by the Martin family and to 'introduce her into good society' betrays a rigidity of outlook and a self-created sense of superiority totally out of touch with the realities of Highbury life; for whether Jane Austen's depiction of that town is true to the social realities of country life in the England of her time, or to a social ideal of her own, Highbury exists in the novel as a world in its own right. The very puddles in its main street and the sharp corner of a particular lane familiar to the reader's inward eye, its inhabitants linked in relationships that have recognisable parallels in every rural community in the world, its activities regulated by the procession of the seasons and diversified by the personalities of various people and the affinities between them, we cannot doubt the validity of Highbury's established manners and customs for a moment. The society around Emma is in a state of lively, animated progression, many Highbury families having risen in the course of a few generations from mere 'respectability' to the possession of 'gentility and property', acquiring fortune and distinction in professions such as medicine, the church, law and military service, and through success in business and trade.

The 'genteel' people of Highbury include families that have declined to poverty from former prosperity, like Miss Bates and her mother, often invited to Emma's home at Hartfield while wealthier families more recently arrived in the sphere of 'gentility' are not. Also among the genteel are successful professional people, like John Knightley, who as the younger son of the Donwell family has become a lawyer, and has married Emma's elder sister Isabella: the physician, Mr Perry, an 'intelligent, gentlemanlike man'; and Mr Elton, the vicar, all of whom are familiar and welcome visitors at Hartfield, by virtue of their relationship (in the special case of John Knightley), their professional and social standing, and their friendship with the Woodhouse family. Two other respectable professions are represented in the person of Mr Weston, formerly an officer in the militia, who has turned after the death of his first wife to trade and business, in which he has made a fortune and has climbed rather higher in the social world than, for instance, Mr Cole, who is also making his way up from somewhat inferior origins through flourishing trade.

For many among the 'genteel' class are ready to progress still further. Mr Elton, we find, hopes to make his fortune through a brilliant marriage and thus enter the class above him, represented in Highbury by the Knightleys of Donwell Abbey and the Woodhouse family at Hartfield, who are allied by blood to 'great' families outside Highbury. Mr Weston is, indeed, already linked to one such family—the Churchills of Yorkshire—by his first marriage and by the Churchills's adoption of his son, Frank.

Emma's belief that she 'can have nothing to do' with the farming class or yeomanry, which is a grade below the 'genteel', is therefore a figment of her own wilful imagination—it is something that she alone 'feels' and wants to feel. Her closest and most intimate friends, Mr Knightley and the Westons at Randalls, have acquaintances everywhere and at every level in Highbury. Marriage with Robert Martin, thinks Emma, must limit Harriet's future to a social circle that *she* has no desire (and pretends she has no power) to enter. Like Emma's conviction that it is her duty to refuse an invitation from the prosperous, rising Coles, and her plans to be 'useful' to Mr Elton by entertaining him at Hartfield and by finding him a wife (for Emma could never think of marrying him herself!), her refusal to notice the Martins and to let Harriet associate with them is an attempt to challenge and check, if she possibly can, the liberality and informality she knows to be general outside Hartfield, and perceives with disapproval even in her closest friends. The individual's relationship with society, always a major preoccupation of Jane Austen (who explored aspects of it in Marianne Dashwood's arrogant isolation from her world and Elinor's tactful diplomacy, Elizabeth Bennet's determination to choose for herself in marriage, and Fanny Price's cultivated mental habit of patience and humility), becomes *Emma*'s great theme, as the novel's spoilt, individualistic heroine is tempted by loneliness to mix more in Highbury life. In the course of a year—during which she falls in love and marries—Emma Woodhouse, who had hitherto pondered exclusively on the factors that *divide* each social rank from those immediately above and below it, comes to feel at last the sense of community that unites them all, and to appreciate her own responsibility to help in maintaining its vigorous life.

The reader who was conscious, while reading *Mansfield Park*, of a striking development in the novelist's symbolic use of a wide range and variety of settings, will recall how the worlds of Portsmouth and London seemed to converge upon Mansfield Park in the first part of the novel, and then to move away once more, drawing the Crawfords, Maria, and Julia to London, and Fanny to her home in Portsmouth. The panoramic vision that played over grandeur, sophistication, and squalor in *Mansfield Park* focuses now in depth on a single country village. It is possible to see, in the mass of selected detail that builds up the atmosphere of Highbury and the interiors of its houses, an intimate connection with material and methods first used in the picture of the Prices' home in Portsmouth. The writing of *Mansfield Park* may well have opened a new world of possibilities to a writer who had in earlier work largely restricted her scope to the 'respectable' classes of society. We remember *Sense and Sensibility*, where we saw so little of the servants at Barton Cottage, despite the smallness of the house and its many inconveniences, which must necessarily have brought the Dashwood family's 'two maids and a man' into close contact with their employers; or *Pride and Prejudice*, where Mrs Bennet so loudly denied Mr Collins's assumption that her daughters had cooked the meal he was eating, so far apart at Longbourn House (apparently) were the worlds of the drawingroom and the servants' hall. But in *Mansfield Park*, many opportunities occur—justified by the need to establish major themes more firmly—to draw pictures of the Prices' maid-of-all-work Rebecca, whose slovenliness and inefficiency do nothing to speed up the 'slow bustle' of Mrs Price's housekeeping; and of Baddeley, 'John Carpenter', and the other servants at Mansfield Park, who support the grandeur of the Bertrams' way of life and are victims, like Fanny, of Mrs Norris's meddlesome interference. In *Emma*, a novel that takes as one of its themes the unity of village life, the lower orders exist as characters in their own right, maintaining their role in a two-way relationship. James, the Hartfield coachman, is the constant object of Mr Woodhouse's concern, and James's daughter Hannah (who has been recommended by Emma for the post of Mrs Weston's maid and gone to live at Randalls) is expected to provide an additional tie between the Westons and the Hartfield family—Mr Woodhouse consoles himself for the loss of 'poor Miss Taylor' by remembering that Mrs Weston 'will be hearing of us' every time James visits his daughter at Randalls. Patty, the single servant the Bates family can afford to employ, shares in their moments of distress and agitation; William Larkins 'thinks more of his master's profit than any thing'; and the Donwell housekeeper, Mrs Hodges, 'cannot bear' that Mr Knightley should deprive himself of apple-tarts by selling or giving away the best cooking apples from his trees.

The domestic side of life attracts a much greater share of our attention in *Emma* than it has seemed to do in any previous novel. The reader soon becomes familiar with the interiors of the Highbury houses; he is introduced to Mrs Goddard's 'neat parlour hung round with fancy-work', he hears from a delighted Harriet of Mrs Martin's '*two* parlours, two very good parlours indeed', he encounters the unexpected step at the turning of Mrs Bates's dark and narrow staircase, and enters many times with Emma the cramped quarters to which it leads. He is soon familiar with the established customs of each household, knows of old Mr Woodhouse's kindly fears for his guests' digestions, guesses at the privations suffered by the Bates family, and admires the grand pianoforte in the Coles's drawing-room, expressive at once of its owners' wealth, their good-humour, and their lack of education—unable to play it themselves, they hope their many visitors will give them pleasure by making use of it. A great deal of space is devoted in *Emma* to such matters, that appear trivial in themselves but serve the comic purposes of the novel at the same time as they create Highbury in the reader's imagination, filling with unimportant incidents and detail the routine of Emma's uneventful life.

Emma's energetic attempts to vary that routine by being 'useful' to her friends provide the novel with its plot, and begin in earnest when her governess's marriage to Mr Weston leaves her intellectually solitary, her days devoted to the care of her father and unenlivened by congenial associates of her own age. Emma's boredom is relieved by a new and temporarily absorbing interest when she meets Harriet Smith, a pretty young woman of unknown parentage, who has been brought up at Mrs Goddard's school in Highbury. Emma decides to patronise and 'improve' Harriet:

She was not struck by any thing remarkably clever in Miss Smith's conversation, but she found her altogether very engaging—not inconveniently shy, not unwilling to talk—and yet so far from pushing, shewing so proper and becoming a deference, seeming so pleasantly grateful for being admitted to Hartfield, and so artlessly impressed by the appearance of every thing in so superior a style to what she had been used to, that she must have good sense and deserve encouragement. Encouragement should be given...The acquaintance she had already formed were unworthy of her...*She* would notice her; she would improve her; she would detach her from her bad acquaintance, and introduce her into good society; she would form her opinions and her manners. It would be an interesting, and certainly a very kind undertaking; highly becoming her own situation in life, her leisure, and powers.

Here is a passage that unites in the close-knit, organic way that has become characteristic of Jane Austen's best writing, the main threads of the novel's interests. We learn something of Harriet's appearance and manners in the first sentence, but we learn much more (indirectly) about Emma, who is summing her up. Harriet may lack wit, but she is *engaging*—that is, she attracts Emma. Why? Because, it soon becomes clear, her deference approximates to Emma's idea of the respect she is entitled to. Harriet's shyness is *not inconvenient*; why? It allows Emma to talk, and to guide the conversation of her guests as she will—Emma prides herself on her talents as a hostess. Harriet does not *push*—that is, she does not try to take the centre of the stage, which Emma has come to regard as hers by right. She is *pleasantly* grateful for being invited to Hartfield—her gratitude for what she clearly regards as an honour pleases and flatters Emma. Thus, Harriet's admiration of the elegance of Hartfield (for which Emma is chiefly responsible) is felt by her hostess to be more discriminating than it really is; and on this mistaken belief in potentialities that need but a little fostering to make Harriet a satisfactory companion for her, Emma founds her attempts to mould a work of art. Part of the comedy of the novel lies in the disappointments Emma must undergo as her Galatea betrays at every turn a perfect vacancy of mind, a complete lack of the divine spark that can bring her to full and intellectually satisfactory life.

Emma's enthusiasm for Harriet should, by its very warmth, put us on our guard. We learn, from Mr Knightley's conversation with her former governess, that Emma has frequently drawn up methodically arranged lists of books she intended to read, only to abandon them after a short time. In music and singing, as in painting, her record has been one of 'many beginnings'. Does she propose to devote to the 'improvement' of Harriet Smith merely this kind of transient enthusiasm? It would seem so, and in her delighted schemes for Harriet's welfare, Emma cannot perceive that the consequences may be dangerous and destructive to them both. It would *certainly be a very kind undertaking*. Emma congratulates herself here on her own generosity, but the placing of these words after the earlier comment on the *interest* that the project holds for her suggests that she will be guided by a spirit of idle self-indulgence, not of true benevolence. Regarding her meddlesomeness as kindness, Emma cannot recognise the impertinence and immorality of what she is about to do. She is quite confident that she can only influence Harriet for the best, believes herself socially and intellectually fitted for the responsibility of forming Harriet's mind, and remembers that the scheme will while away the lonely hours occasioned by her governess's marriage.

In whatever light she chooses to look at it, there is no doubt that Emma has selected in Harriet Smith a sacrifice to her own vanity and boredom. Her benevolent intentions are given a dangerous twist by her delight in matchmaking; in the course of misdirecting Harriet's emotional life, Emma makes enemies for herself by assuming an insight into the thoughts and motives of Highbury people that she does not possess, spreads her errors over an unexpectedly and embarrassingly wide area, and proves herself totally unfit for the role of judge and social arbiter that she has secretly assumed.

Emma's vain inclination to impose her imagination and her will on reality leads her to make a major error: Harriet Smith, whom she has chosen to be her own friend and confidante, *must* (she thinks) be a gentleman's daughter, and her beauty will enable her to pick and choose from among many suitors. She must, therefore, deserve a better fate than marriage with Robert Martin, the young farmer who admires her. Emma makes up her mind that Martin is poor and dependent—'has his fortune entirely to make'—and persists in thinking of him as 'illiterate and vulgar' because she wants to believe him so, although she has read his well-written letter to Harriet, and heard Mr Knightley describe him as a sensible, reliable, prosperous young man. Emma separates Harriet from Martin and the 'yeomanry' he represents, and attempts to match her with the 'genteel' vicar, Mr Elton. Despite Mr Knightley's timely warning that Mr Elton is too 'well acquainted with his own claims' to make an imprudent marriage, Emma imagines him to be passionately in love with Harriet. Mistaking his flattery of herself for an indirect courtship of her friend, Emma looks forward to their marriage as yet another proof of her power and her benevolence, another reason for self-congratulation.

Emma's imagination leads her to excesses that cease to be comic, when a Highbury acquaintance of her own age, Miss Bates's niece Jane Fairfax, comes back to the village with what seems to Emma an increase of her habitual cold reserve. Accomplished and of gentle birth, Jane's poverty has marked her out for a future as a governess. Emma, always willing to imagine a fault in Jane Fairfax, whose accomplishments are superior to her own and whose praises sound perpetually and irritatingly in her ears, amuses herself by attributing the change in her to a secret love-intrigue of her own fabrication. This baseless fancy she is foolish enough to confide to Mr Weston's son Frank Churchill, the heir to the 'great' name and fortune of his mother's family; failing in her efforts to establish Harriet at the vicarage, Emma has looked even higher, and hopes to interest Frank Churchill and Harriet in each other. Emma imagines that Frank has been a little in love with her, that at her prompting he will be ready to fall in love with Harriet, and that he shares her opinions of Jane Fairfax: she is wrong on all three counts, for he is secretly engaged to Jane.

The intricacies of this plot are tightened further when Harriet confides shyly to Emma that she has fallen in love herself—with Mr Knightley, the leader of Highbury society and Emma's particular ally and friend, and believes her love to be returned. Struggling to sustain this unexpected blow, Emma discovers her own love for Mr Knightley, and realises that she has been brought to the brink of what may well be permanent misery and regret by nothing but her own vain self-will. She perceives, too, that the 'gradations of rank' and the established customs of society maintain a kind of ordered coherence in the world she knows, an order that she has been trying, for her own idle amusement, to destroy.

Emma's exploits, which have made Mr Elton and his bride her enemies, hurt Jane Fairfax, Miss Bates, and Harriet in spirit, and seem to have estranged even Mr Knightley besides bidding fair to ruin her own prospects of happiness, are brought to an end by Harriet's confession. There is nothing more that Emma can do, for herself or for Harriet, beyond repenting past errors most sincerely and determining to act more sensibly and kindly in future. The news of the death of Mrs Churchill, Frank's capricious aunt, now reaches Highbury; his engagement to Jane Fairfax can be openly announced, and a marriage planned. The elimination of Frank Churchill as a suitor for Emma leads to explanations and a better understanding between Emma and Mr Knightley. Harriet Smith, who has retained her attachment to the devoted Martin in spite of Emma's attempts to remould her tastes and heighten her expectations—and in spite of her own admiration for Mr Knightley—cannot resist accepting Martin's second proposal of marriage. Three happy marriages, founded on mutual affection, adapted to the needs of six very different intellects and personalities, maintaining without outrage the traditional gradations of society, replace the dangerous and unequal alliances fancied or connived at by Emma Woodhouse for herself and her Highbury friends.

Emma's 'vain spirit' has been responsible for her two major errors of judgment, which the experiences of twelve months, assisted by the rebukes of Mr Knightley and the occasional pricking of her own active conscience, succeed in correcting. One of her errors, as we have seen, is her misconception of her own social role. The other springs from her reluctance to acknowledge her own imperfections. To compensate for the lack she suspects in herself of a truly generous nature, Emma embarks on the misguided course of action that provides the plot of the novel, and has its source in vanity and boredom, not in true unselfishness.

Her words to Harriet, quoted at the beginning of this chapter, mark the undertaking of a task that Emma believes appropriate, in the light of its apparent generosity and air of charitable patronage, to her own high social position. She will set herself to systematically destroy every shred of respect and admiration felt by Harriet for Martin. In succeeding conversations on the same subject she ruthlessly pursues this objective:

'I want to see you permanently well connected—and to that end it will be advisable to have as few odd acquaintance as may be; and, therefore, I say that if you should still be in this country when Mr Martin marries, I wish you may not be drawn in, by your intimacy with the sisters, to be acquainted with the wife, who will probably be some mere farmer's daughter, without education.'

'To be sure. Yes. Not that I think Mr Martin would ever marry any body but what had had some education—and been very well brought up. However, I do not mean to set up my opinion against your's—and I am sure I shall not wish for the acquaintance of his wife. I shall always have a great regard for the Miss Martins, especially Elizabeth, and should be very sorry to give them up, for they are quite as well educated as me...'

Emma has told herself that she will only probe the extent of Harriet's attachment to Martin before advancing her own alternative, Mr Elton. But her method is studied and cruel, her sentences being blows aimed successively at Martin's uncouth, 'clownish' appearance, his supposedly inferior status, his unsuitable age, his presumed lack of funds, finally—and outrageously, considering Harriet's intellectual poverty—his poor chances of marrying an educated woman worthy of Harriet's regard. Harriet lacks the resources to withstand or meet such an attack; her reply suggests that she has already inwardly bidden the Martins farewell in obedience to Emma's superior judgment, but its uncertain grammar (a classic example of Jane Austen's acute ear for the niceties of social and intellectual distinction as expressed in speech), its hesitancy, and its betrayal of a tenacious affection for the Martin family should have indicated to Emma that on this last point, if not on all, she has gone too far.

Emma's methods are unfair, not only to the absent Martin and the defenceless, slow-witted Harriet, but *to herself*. Her arrogant self-will exists side by side with a compassionate,

charitable spirit that includes the destitute as well as the impover-
ished respectable folk of Highbury. She could not have spoken
in this way without deliberately silencing her conscience. But—
typical of her contradictory impulses of selfishness and generosity—Harriet must for her own good be separated from the
Martins, and Emma will distort her own sense of what is right
and just in order to do it.

The recurring theme of moral education, explored in Emma's
progress to a clearer judgment and a repentant, humble frame of
mind, together with the reintroduction of a matchmaking *motif*,
seem to relate *Emma* to *Pride and Prejudice*, whose heroine
underwent a rather similar emotional and moral education.
Talented and intelligent, mentally superior to the majority of
their acquaintances, Emma and Elizabeth are led by vanity into
error—except that, where Elizabeth was misled by her vain
prejudices, Emma is tricked by her vain self-will. Learning that
humility is safest when dealing with other people, that society
will not be moulded to their will and that they are themselves
fallible members of that society; taught by experience to check
their headstrong and ill-directed behaviour, recalled by their
conscience to a proper value of humility and selfcontrol, we see
further that the history of each heroine is conceived and presented
almost entirely in terms of lighthearted comedy. An illnatured
remark made by Emma to Miss Bates is the worst cruelty
inflicted upon anybody in *Emma*, and Jane Fairfax's secret
engagement the only source of mystery.

But striking as these similarities between the two novels are,
a single dissimilarity exists that seems still more remarkable,
sets *Emma* quite apart from *Pride and Prejudice*, and appears to
provide the key to its technical perfection. There is a strong
sense of personal involvement and identification of the author
with the heroine in *Pride and Prejudice*—emerging in Elizabeth's
defying of the pride and power of rank as she sees it embodied
in Darcy and the de Bourghs, and in her gallant defence of her
right to control her destiny in marriage against the interference of
society as represented by her mother and Lady Catherine—that
is entirely absent or perfectly submerged in *Emma*. The defence

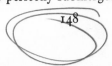

of feminine selfrespect is certainly undertaken in *Emma*, and in words strikingly similar to those used by Fanny to Edmund in *Mansfield Park* (see Chapter 7), but it is undertaken by the heroine on a friend's behalf, not her own:

'Oh! to be sure,' cried Emma, 'it is always incomprehensible to a man that a woman should ever refuse an offer of marriage. A man always imagines a woman to be ready for anybody who asks her.'

Emma's support of Harriet's right to refuse Martin's proposal of marriage is justified in theory, but false in practice, as Mr Knightley points out. Harriet is incapable, by her very nature, of an independent or rational judgment, and energy expended in encouraging her independence is misdirected. The defence of women's rights is more publicly and spectacularly undertaken later in the novel by Mrs Elton, a woman who is as anxious to shine in Highbury society as Emma can be to guide and control it:

'No, indeed, I shall grant you nothing. I always take the part of my own sex. I do indeed. I give you notice—You will find me a formidable antagonist on that point. I always stand up for women...'

The whole question of female intelligence and independence seems to be in doubt and even in danger of ridicule, when it is applied to a Harriet Smith or supported by a Mrs Elton. For Mrs Elton is a vulgar caricature of Emma herself, and although Emma despises her, we recognise her own faults, carried to an extreme point, in Mrs Elton's personality.

The undertone of coquettishness in Mrs Elton's conversation gives the clue to her character. Vain, self-satisfied, under-educated by Emma's standards, she would like to take the lead in Highbury society. This is the motive behind her eagerness to defend her sex, which leads her to assume (unasked) the 'duty' of protecting and patronising Jane Fairfax:

'I know you, I know you; you would take up with any thing; but I shall be a little more nice, and I am sure the good Campbells will be quite on my side; with your superior talents, you have a right to move in the first circle. Your musical knowledge alone would entitle you to name your own terms, have as many rooms as you like, and mix in the family as much as you choose; that is—I do not know—if you knew the harp, you might do all that, I am very sure; but you sing as well as play; yes, I really believe you might, even without the harp, stipulate for what you chose...'

The 'patronage' Mrs Elton bestows on Jane Fairfax is impudent and unconsciously cruel; it is also selfish, for however satisfactory the post may be that she will find for Jane to enter as a governess, her persistent calculation of the market value of Jane's accomplishments and her attitude of solicitous benevolence serve only to elevate her own status and talents at Jane's expense.

Mrs Elton's tacit rivalry with Emma is clear from the time she enters Highbury as Mr Elton's bride. Not only has Mr Elton met and married her a few weeks after his humiliating rejection by Emma, so that every meeting between the two women is coloured by the past in some way, but her eagerness to 'bring' Jane Fairfax forward is at once an echo of Emma's own enthusiasms regarding Harriet Smith, and a reproach to Emma's neglect of Jane:

'Jane Fairfax is absolutely charming, Miss Woodhouse. I quite rave about Jane Fairfax...So mild and ladylike—and with such talents!...And her situation is so calculated to affect one! Miss Woodhouse, we must exert ourselves and endeavour to do something for her. We must bring her forward... She is very timid and silent. One can see that she feels the want of encouragement. I like her the better for it. I must confess it is a recommendation to me. I am a great advocate for timidity—and I am sure one does not often meet with it. But in those who are at all inferior, it is extremely prepossessing...'

Emma is disgusted and angry at Mrs Elton's patronage of Jane, but the line that separates her own exploitation of helplessness from her rival's is very thin. Mrs Elton's pretensions to taste and intellect infuriate Emma at nearly every encounter, but we recognise while she does not—or shuts her eyes to the evidence—that their vanity is a common characteristic, and frequently expressed in similar ways. Emma prides herself on the possession of 'an active, busy mind, with a great many independent resources', but reacts with violent energy to Mrs Elton's coy revelations on the same subject:

'When he was speaking of it in that way, I honestly said that *the world* I I could give up—parties, balls, plays—for I had no fear of retirement. Blessed with so many resources within myself, the world was not necessary to *me*. I could do very well without it. To those who had no resources it was a different thing; but my resources made me quite independent...'

Emma cannot laugh, as the reader can, who knows that a true and generous sympathy redeems Emma's meddling, while Mrs Elton's pretensions to patronage originate in an anxious self-love that renders them comic, even pathetic. *She* cannot regard Mrs Elton as anything but an interloper,

'A little upstart, vulgar being, with her Mr E., and her *caro sposo*, and her resources, and all her airs of pert pretension and under-bred finery. Actually to discover that Mr Knightley is a gentleman! I doubt whether he will return the compliment, and discover her to be a lady.'

Jane Austen's ironic presentation of Mrs Elton as a champion of defenceless feminine virtue and worth renders such championship suspect, comic in itself, and irrelevant to the real needs of the helpless, suggesting that her primary concern in *Emma* is elsewhere. Neither Jane Fairfax (who must, perforce, consider her own accomplishments as financial 'resources' rather than social assets) nor Harriet Smith (who has never known want, but has no accomplishments to speak of) derive much real assistance from their eager patrons—indeed, nothing but tact and sympathy can usefully be extended to two such different women, who have so little in common beyond their gentle manners and their social disadvantages, even these last arising from entirely different causes.

The discriminating eye that observes Jane Fairfax and Harriet Smith in their different dilemmas, the searching irony directed at the contradictions of Emma's character, the sympathy that follows all three, seem to confirm our impression of the wider-ranging moral vision that governed the characterisation of Fanny Price, Mary Crawford, and Maria Bertram in *Mansfield Park*. It may have been that Jane Austen, learning more about life as she matured in years and experience, was unwilling to generalise (as she had done in *The Watsons*, for example) on the subject of the social disadvantages of women, among whom she had come to discern differences in nature, in intellect, in manners and in education that set them very far apart from one another. The interests of *Emma* include the situation of the single woman in society—explored in Jane Fairfax, Harriet Smith, Miss Bates, and in Emma herself—but they are by no means restricted to it.

It is not a 'social problem' that is at the heart of the novel, but the human, everyday problem of disciplining oneself to meet the demands of ordinary life. The confident ease that characterises *Emma* has been made possible by the fact that Jane Austen has been able to proceed, less emotionally hampered by personal problems and uncertainties than ever before, to the creation of a work of art.

It is as a masterpiece of comic art that *Emma* must be viewed. Faults are found in the heroine, but 'in a joke—it is all a joke', and reform is never out of sight. Emma makes enemies, but they are incapable of doing real damage. Frank Churchill's irresponsible treatment of Jane and Emma, and Emma's of Harriet are the gravest crimes committed, and all spring from real affection and good, though misguided, intentions; Emma's governess is a friend, not a tyrant, and her teaching (unlike that of Mrs Norris) is powerless to warp her pupil's nature—or even, indeed, to discipline and control it, for Emma, 'highly esteeming Miss Taylor's judgment', is 'directed chiefly by her own'. Where Fanny Price's moral superiority to Mary Crawford and Maria Bertram was never in any doubt, Emma Woodhouse is never permanently certain of her moral superiority to anybody—not even to Mrs Elton.

Consider, for example, Emma's relationship with Jane Fairfax and Harriet Smith. Emma knows very well that Jane, who possesses real refinement of mind and manners, and is truly cultivated and accomplished, would be a more appropriate companion for her than Harriet, who to all but infatuated eyes 'is pretty, and...good tempered, and that is all'. Why, then, does Emma reject the opportunity of Jane's friendship and make a fuss of Harriet? She tells herself that Harriet is worth a hundred Jane Fairfaxes, underrates even her own intelligence as being inferior to 'all the charm and all the felicity' of Harriet's tender heart. She complains at the same time that Jane is so distant in her manner (and her aunt, Miss Bates, so tiresome!) that nobody could desire a closer acquaintance. In adopting this attitude Emma exaggerates Harriet's virtues, and her dislike of Jane Fairfax has roots in jealousy. Far from becoming close friends,

as their neighbours wish them to do, each turns for companionship to the other's (and her own) opposite—Emma to Harriet,
Jane to Mrs Elton. Emma rules Harriet, Mrs Elton patronises
Jane. The indifference and dislike that prevail among the members of this quartet are only thinly covered by the requirements
of social politeness.

In her relationship with Harriet, certain other features of
Emma's personality become clear. Her arrogant self-importance,
politely and wisely concealed when visiting neighbours in Highbury, is openly indulged before Harriet, who would not dream of
criticising her. Harriet, it seems, is even ready to regulate her own
life according to Emma's deluded doctrines. Their relationship
exposes and indulges Emma's love of power, and her desire to
dominate her world. Harriet is an easy victim, and in return for
adoration and obedience Emma gives Harriet her affection and
her patronage. We begin to feel that although Emma's dislike of
Mrs Elton and Jane Fairfax is somewhat justified by the vulgar
pretensions of one and the reserved manners of the other, both
these ladies might have got on better with Emma had they
deferred to her as Harriet artlessly does. Mrs Elton, Jane, and
Harriet help to define Emma, whose real generosity of spirit
shines out clearly beside Mrs Elton's anxious attempts at patronage; whose natural, unaffected, open relationships with Mr
Knightley and Frank Churchill contrast with the obscure mystery
that surrounds Jane; and whose wit and intelligence—though
they often lead her into error—sparkle all the more brightly
because they play beside, and over, Harriet's dull good nature.
Her comically confused motives and attitudes, her good intentions and her ill-judged actions, all bring Emma close to our
experience of people in real life.

And it is real life that is the subject of *Emma*, emerging in the
heroine's gradually achieved ability to see society in true perspective, and to do justice to its positive virtues. While each earlier
novel accurately reproduced in fiction the outlines of the social
world that Jane Austen knew, in *Emma* the 'gradations of rank'
within a single village are drawn with careful, even loving detail.
Jane Fairfax, caught helplessly between the ranks though she is—

fitted by her talents to move in the highest but doomed by her poverty to join the numbers of the 'respectable' employed—cannot for all the pathos of her situation in the context of the time, monopolise the reader's sympathy, which is demanded by the dilemmas of many others; Harriet Smith, fated by the accident of her birth to attract Emma's dangerous charities and Mr Elton's sneers; Miss Bates, depressed to the level of becoming an object of her neighbours' charity; Mr Weston, whose high-born first wife could not forgive him his merely 'respectable' origins; Mr Elton, whose talk of love and proposal of marriage are treated by Emma as social impertinence; Emma herself, isolated at Hartfield by her father's ill-health and her own mistaken ideas of social decorum. The task of adaptation to the requirements of social life must be accepted by many of the characters in *Emma*, and not only by the central figure, as a form of necessary self-discipline that brings its own rewards. And so, although Jane Fairfax eventually marries Churchill, it is not before she has prepared herself for a future as a governess, and accepted her first post. Mr Weston finds happiness in a second marriage, but must bear the knowledge that his son is being brought up by those who despise and dislike him. Emma marries Mr Knightley and is restored to a good understanding with Jane Fairfax, but not before she has endured a private purgatory of shame and regret.

In the working out of these personal histories, in each description of people victimised in some way by society, there is discernible no shrillness of tone or bitterness of feeling, although irony remains Jane Austen's chosen method:

Human nature is so well disposed towards those who are in interesting situations, that a young person, who either marries or dies, is sure of being kindly spoken of.

All—except for Jane Fairfax, who though not sentimentalised yet attracts the most sympathy—are presented with lively irony. 'You and Mr Elton are one as clever as the other', cries poor Harriet enthusiastically, misled by Emma and soon to be insulted by Mr Elton. The 'unmanageable good-will of Mr Weston's temper' assembles the ill-assorted explorers to Box Hill, on an excursion of pleasure that brings regret and resentment to every member of the party but himself and the dull-witted Harriet. We have a memorable glimpse of Mr Elton as Emma and Harriet pay their wedding visit to his wife:

...when she considered how peculiarly unlucky poor Mr Elton was in being in the same room at once with the woman he had just married, the woman he had wanted to marry, and the woman he had been expected to marry, she must allow him to have the right to look as little wise, and to be as much affectedly, and as little really easy as could be.

Emma herself is treated throughout with an irony that never, even in her saddest and most repentant moments, becomes clouded or changes into sentimentality. As for Miss Bates, who of all the spinsters in the novel, is the nearest to her creator in age and situation, being 'neither young, handsome, rich, nor married',

Miss Bates stood in the very worst predicament in the world for having much of the public favour; and she had no intellectual superiority to make atonement to herself, or frighten those who might hate her, into outward respect.

Emma, who enjoys most of the advantages lacked by her less fortunate neighbour, is sometimes haunted by the idea that she might herself become one day (as Harriet puts it) 'an old maid at last, like Miss Bates!' It is evident that Jane Austen had no illusions about small town popularity; intellect in a poor, plain spinster might help *her* bear her situation more patiently, but a display of it would inevitably excite fear and dislike in others. Taken by itself, it is a searing passage that reminds us that the novelist was probably coping at the time with the special problems of an intelligent single woman who must live in a society that has no value for her intelligence and offers her no respectable alternative to marriage. And yet, the character of Miss Bates herself as she comes before us in speech and action is far from being an indictment of society; she has neither money nor wit with which she can impress and control the social world of Highbury, but she offers it love, gratitude, and a tranquil, contented frame of mind —*and receives love and respect in return*:

'...and then the baked apples came home, Mrs Wallis sent them by her boy; they are extremely civil and obliging to us, the Wallises, always—I have heard some people say that Mrs Wallis can be uncivil and give a very rude answer, but we have never known any thing but the greatest attention from them. And it cannot be for the value of our custom now, for what is our consumption of bread, you know?'

Highbury has consistently honoured Miss Bates, whose quiet '*now*' simultaneously summarises and dismisses the painful story of the family's descent in the world. It has never ceased to praise and welcome Jane Fairfax, or to be kind to Harriet Smith. Emma will perceive that Highbury is by no means the 'inferior society' she had thought it to be. While Emma discusses with Harriet her own intention to remain single, she has Miss Bates in her thoughts:

'Never mind, Harriet, I shall not be a poor old maid; and it is poverty only which makes celibacy contemptible to a generous public! A single woman, with a very narrow income, must be a ridiculous, disagreeable, old maid! the proper sport of boys and girls; but a single woman, of good fortune, is always respectable, and may be as sensible and pleasant as anybody else...'

Harriet's response to this is 'Dear me!' She has not understood half of what Emma has been saying. But in any case, Emma has really been thinking aloud, too intent on her own reflections to adjust her speech to Harriet's understanding. She has been speculating on what life must be like for the shabby-genteel, just as she delighted in Harriet's descriptions of the Martin family of Abbey-Mill Farm, 'amused by such a picture of another set of beings'. Emma has never known want herself, and her own impatience with Highbury society makes her exaggerate and distort her picture of its treatment of the poor spinster. It does not take long for her good sense to remind her that Miss Bates 'is very much to the taste of everybody, though single and though poor'. The firm control of tone, the exquisite poise, above all the good sense with which Jane Austen reflects on spinsterhood and the money values that govern society, without allowing the subject to break up the carefully contrived smoothness of the novel's surface, indicate a maturity of outlook that has made the technical artistry of *Emma* possible.

Miss Bates is a character of great importance to Jane Austen's purposes in *Emma*. She is 'a great talker upon little matters', and like Anne Steele's chatter in *Sense and Sensibility* and Lydia Bennet's in *Pride and Prejudice*, her talk reveals (if Emma would only attend!) matters basic to the plot:

'...My dear sir, you are too obliging. Is there nobody you would rather? I am not helpless. Sir, you are most kind. Upon my word, Jane on one arm, and me on the other!...Well, where shall we sit? where shall we sit?...Oh! do you recommend this side? Well, I am sure, Mr Churchill—only it seems too good—but just as you please...'

In the flow of Miss Bates's chatter at the Crown Inn lie scattered the evidences, unconsciously absorbed and relayed without prior analysis, yet perfectly accurate, of Frank Churchill's attentions to Jane Fairfax during the very period that Emma, misled by his gallantry, fancies him to be attached to herself. The strained, unhappy course of Jane's relationship with Frank Churchill must, by the nature of things and by the scheme of the novel be hidden from Emma, but the misunderstandings between them that reach a point of crisis at Donwell Abbey and culminate, after the expedition to Box Hill, in Jane's acceptance of a post as governess are all outlined, and in their proper sequence, in her aunt's conversation with Emma on the following day. Ironically enough, Emma, who has concocted a fantasy involving Jane without the help of any real facts other than the mysterious gift of a piano, cannot interpret them correctly when they are presented to her, so preoccupied is she with her own need to make amends to Miss Bates. Again, Miss Bates's talk, flowing naturally and un-trammelled with the movements of her mind, establishes her sim-plicity and generosity of heart so effectively that Emma's rude remark to her on Box Hill seems indefensibly brutal and unfair:

'Oh! very well,' exclaimed Miss Bates, 'then I need not be uneasy. "Three things very dull indeed". That will just do for me, you know. I shall be sure to say three dull things as soon as ever I open my mouth, shan't I? (looking round with the most good-humoured dependence on every body's assent). Do not you all think I shall?'

Emma could not resist.

'Ah! ma'am, but there may be a difficulty. Pardon me—but you will be limited as to number—only three at once.'

The character of Miss Bates and her mannerisms of speech (she seldom, when in full flow, finishes a sentence, and this well-known idiosyncrasy gives point to Emma's rejoinder) are thus made to contribute to the disciplining of Emma and the curing of her social arrogance; at the same time they serve the themes of the novel in yet another way by reflecting, through her universal goodwill and the pictures created in the reader's imagination by her incessant talk, the integrated organic world of Highbury.

Miss Bates's amusing monologues are filled with scraps of information of whose significance she is unconscious or only partly aware, little sketches of other people as they move, pause, and gesture, half-reported dialogues and apparently trivial exchanges of all kinds; in her speech Highbury comes to magnificent life. The Westons of Randalls, the Knightleys of Donwell Abbey, and the Woodhouse family of Hartfield jostle each other in her conversation, and rub shoulders in the most democratic way with the newly-rich Coles, Mr Samuel Larkins, and Mrs Goddard the school-mistress. There is created for us a vivid impression of a populated world, a society engaged in various well-defined, long-established activities that only occasionally include or concern the principal characters: that microcosm of the real world that Jane Austen characteristically works to project.

The setting itself is vividly realised, and its every feature soon seems as familiar to the reader as Highbury's main street appears to Emma, who stands looking out on it idly as Harriet hesitates over choosing muslins at Ford's:

Much could not be hoped from the traffic of even the busiest part of Highbury; Mr Perry walking hastily by, Mr William Cox letting himself in at the office door, Mr Cole's carriage horses returning from exercise, or a stray letter-boy on an obstinate mule, were the liveliest objects she could presume to expect...

She looked down the Randalls road. The scene enlarged; two persons appeared; Mrs Weston and her son-in-law; they were walking into Highbury; to Hartfield of course.

Unobtrusively, almost unconsciously, the reader comes to share Emma's intimate knowledge of her village, he becomes familiar with the houses that face the street, learns to expect certain events to occur at that hour of the day. With Emma he dismisses as uninteresting (because customary) the appearance of the doctor, the lawyer, the letter-boy, and the horses; sharing Emma's quickening interest, he welcomes the unexpected; and as the Randalls party approach, he speculates with Emma concerning their probable objective. *To Hartfield of course.* That *of course* tells us something of Emma's opinion of her own importance and attractions, and of the contempt in which she holds the village; but we learn from it too that in Highbury everybody knows the other's business, so that an unusual occurrence becomes a topic of endless pleasurable speculation. And so it does, for 'all manner of solemn nonsense was talked on the subject' of Mr Weston's remaining single by his friendly neighbours, his son Frank is 'one of the boasts of Highbury', his 'merits and prospects a kind of common concern'. There is 'not a dissentient voice' in the village on the question of the propriety of a visit from Frank to his father on his second marriage. Such an atmosphere of close, even stifling intimacy has been created that we do not need to ask why Emma chooses to keep aloof from Highbury society in general, limiting her circle to her own family, the Westons, and her brother-in-law, Mr Knightley.

The 'gradations of rank' in Highbury, summarised in this chapter for our convenience, are presented in the novel with a rich complexity that in itself contradicts Emma's wilful desire to see only a part and not the whole. The deftness with which the characters are moved within and across them, indicates a perfect familiarity with their subtleties; the fastidious care with which situations are built upon them reveals a healthy respect for their usefulness in regulating life in a known, familiar society, together with an ironic enjoyment of the shading they lend the ordinary exchanges of everyday life.

We can look, for instance, at Mr Elton's proposal of marriage to Emma, made in the carriage as they return together from the Westons' dinner-party at Randalls on Christmas Eve. He hopes to marry into the rank above his, but he *talks* of love. *She* has intended him to marry a wife whose claims to rank of any kind are obscure and uncertain. Her refusal is given in the manner of a social snub:

'Encouragement! I give you encouragement! sir, you have been entirely mistaken in supposing it. I have seen you only as the admirer of my friend. In no other light could you have been more to me than a common acquaintance...'

If Elizabeth Bennet's tête-à-tête with Mr Collins in *Pride and Prejudice* was excellent social comedy, Emma's with Mr Elton reaches greater depths of subtlety:

He was too angry to say another word; her manner too decided to invite supplication; and in this state of swelling resentment, and mutually deep mortification, they had to continue together a few minutes longer, for the fears of Mr Woodhouse had confined them to a foot pace. If there had not been so much anger, there would have been desperate awkwardness; but their straightforward emotions left no room for the little zigzags of embarrassment.

The reader's amusement at the discomfiture of both deluded actors in this scene must be tempered with sympathy; Mr Elton, as much and even more than Emma, must be pitied in his vanity and in the shock of his disillusionment. The slowness with which their carriage moves, as it turns the well-known dangerous corner into Vicarage Lane in deep snow, makes their discomfort seem endless. The last phrase, *the little zigzags of embarrassment*, distils a lifetime's experience of social intercourse, in the same way that the entire scene grows out of the social structure and the familiar geography of Highbury.

Jane Austen's picture of social life in Highbury, like her picture of Emma herself, must be viewed from many angles to be seen in true perspective. There Emma Woodhouse, an heiress to thirty thousand pounds, and Jane Fairfax, who has been trained to earn her living as a governess, can meet on equal terms. 'There are few places with such society as Highbury,' says Miss Bates; 'we are quite blessed in our neighbours'. And certainly, the village is so closely and happily integrated, so much a community, that long residence there brings more honour than a long purse. Wealth, on the other hand, however newly acquired, does not disqualify families such as 'the worthy Coles' from notice. Mr Woodhouse, 'whose talents could not have recommended him at any time', is appreciated in Highbury for his kindliness and good temper. There is a significant lesson to be learned from the fact that Jane Fairfax's talents are recognised by Mrs Elton, Mrs Cole, and others whom Emma professes to despise; their claims to taste may be small, but they all praise Jane without exception and without jealousy—and Emma does not. We begin to doubt the justice of Emma's frequent condemnations of Highbury people. Jane Fairfax's dejected reference to 'offices for the sale of the human intellect' (of which Mrs Elton is proposing to become herself an agent!) allows us a brief glimpse of the brutal, commercialised world outside Highbury, and we see the village for a moment as *she* sees it, as a haven of respite from the inevitably unpleasant future that waits for her outside.

A greater sympathy for Jane Fairfax and a better ability to share the liberality of Mr Knightley's point of view, both achieved with much effort, are the steps by which Emma comes to a rational point of view herself. She can congratulate Frank Churchill on their common destiny, 'which bids fair to connect us with two characters so much superior to our own.'

Jane Austen's treatment of Mr Knightley seems to derive from and improve upon her portrait of Edmund Bertram in *Mansfield Park*. His relationship with Emma, developing over many years of intimate knowledge and affection to a strong and sympathetic, loving understanding, is similar in this to Edmund's with Fanny, but it is more complex than theirs and less unequal. Mr Knightley is perfectly aware of the weaknesses that underly Emma's loveliness and grace of manner, and although he loves her he cannot see her 'acting wrong, without a remonstrance'. He has weaknesses of his own, too, among them a decided self-satisfaction (although his has more justification than Emma's) and an uncharitable prejudice against Frank Churchill (justified to some extent, as events will prove). His blunt manners, his penetrating judgment, and his 'general benevolence' (for which his brother's dislike of company and Mr Weston's gregariousness are useful foils) help to build up an impression of an attractively masculine personality. His wit, unlike Emma's, is never unkind, and his mature steadiness suitably complements the contradictory impulses that govern Emma's nature, although in many things they are alike.

The quality of their relationship is established by a succession of subtle touches, from which the reader can draw a conclusion regarding Mr Knightley and Emma that is hidden from them, so used have they become over the years to their comfortable friendship. We have the hint, for instance, let slip without fuss by Mr Knightley in a conversation with Mrs Weston about Emma's friendship with Harriet, that he has kept by him for some time a list of books that Emma had drawn up at the age of fourteen; Mrs Weston does not pay much attention to this, and neither does Mr Knightley himself recognise its real significance —at the time. But it is one of the very few glimpses the reader has of Mr Knightley away from Hartfield and Emma, or the houses of Highbury, and it is not easily forgotten. On her side, Emma has been long used to measuring each new acquaintance against a standard unconsciously derived from her admiration and respect for Mr Knightley. Although she does not pause to examine the reason for her feelings, she is indignant when Harriet dares to compare him with Mr Elton, resents Mrs Elton's familiarities with his name, will not tolerate for a moment Mrs Weston's kindly suggestion that Jane Fairfax would make him a suitable wife, and wonders aloud that she has herself been 'somehow or other safe' from the danger of falling in love with Frank Churchill. The arrival of Frank in Highbury and Jane Fairfax's return there, with all the social meetings, misunderstandings, and forming of alliances that result from them, awaken Mr Knightley to the realisation that his protective guardianship of Emma has become indistinguishable from love; and when Harriet shyly confides to Emma that she thinks Mr Knightley may come to love her, Emma knows at last that she loves Mr Knightley herself.

The deep, unspoken understanding that links them together despite their conflicting natures and opinions is apparent from the first time we see them together at Hartfield, on the evening of Mrs Weston's wedding-day. Even the bitter quarrel that follows soon after over their respective plans for Harriet Smith and Robert Martin does not shake their regard for each other. Chapter 12 of the first volume, which is devoted to a description of a quiet evening at Hartfield, on the occasion of a Christmas visit to their Highbury relations by Mr and Mrs John Knightley, opens with a brief exchange between Emma and Mr Knightley that makes this clear. The rest of the chapter details a conversation between Mr Woodhouse and his elder daughter, Isabella. It is an exchange rich in comedy, for Isabella is very like her father, who judges people by their solicitude for—and effect on—his health. Isabella enjoys a similar range of illnesses and nervous worries to his, and she is equally dependent on a favourite family doctor; but Emma cannot enjoy it. She spends her time trying to guide their conversation away from topics that she knows must depress her father or provoke her brother-in-law; but when she fails, and John Knightley's impatient temper twice threatens to wreck the peace and tranquillity of their family meeting, it is hastily and successfully smoothed away—first by Emma, and then by Mr Knightley. The scene provides the reader with a view of Emma's personality that her conversations with the pliant Harriet and her unkind remarks at the expense of Highbury people do not afford. It illustrates her quicksighted, unselfish devotion to her father, her loyalty to her family as a whole, and indicates too the identical interests and shared sense of responsibility that unite her with Mr Knightley and raise them both above the others.

Emma's marriage with Mr Knightley is a token of her partial abandonment of her earlier preconceptions, and of her readiness to accept a more liberal, just outlook on life. It is thus in harmony with the general tenor of a novel that shows at every turn the effects of a wider experience of life and a more sympathetic outlook than Jane Austen has expressed in any other work we have examined so far. Good and agreeable manners, such as those of Mr Elton and of Frank Churchill, can deceive; they disguise a mean and revengeful spirit in one, and a lack of real delicacy of feeling in the other. Bluntness, on the other hand, may be the outward characteristic of a thoughtful and sensible man such as Mr Knightley; and Robert Martin's lack of polish does no harm to his character or to his manners, which reveal his 'sense, sincerity, and good-humour'. The apparently chilly reserve of

Jane Fairfax hides a loyal, even heroic spirit, while Harriet Smith's dull wit and pretty face are as much her own as her affectionate heart. Mrs Elton, a vain and selfsatisfied social climber, has manners that please nearly everyone in Highbury. Mr Weston is sociable without the power of discrimination or the advantage of social tact; John Knightley regards a dinner-party as an unjustified invasion of his domestic privacy. Emma herself, despite all the faults that provide the novel with its material, has many claims to the reader's respect. Beautiful but devoid of personal vanity, she feels deeply for others while Mrs Elton only talks of doing so. She acknowledges her inferiority in accomplishments to Jane Fairfax, and occasionally believes herself even inferior to Harriet. She is impervious to the flattery of Churchill's and Mr Elton's attentions, repents her own foolishness, tries to make amends. It is her own uneasy awareness that Highbury does not accept her own valuation of herself that makes Emma so critical and impatient with its ways of living and thinking, provokes her into trying to dictate social laws to it, and brings her at last to see it as it really is.

The scene at Hartfield we have just been examining is one of many that, by means of presenting groups and pairs of characters engaged in conversation and the ordinary activities of daily life, establish standards of sensible, correct behaviour, of right feeling and judgment. It is matched by other scenes elsewhere in *Emma*: half a chapter in which Mr Weston tells the newly-arrived Mrs Elton of his son Frank, in the intervals of her telling *him* of her brother-in-law Mr Suckling's house at Maple Grove, neither of them in the least interested in what the other has to say; Harriet Smith's preparation of a riddle-book, and her efforts to get her sober, practical farmer to read sentimental novels; Frank Churchill's word-games at Hartfield; Mrs Elton's 'apparatus of happiness'—a large bonnet and a basket—for gathering strawberries at Donwell; and the expedition to Box Hill, where an inexplicable tension broods over the ill-assorted guests' attempts at polite accord, and where an over-wrought, over-excited Emma insults the harmless Miss Bates.

The village, like societies everywhere, could certainly produce its own illustrations of the cardinal sins, in Mr Elton's greed and his wife's envy, in Emma's pride and her father's 'habits of gentle selfishness', in Mr Weston's sleepiness of mind—but the reader's response to these characters is complex, not simple. There are no saints or sinners in Highbury, only real people who do right in some ways and err in others. They all have a place in its society.

# 9

# 'PERSUASION'

How eloquent could Anne Elliot have been, how eloquent, at least, were her wishes on the side of early warm attachment, and a cheerful confidence in futurity, against that over-anxious caution which seems to insult exertion and distrust Providence! She had been forced into prudence in her youth, she learned romance as she grew older—the natural sequel of an unnatural beginning.                                                                    *Persuasion*, Vol. 1, Chapter 4

In her last completed novel, unpublished and probably only partly revised for publication at the time of her death in 1817, Jane Austen explores a human situation, the dilemma of a young woman whose prudence has been mistaken for moral weakness by the person upon whom her happiness depends. Persuaded by her godmother, Lady Russell, to abandon her engagement to marry the brilliant but penniless young naval officer she loves, Anne Elliot throws away her best chance of personal happiness and finds (since 'no second attachment...had been possible to the nice tone of her mind, the fastidiousness of her taste, in the small limits of the society around them') eight years pass by in enduring the selfishness and indifference of her father and her two sisters. Anne blames neither herself nor Lady Russell for her present unhappiness; at the age of eighteen, inexperienced enough to accept the judgment of an older person as likely to be superior to her own, bound by affection, respect, and duty to her advisor, and convinced besides that she can only hamper her lover's career by marrying him without her family's countenance and financial support, Anne could not, probably, have acted otherwise than she did. But Lady Russell, though a sensible and intelligent woman, has 'prejudices on the side of ancestry', and Anne's regrets at having conformed at eighteen to a social code she sees clearly at twenty-seven to be worthless and shallow are as severe as if she had been guilty herself of pride and worldly materialism. Wentworth parts from her, angry and resentful of her 'weakness' and her apparent lack of confidence in him and in her own judgment. The chief interest of *Persuasion* rests in a sympathetic and sensitive exploration of Anne Elliot's feelings in her unhappy situation: the more unhappy in that no effort of hers *now* can win back the happiness she has voluntarily sacrificed. Like Emma Woodhouse on learning that Harriet believes Mr Knightley to return her love for him, Anne must teach herself to expect Captain Wentworth's marriage to another woman, Louisa Musgrove; unlike Emma, Anne cannot enjoy even the bitter consolations of self-blame and repentance. She has learned that 'prudence' has two sides to it, one shaped by good sense, and the other separated by so thin a line from materialism that the individual who is guided by it can be as wholly deprived by it as by a blatantly materialistic outlook, of personal fulfilment through love, hope, and energetic effort. Mistaking the second for the first, Anne Elliot has helped to maintain, by her actions, a social code to the unjust and inhuman aspects of which she is privately, but intensely, opposed.

Lady Russell, who provides the means by which this code of values disrupts and blights Anne's emotional life, is not its embodiment or symbol in the novel so much as its representative and apologist. Vanity and pride of rank concentrate their forces at Kellynch-hall, where the widowed baronet Sir Walter Elliot and his eldest daughter, Elizabeth, maintain a little court of hypocritical toadies; with an auxiliary at Uppercross Cottage in the same county, for the family pride is strong in the youngest Elliot, Mary, who has married Charles Musgrove, the heir to Uppercross Great House. Jane Austen captures in dialogue the essential qualities of Sir Walter's personality and his daughters', that menace Anne's peace and her discriminating mind:

'Wentworth? Oh! ay, Mr Wentworth, the curate of Monkford. You misled me by the term *gentleman*. I thought you were speaking of some man of property: Mr Wentworth was nobody, I remember; quite unconnected; nothing to do with the Strafford family. One wonders how the names of many of our nobility become so common.'

'Very well,' said Elizabeth, 'I have nothing to send but my love...'

'Yes, I made the best of it; I always do; but I was very far from well at the time; and I do not think I ever was so ill in my life as I have been all this morning—very unfit to be left alone, I am sure...So, Lady Russell would not get out. I do not think she has been in this house three times this summer.'

Sir Walter's small-minded snobbery, Elizabeth's careless insincerity, Mary Musgrove's shift from querulous self-pity to pique—all aspects of the Elliot traits of cold-hearted selfishness and insensitivity—are admirably caught in these lightning portraits. And in Mrs Clay, Elizabeth's confidante, we recognise the hypocritical servility upon which their selfishness feeds:

'Indeed I do say it. I never saw any body in my life spell harder for an invitation. Poor man! I was really in pain for him; for your hard-hearted sister, Miss Anne, seems bent on cruelty.'

Such exposure, through irony, of social and moral weakness in the Elliot establishment is, however, but a secondary interest in *Persuasion*, whose primary artistic aim is the successful creation of Anne Elliot. Sir Walter and Elizabeth are respected only by each other, and by the social climbers of Bath. They are as indifferent to Mary Musgrove as they (and Mary herself) are indifferent to Anne. The respect that even an apologist for rank like Lady Russell has for them is tempered by her good sense and her honesty. They are patronised by their social superiors, Lady Dalrymple and Miss Carteret, manipulated by their familiars, Mrs Clay and Mr William Walter Elliot, and regarded with indifference or contempt by every person of sense. Their influence outside Kellynch is negligible, and they are important to the novel because circumstances have confined Anne to Kellynch and to their company. Their selfishness towards Anne necessitates a degree of self-discipline in her that recalls the struggles in a similar direction of Fanny Price and Elinor Dashwood; and wins our respect for the firm principles that prevent her using marriage as a means of escape from such a family.

Almost as selfish as the Elliots, though free of their false pride and the indifference that separates one from the other, are the Musgrove family at Uppercross. Anne values the informal manners of Mary's relations, carried though they sometimes are to unwise excess; but the Musgroves' deepest affections and loyalties are concentrated within their own family circle, and with

a corporate expression of that selfish benevolence that character-
ised Lady Bertram's exploitation of Fanny in *Mansfield Park*, they
have little time for matters outside their own concerns. Their
affection for Anne arises more from an appreciation of her
usefulness and her tactful sympathy in their family affairs, than
from any real understanding of her mind and nature.

In complete contrast to these two linked worlds of selfish pride
and self-centred benevolence is a third into whose freer, fresher
atmosphere Anne will finally escape with Wentworth, who is its
chief representative in the novel. His is a world ruled by energetic
activity, by selfless devotion to duty and to intimate personal
relationships; and the relaxed informality of Uppercross is perhaps a step towards it from the chilly world of the Elliots that
Anne has been forced to inhabit. The impression of energy and
sense created by Wentworth's personality is supported by those
of his sister and her husband, Admiral Croft, who provide Anne
with an example of brave endurance and of mutual love in married
life that she adopts as a personal ideal; and by the Harvilles,
Wentworth's friends, at whose unpretentious house in Lyme
Regis Anne discovers 'a bewitching charm in...hospitality so
uncommon, so unlike...dinners of formality and display'. The
Harvilles' simplicity and warmth contrasts with the cold insincerity and indifference that the Elliots display towards each other.
When the Crofts meet Charles and Mary Musgrove, they make
Mary seem even shallower, her marriage emptier than ever of
true affection and generosity. When Sir Walter is forced by his
own extravagance to let Kellynch-hall and settle in Bath, his
house is rented by Admiral Croft, who performs the manorial
duties of the place a great deal better than the owner has ever
done. The Crofts' abilities and their integrity, like Wentworth's
independent spirit, illustrate (as in *Emma*) the changes taking
place in English society. The energy and the success of the naval
families counter and defeat the rigidity of the Elliots' social code;
and Anne Elliot, whose personal happiness has been caught up
in the conflict—and whose sense of family loyalty does not allow
her to seek the sympathy of the Elliot's many critics—is able at
last to identify herself with a way of life that has its share of

dangers and anxieties but is infinitely more congenial to her than life at Kellynch-hall or at Uppercross Cottage, where good sense is perpetually sacrificed to pride and selfish insensitivity.

The three worlds converge when the Elliots, the Musgroves, the Crofts, and the Harvilles assemble in Bath; and from their social meetings there and in the course of the novel, firm standards of moral and social propriety arise and are established. Anne's devotion to her invalid friend, the widowed Mrs Smith, contrasts effectively with the relentless pursuit of Lady Dalrymple by Sir Walter and Elizabeth, encouraged by Lady Russell and Mr Elliot. Mrs Musgrove personifies Christmas hospitality as she presides at the centre of the 'fine family piece' in Vol. 2, Chapter 2, protecting the little Harvilles from her own spoilt grandchildren, creating an atmosphere that invites Anne's regretful comparisons with 'the sad want of such blessings' in her own home; and the 'heartiness, and...warmth, and...sincerity' that Anne's visit calls forth from the Musgrove family at Bath can be compared a little later on in the same scene with their response to the visit of Sir Walter and Elizabeth,

> whose entrance seemed to give a general chill. Anne felt an instant oppression, and, wherever she looked, saw symptoms of the same. The comfort, the freedom, the gaiety of the room was over, hushed into cold composure, determined silence, or insipid talk, to meet the heartless elegance of her father and sister.

Sir Walter imagines that the Crofts will hasten to take advantage of their acquaintance with him, and plans anxiously how he may avoid introducing them to Lady Dalrymple, but the Crofts consider 'their intercourse with the Elliots as a mere matter of form, and not in the least likely to afford them any pleasure'.

This aspect of Jane Austen's technique recalls her methods in *Mansfield Park*, with its contrasted worlds of Mansfield, London, and Portsmouth. The expeditions to Sotherton Court and to Box Hill in *Mansfield Park* and *Emma*, during which characters make such important discoveries regarding themselves and others, are matched in *Persuasion* by the journey from Uppercross to Lyme Regis, undertaken by Louisa and Henrietta Musgrove, Mary and Anne, escorted by Captain Wentworth and Charles Musgrove.

At Lyme the sharp sea breezes accompany an unexpected renewal of Anne's physical attraction for Wentworth; there she is seen for the first time and admired by Mr Elliot; and there Louisa Musgrove, in an excessive indulgence of the wilfulness that Wentworth has been encouraging in her—believing it a valuable counter to the 'weakness' he abominates in Anne—falls on the hard pavement of the Cobb, and plunges her family and friends into protracted anxiety and fear for her health. At Lyme Anne's calm resourcefulness, displayed to advantage while the others are striking attitudes of helpless despair around the unconscious Louisa, is recognised and properly valued by others for the first time. The expedition is an important contribution to the plot, for Louisa's convalescence at Lyme in the Harville's house ends in her engagement to Wentworth's brother-officer and friend, Captain Benwick, leaving Wentworth 'unshackled and free' at last to propose a second time to Anne. Most important of all, the expedition to Lyme marks a turningpoint in Wentworth's relationship with Anne; for when, as he prepares to break the news of Louisa's accident to her parents, he tells Anne 'I have been considering what we had best do'—that *we*—as Anne fully realises—is 'a proof of friendship, and of deference for her judgment', implying moreover that they are as one in their affectionate concern for the Musgrove family. From this point on, Wentworth (who has been treating Anne with studied indifference) must admit even to himself that his early regard for her is unaltered:

He had imagined himself indifferent, when he had only been angry; and he had been unjust to her merits, because he had been a sufferer from them.

The beauty of Lyme and its atmosphere of health and freshness are peculiarly identified with Anne Elliot, and in harmony with her character; and while her late-flowering romance finds a melancholy echo in the autumn scenes at Uppercross, her reunion with Wentworth is part of a spring morning in Bath.

For we will find the techniques that have been tried and perfected in earlier writing put to strikingly new artistic uses in *Persuasion*. Never before has Jane Austen so clearly subordinated every other concern, so skilfully bent every technical device, to the convincing creation of a single character. Her ability to subject to this artistic intention even the didactic elements that provided the structural backbone of her earlier novels (not excluding *Emma*) illustrates a greater maturity of outlook and a more objective approach to life than she has hitherto been able, perhaps, to bring to her writing. The moral lessons *Persuasion* teaches are three: the duty of each individual to exert discriminating judgment and publicly assert high principles when the need arises, the inestimable value of trust and constancy in personal relationships, and the futility of vanity and social pride. But Anne Elliot's judgment, when we meet her for the first time, is already penetrating and reliable, her principles steady, her actions ruled by humility, and her joyless existence illuminated by her constancy to Wentworth. Not even Fanny Price was so little in need of moral discipline. Anne's progress is made towards a greater confidence in her own judgment, and in the validity of her own ideals.

Having been once misled by Lady Russell's counsel, Anne takes care—when Charles Musgrove proposes marriage to her—to leave 'nothing for advice to do'; she refuses Charles, although Lady Russell would have liked the match. Admiral Croft's manners may not suit Lady Russell, but they delight Anne, who warms to his 'goodness of heart and simplicity of character'; Lady Russell considers Lady Dalrymple 'an acquaintance worth having'—Anne is more fastidious. The novel moves forward to the point when Anne, having grown in confidence herself, can recognise Wentworth's claim upon her loyalty to be more important than the satisfaction of her family's empty vanity. She is able to defy their known prejudices and publicly acknowledge her acquaintance with Wentworth at Bath 'in spite of the formidable father and sister in the background', and feel 'equal to every thing which she believed right to be done'. Given at last the second chance she had never dared to hope for, Anne can confidently take the step she withdrew from eight years before, of marriage with Wentworth.

The effect of a continuous process of growth in Anne is partly achieved through Jane Austen's presentation of her as an interested (though sometimes unwilling) observer of marriage and of married life. Her dead mother's uncomplaining loyalty to a foolish husband, her sister Elizabeth's campaigns for matrimonial aggrandisement, the mutual disenchantment of Charles and Mary Musgrove, the warm and loyal attachment between the Crofts, the Harvilles, and the Musgroves, Captain Benwick's ability to find speedy consolation for his fiancee's loss in Louisa Musgrove, even the relationships between Harriet Musgrove and Charles Hayter, and between the Smiths, provide Anne with material to ponder. She reluctantly witnesses Mary's selfishness and Charles's irresponsibility as they dispute the rival claims of a dinner party and the care of their sick child; the nature of Anne's own 'generous attachment' to Wentworth is implicitly defined by contrast with Mary's querulous selfpity. Mrs Croft voices Anne's deepest convictions when she declares affectionately:

'...the happiest part of my life has been spent on board a ship. While we were together, you know, there was nothing to be feared'.

Even placid Mrs Musgrove has known the rigours of separation, for

'Mr Musgrove always attends the assizes, and I am so glad when they are over, and he is safe back again.'

Anne Elliot's respect for her mother's memory, her affection for Mrs Musgrove and her admiration of Mrs Croft shape her ideal of love and marriage. She is quick to see and interpret the glance of accord that passes between Captain Harville and his wife, and she is delighted by the domestic happiness of the Crofts who bring with them to Bath 'their country habit of being almost always together'. Unlike her sister Elizabeth, who had

while a very young girl, as soon as she had known him to be, in the event of her having no brother, the future baronet, meant to marry [Mr Elliot]

Anne possesses a fastidious moral delicacy that links her with Elizabeth Bennet and Fanny Price. Her unfaltering constancy to Wentworth expresses quietly but firmly her ideal of morality in personal relationships.

The sympathetic evocation of a personality in which intelligence is married to intense feeling is not new to Jane Austen's work, although to meet Anne Elliot after Emma Woodhouse might startle a reader into believing this to be a total change of interest. An attempt made in this direction as early as *Sense and Sensibility* was hindered by the need to fit Marianne Dashwood's sensitive, passionate nature into the comic stereotype demanded by a rigid conception of 'sensibility'. In *Mansfield Park*, as we have seen, the attempt was repeated, and with greater success, although Fanny Price loses something through contrast with the more vivid personality of Maria Bertram and the wit and vivacity of Mary Crawford. In *Persuasion*, the experiment is at last completely successful. Like Marianne Dashwood, Anne is emotional and sensitive. To the better regulation of her rioting emotions each trial of mind and temper is consciously directed by Anne herself, who is aware (as was Fanny Price) of the dangers of selfpity, and in order to occupy her mind is 'glad to have any thing marked out as a duty'. Finally, like Elinor Dashwood and Elizabeth Bennet, Anne possesses a fine sense of the absurd. The analogy of chemistry comes readily to mind, for Jane Austen displays to a marked degree the love and use of logic, the capacity to learn by patient trial and error, the reliance on order, and the distrust of emotionalism that characterise the scientific mind. In Anne her chemistry has produced at last the incorruptible blend, in perfectly judged proportion, of wit and a gentle nature, understanding and a passionate heart. There is no longer any need to punish a heroine for an unruly intelligence that makes her unfit for society. Anne's intelligence helps her to win the resolution and resignation of spirit that makes her situation bearable, and creates in her something of

that elasticity of mind, that disposition to be comforted, that power of turning readily from evil to good, and of finding employment which carried her out of herself

that her friend Mrs Smith enjoys by a happy gift of nature.

The sweetness of Anne Elliot's character is the result of a necessary sanity and steadiness, not of an incredible saintliness. Anne shares with Fanny Price a bitter sense of isolation and neglect, doomed as she seems to be slighted and exploited, like

Fanny, by her nearest relations and friends. But Anne has had time to build a defence against depression, she has mastered 'the art of knowing our own nothingness beyond our own circle'. Selfishness in those around her can hurt her, but it does not surprise and cannot permanently depress her. She has, on the contrary, learned to wring a wry amusement from its manifestations, and a continuous stream of ironic reflection plays in secret upon both important aspects of her personality—her unfailing courtesy, and her sympathy for other people. Anne perceives with some amusement, for instance, the cause of Henrietta's concern for old Dr Shirley's infirmity, but generously concedes

how desirable it was that he should have some active, respectable young man as resident curate, and was even courteous enough to hint at the advantage of such resident curate's being married.

No wonder Henrietta is 'very well pleased with her companion'! The same generous courtesy, coupled with a sense of filial duty prevents Anne retorting to Sir Walter's sneering crudities on the subject of Mrs Smith, that *her* friend

was not the only widow in Bath between thirty and forty, with little to live on, and no sirname of dignity.

Leaving Kellynch-hall to spend two months at Uppercross in the neighbourhood of the Musgrove family, Anne prepares 'to clothe her imagination, her memory, and all her ideas in as much of Uppercross as possible'. She has learned, in fact, how to conform without hypocrisy. Her sympathetic presence is as necessary to her discontented, petty-minded sister Mary as it is welcome to Mr and Mrs Musgrove, and their gay, lively daughters. The difference between Anne and Mrs Clay, who has supplanted her in the affections of her father and Elizabeth and who also knows 'the art of pleasing; the art of pleasing, at least, at Kellynch-hall', is that Anne's interest in others is motivated by no selfish schemes of a materialistic kind but has been developed in order to control her own melancholy feelings. And so Anne attempts to fill her life with 'duties'; she catalogues the books and pictures at Kellynch-hall, carries out Elizabeth's directions regarding the garden, arranges her books and her music, visits in the parish, nurses her young nephew, redirects Captain Benwick's reading along more sensible lines, and plays country dances by the hour for the lively Musgroves. Unembittered although still in love, Anne shows gentleness under affront, and inexhaustible tact in smoothing away clashes and difficulties between Uppercross Cottage and the Great House; and if her eyes fill with tears as Wentworth dances with Louisa Musgrove, that fact is known to nobody. Her tears, like her offer to play 'as usual', are the measure of the selfcontrol Anne has achieved. Her methods of self-discipline, despite some agitation at seeing Wentworth again, are justified and confirmed by every proof Wentworth gives her of his apparent indifference. By the time his entanglement with Louisa is at an end, Anne has prepared herself for a future without him; and although she has not ceased to love him, her emotional education is complete.

It is Anne Elliot's controlling good sense, her determination to guard her own peace of mind, that holds the reader's respect, even when her situation invites sympathy or her acute emotional agitation provokes amusement. Anne's good sense defines the play of her feelings, and in no other novel does a heroine, silly or sensible, reach the emotional intensity which she sustains when she gives eloquent expression at last to the thoughts kept secret so long, and reserves for her sex in the hearing of her lover the single unenviable privilege 'of loving longest when existence, or when hope is gone.' A declaration of such deeply felt, passionately expressed emotion as this gives the Jane Austen heroine a new dimension. Our response to it is the stronger for our awareness of Anne's habitual restraint.

A very great deal of Jane Austen's artistic effort in this novel is devoted to communicating, with sympathy and immediacy, the emotional side of her heroine's nature. Our sympathy and understanding are won for Anne from the very beginning because we share her station of passive listener and observer throughout the brilliant opening description of her father's religious reverence for the commandments of rank as embodied in that 'book of books', the *Baronetage*; and again, during the conversations with Mr Shepherd the lawyer that rapidly succeed it, concerning the letting of Kellynch-hall. We learn that Sir Walter turns to the *Baronetage* as some men turn to the Bible, for consolation and support, the need for which occurs more frequently as he becomes more distressed for money. When Mr Shepherd suggests that a wealthy Admiral might prove an ideal tenant, to be met by Sir Walter's sneers regarding the social obscurity and poor personal appearance of seagoing men, Anne's quiet voice is heard for the first time, in a gentle defence of the navy. The second time she speaks it is, significantly, to give her father a concise and accurate summary of Admiral Croft's career:

'And who is Admiral Croft?' was Sir Walter's cold suspicious inquiry.

Mr Shepherd answered for his being of a gentleman's family, and mentioned a place; and Anne, after the little pause which followed, added—

'He is rear admiral of the white. He was in the Trafalgar action, and has been in the East Indies since; he has been stationed there, I believe, several years.'

We note that Anne is surprisingly well informed regarding the movements of naval men and vessels, for a provincial young lady with no family connections in the navy; even the Musgroves, who had at least a midshipman in their family, are 'unobservant and incurious...as to the names of men and ships'. Anne's ability to provide, without notice, an accurate account of Wentworth's brother-in-law's career illuminates for a moment the mental activity that goes on in the privacy of her calm silence. Every detail that she can gather from newspapers and navy lists about Wentworth and his relations is precious to Anne, who follows with secret devotion a career in which she can no longer hope to share. When the reader reviews this conversation in the light of Anne's revealed interest in the navy, of a third interposition in which she provides the forgetful Mr Shepherd with the name 'Wentworth', and of the history of her romance that follows soon after, Sir Walter's vain and foolish remarks acquire the appearance of a form of subtle—because probably unconscious—torture; for the reader has learned to listen with Anne's ears, and is in the secret of her private ideals and emotions.

Anne's personality and her dilemma—her sensitivity and her hidden love for Wentworth—have been so well established by these means in the novel's early chapters that when she comes to Uppercross and meets Wentworth once more after their eight years' separation, the reader responds sympathetically to the flood of deep emotion beneath her composure:

> ...a thousand feelings rushed on Anne, of which this was the most consoling, that it would soon be over. And it was soon over. In two minutes after Charles's preparation, the others appeared; they were in the drawing-room. Her eye half met Captain Wentworth's; a bow, a curtsey passed; she heard his voice—he talked to Mary, said all that was right; said something to the Miss Musgroves, enough to mark an easy footing: the room seemed full—full of persons and voices—but a few minutes ended it. Charles shewed himself at the window, all was ready, their visitor had bowed and was gone... the room was cleared, and Anne might finish her breakfast as she could...
> Mary talked, but she could not attend. She had seen him. They had met. They had been once more in the same room!

To Anne, the seconds have passed as in a dream, her inward sensations so strong as what she has unconsciously longed for comes to pass, that ordinary conversation becomes indistinct, a familiar family party seems a tumultuous, anonymous crowd. When she and Wentworth begin to meet regularly in company at Uppercross, as they must soon do, any conversation that takes place within Anne's hearing registers with the reader as likely to affect her feelings in a manner that he can guess at through his established understanding of her mind and character. The dinner party at the Great House in Vol. 1, Chapter 8, finds Anne in her accustomed role of passive listener, comparing Wentworth's gay ridicule of Louisa Musgrove's ignorance regarding the accommodation available on a ship with his amusement in the early days of their acquaintance, of her own ignorance on similar subjects; hearing his many references to the year he received his first appointment—which was also the year of their parting; listening to Mrs Croft's descriptions of life as a sailor's wife, which Anne would herself so gladly experience, if she could. There is nothing in the conversation that bears a reference to their relationship, but Anne's knowledge of Wentworth's mind and habits of thought, her familiarity with every detail of his career, and her love for him—still alive and seemingly unrequited —create a *rapport* with Wentworth that is not unlike our own sympathetic understanding of her, and provide each turn of talk with an emotional undertow that is immediately apparent to us. Much of the novel is seen by us through Anne's eyes, and ordinary events receive an emotional heightening because we are aware of the intensity of her feelings.

Jane Austen uses Mrs Clay's furtive behaviour, explained later by the revelation of her liaison with Mr Elliot, as a further means of communicating the ceaseless, silent questioning of her own and her lover's feelings that goes on in Anne's mind, unseen and quite unguessed at by her family and her friends. Intent on her own thoughts, sunk in 'the broodings of this restless agitation', any detail that catches her attention or awakens her curiosity must be unusual and arresting. Jane Austen accumulates a number of such details; and while, with each one, we understand more of the intense emotion Anne is experiencing, we are carried by stages further along in the development of the plot. There is, for example, a very odd 'point of civility' to be settled between Anne and Mrs Clay, as to which of the two will walk home in the rain and which will ride with Elizabeth in Lady Dalrymple's carriage. Anne, as we know, would rather get wet than bear the company of her relations the Dalrymples, who are 'nothing' to her. But Mrs Clay? She has not shown herself so pressingly eager to be of service to Anne at any previous time; and would it not have been most natural for her to wish to accompany Elizabeth home in all the glory of the Dalrymple carriage? But there is a bonus attached to the wet walk home—the company of Mr Elliot. And though we know Anne's mind, there is no adequate reason for the 'generosity so polite and so determined' with which Mrs Clay insists that she is wearing the thicker boots. Surely these inconsistencies must strike Anne? They do not. She has no time to reflect longer on the implications of this interesting incident because just then she glimpses Captain Wentworth through a window in the shop, and the moment of speculation is gone for ever:

For a few minutes she saw nothing before her. It was all confusion. She was lost.

On their walk home to Camden-place, Elliot's conversation is filled with 'insinuations highly rational against Mrs Clay'. He could be sincere; he could, on the other hand, be covering up Mrs Clay's recent eager indiscretion. Anne hardly attends to what he is saying, for 'just now she could think only of Captain Wentworth'.

From now on such incidents become more frequent, and Anne's inability to perceive what is before her eyes and interpret it correctly reveals the extent of her own preoccupation. She is surprised that Mrs Clay can assume 'a most obliging, placid look' at the prospect of Elliot's evening visit, but puts it down to good acting, having been diverted from her half-suspicions by Mrs Smith's assurance that Mrs Clay's objective is Sir Walter himself. Anne does not believe it can be Mr Elliot whom Mary spies 'deep in talk' with Mrs Clay at a street corner (when he is supposed to be at Thornberry-park) until she sees him herself, and does not even then recollect that Mrs Clay had left Camden-place directly after breakfast that morning on a self-imposed errand. Anne's personal problems keep her mind occupied with thoughts of the morrow's card party, but she does remember to ask for an explanation of that strange tête-à-tête, only to have her suspicions lulled by Mrs Clay's plausible chatter:

'Oh dear! very true. Only think, Miss Elliot, to my great surprise I met with Mr Elliot in Bath-street! I was never more astonished...He had been prevented setting off for Thornberry, but I really forget by what—for I was in a hurry, and could not much attend, and I can only answer for his being determined not to be delayed in his return. He wanted to know how early he might be admitted tomorrow. He was full of "tomorrow"...'

Anne tells herself that Elliot has perhaps been censuring Mrs Clay's designs on Sir Walter—an odd explanation, when one comes to think of it. But the truth is that Anne's attention is very far away from Mrs Clay and Mr Elliot, and so is the reader's, for every moment increases the suspense that attends the scenes leading up to Wentworth's meeting with Anne at the White Hart Inn. When Mrs Clay ends up under Elliot's protection in London, the reader who comes to *Persuasion* for the first time is as surprised as the other characters in the novel are by the event, but on looking back he will discover that Jane Austen has scattered clues enough. To do more would have focused the interest of this last section of the novel on a Sir Walter–Mrs Clay–Elliot triangle, rather than on the steadying relationship of Wentworth and Anne. Such a triangle might have had richly comic possibilities, but it is hardly surprising—knowing Jane Austens' preferences in selecting her materials as we do—that she did not choose to explore them. If she had, the carefully built up structure of *Persuasion* would have been distorted, the aura of 'high-wrought love and eternal constancy' that has been created about Anne's personality would have had to give way to a coarser atmosphere, and with it must have disappeared the delicate mist of inward preoccupation through which Anne gazes at her immediate world in the novel's final pages. In its very remoteness from Anne's consciousness, the liaison between Elliot and Mrs Clay helps to emphasise the extent of the gap separating Anne's moral fastidiousness, her loyal constancy to Wentworth, and her sensitive mind from the crudity, the fickleness of purpose, and the double-dealing of this unattractive pair.

Is her emotionalism Anne Elliot's only weakness? Jane Austen described this character jokingly as 'almost too good for me', but her virtues are hardly superhuman and her failings are common enough. The latter include delight in the discovery that she has regained her former power over Wentworth:

Jealousy of Mr Elliot! It was the only intelligible motive. Captain Wentworth jealous of her affection! Could she have believed it a week ago—three hours ago! For a moment the gratification was exquisite.

But whereas a vain coquette, such as Isabella Thorpe in *Northanger Abbey*, would have done everything in her power to prolong Wentworth's agony of uncertainty, Anne's very next wish is to end it at once with an assurance of her love. Anne's triumphant joy—it lasts only *for a moment*—is endearing, occurring in a character generally so far above pettiness. It emphasises her humanity, and the reader triumphs briefly with Anne at this point in her story, having shared her trepidation, her indecision, her misgivings, her longing to look again on Wentworth, and the acute embarrassment in his presence that have preceded it.

She now felt a great inclination to go to the outer door; she wanted to see if it rained. Why was she to suspect herself of another motive? Captain Wentworth must be out of sight.

*Why was she to suspect herself of another motive?* Critics have noted the smoothness with which the narrator's comments slide easily into Anne's. In this passage we can hear Jane Austen's dryly amused tone through Anne's exasperation with her own conscience. It is a tone that we hear often:

> She hoped to be wise and reasonable in time; but alas! alas! she must confess to herself that she was not wise yet.

> She had some feelings which she was ashamed to investigate. They were too much like joy, senseless joy!

> ...by some other removals, and a little scheming of her own, Anne was enabled to place herself much nearer the end of the bench than she had been before, much more within reach of a passer-by.

Anne is treated ironically in these and other parts of *Persuasion*, although not with the astringent narrative tone employed by Jane Austen throughout her writing of *Emma*.

It is significant, in this connection, that the heroine of *Persuasion* exemplifies 'the loveliest medium', the coexistence in a central character of a controlled intelligence and deep-flowing emotions. Anne does full justice, for instance, to the Musgroves' warm and generous affections although she is perfectly conscious of their insensitivity. Her selfcontrol makes her welcomed at Uppercross; if she did not deliberately keep her opinions in check we would not find Mrs Musgrove saying, as she does:

> 'I am sure neither Henrietta nor I should care at all for the play, if Miss Anne could not be with us.'

The successful evocation of Anne's character, with its hidden play of inward irony and intense feeling, its ceaseless striving after outward and emotional control, has an effect on the novel as a whole. The distinctive atmosphere of *Persuasion* derives from Anne, its quiet restraint suggesting that Jane Austen, like her heroine, had acquired with experience a better sense of perspective, a more patient tolerance, and a firmer grasp of her emotions. It would seem that for Jane Austen there was no longer any urgent personal need to castigate society, nor to discipline one part of her nature by subjecting it to another. Anne's source of happiness is 'in the warmth of her heart', which her good sense and reason have prevented from petrifying into the cold ashes of bitterness such as Elizabeth's, or of selfpity such as Mary's. *Persuasion* tranquilly states Jane Austen's newly achieved ability to accept the coexistence of opposed characteristics in a single personality, and her commitment to an exploration of character as her new artistic goal.

The major artistic triumph achieved in creating Anne Elliot tends to obscure somewhat a minor one, Jane Austen's presentation of Frederick Wentworth, a hero with disadvantages. Wentworth possesses the pennilessness and attractive manners that Jane Austen combined so inauspiciously in Willoughby and George Wickham, the handsome adventurers of *Sense and Sensibility* and *Pride and Prejudice*. Anne falls in love with 'a remarkably fine young man', handicapped by 'a great deal of intelligence, spirit and brilliancy'—for these qualities do him no service with the person who guides Anne's decisions at the time. It has been pointed out with some truth that Wentworth represents a class, that his personality evinces 'all the new bourgeois virtues—confidence, aggressiveness, daring, an eye for money and the main chance'.[1] These virtues, shared with the Crofts and the Harvilles, place him in permanent opposition to the settled and rigid values of the Elliot establishment. *Persuasion*, like *Emma*, reflects without distortion the economic and social pressures that work upon its characters, but it would be overstating the case to declare that its chief interest lies in its value as a social document. Jane Austen's interest in Wentworth is the artistic one of creating the illusion of a convincingly human personality—in this case that of a man of worth and integrity, swayed by his pride and by his emotions. Wentworth's struggle to succeed in his profession is over by the time he reappears in the novel as an eligible suitor to Louisa Musgrove; and at no time does Jane Austen suggest that his earlier unsuitability to marry among the Elliots originated in anything but his lack of funds— for Sir Walter's views on rank are ignored or ridiculed by every unprejudiced person of sense. Similarly, Wentworth experiences no difficulty in fitting into the elegant pursuits of Bath and even

[1] Marvin Mudrick, *Jane Austen: Irony as Defense and Discovery* (1952).

Elizabeth Elliot regards a man of such presence as a social asset, although he prefers to spend his time in sensible company. Jane Austen demonstrates, through Wentworth, the obtuseness of a society that recognises true worth only when it is united to wealth and success. To Anne goes the credit of never having doubted the worth that society belatedly acknowledges, of penetrating the cloud of obscure suspicion that Wentworth's lack of name and prospects and his attractive personality had raised between him and Lady Russell.

A portrait of Wentworth is painted in Vol. 1, Chapter 4, of which the keynote is confidence and independence of mind. He is clearly not a man to view caution kindly, even caution exercised in his own interests. He is aware that always beside Anne, guiding (and he has every excuse for thinking, controlling) her decisions, is the figure of Lady Russell. Wentworth leaves Anne in anger, determined to forget her. An interesting parallel is drawn here:

'It was a great object with me, at that time, to be at sea, a very great object. I wanted to be doing something.'

While Anne had been contriving occupation for her mind at home, Wentworth has been seeking distraction in activity. In the long interval that elapses before Wentworth makes his second appearance in Anne's life, his character and memory are kept alive for the reader by a series of subtle touches. Their angry parting has given Anne no cause to hope for a renewal of their engagement to marry, but their brief and intense association has provided her with a standard of masculine worth that she can never relinquish. Despite the urging of her friends and her own delight in domesticity, Anne remains faithful—not to a sentimental memory, but to a standard of excellence that she will not trade for an inferior article. Wentworth's character grows in the reader's estimation, its qualities defined and elaborated by implication as Anne coolly sums up the people she meets. Charles Musgrove, who proposes marriage to her before he finally marries Mary, is likeable enough, but Anne rejects him; and during her stay at Uppercross Cottage the reader finds Charles unpleasantly selfwilled and casual, even irresponsible.

Mr Elliot, who seems to Lady Russell to be the perfect husband for Anne, strikes her god-daughter as

rational, discreet, polished, but...not open. There was never any burst of feeling, any warmth of indignation or delight, at the evil or good of others. This, to Anne, was a decided imperfection...She prized the frank, the open-hearted, the eager character beyond all others. Warmth and enthusiasm did captivate her still.

Anne's estimation of each new suitor is made with implicit reference to the standard provided by Wentworth, and her doubt or mistrust becomes an indication (since we have learned to respect her judgment) of his worth. Wentworth returns, and they meet again. Jane Austen allows the reader a glimpse into Wentworth's mind as he reflects on that meeting, in a passage that is subtly ambiguous throughout:

He had not forgiven Anne Elliot. She had used him ill; deserted and disappointed him; and worse, she had shewn a feebleness of character in doing so, which his own decided, confident temper could not endure. She had given him up to oblige others. It had been the effect of over-persuasion. It had been weakness and timidity.

He had been most warmly attached to her, and had never seen a woman since whom he thought her equal; but, except from some natural sensation of curiosity, he had no desire of meeting her again. Her power with him was gone for ever.

It was now his object to marry...He had a heart for either of the Miss Musgroves, if they could catch it; a heart, in short, for any pleasing young woman who came in his way, excepting Anne Elliot.

Although presented as narrative, the passage carries the rhythms of Wentworth's characteristically energetic speech, and lays bare, through the very words he uses, the emotions that he will not admit to himself. Through what is on the surface an impartial, detached account of Wentworth's state of mind that is professedly casual in its final attitude to Anne, there breaks his resentment at her 'betrayal' of him, and clear indications (because he deliberately attempts to suppress and ignore them) of his interest in Anne's welfare and his constant love for her. Still in love, full of hurt pride, Wentworth is ready to marry on the rebound. So begins his relationship with Louisa Musgrove, coupled with a rather graceless determination to prove his indifference to Anne.

But it is soon clear that Anne has given Wentworth in her turn an unchanging standard of feminine perfection. His original opinion of her character alters no more than her estimation of his. She is 'not out of his thoughts' when he describes his ideal life-partner to his sympathetic sister, Mrs Croft. Any mention of her name attracts his close attention. A real tenderness breaks through his elaborate pretence of indifference at least twice while they are both at Uppercross, when he rescues her from her young nephew's playful torture, and again when, perceiving her exhaustion during a long walk back from Winthrop, he arranges for her relief. At Lyme he is dragged out of his carefully constructed armour by Elliot's open admiration of Anne, and by the quiet competence she alone shows when Louisa falls on the Cobb. Wentworth is consistently, if we overlook his histrionics on the Cobb, true to life. His faults are not glossed over, and the vitality and warmth that captivate Anne are registered in his fluent, vigorous speech, his generous thoughts and actions. Even at the close of the novel, when all is in train for a happy ending, there is no easy solution for Wentworth, no 'perfect friendship' possible for him with Lady Russell. He is aware that he has been his own enemy in allowing his pride to keep him away from Anne so long, but the memory remains with him of how Lady Russell's influence first estranged them.

*Persuasion* is the only one of Jane Austen's novels that can, with some assurance of accuracy at least, be studied in the process of its creation, for a cancelled chapter of the novel survives with the material that Jane Austen substituted for it—Chapters 10 and 11 of the second volume that we know. The alterations she made in her original draft have been subjected to analysis and criticism, changes which show her to have been acutely sensitive to niceties of tone and atmosphere. For example, the passage describing Anne Elliot's reaction to the revelation of Elliot's true character read originally as follows:

...pained for Lady Russell & glancing with composed Complacency & Lenient (?) Triumph upon the fact of her having been right & Lady R wrong herself the most discriminating of the two. *She* had never been satisfied. Lady Russell's confidence had been entire.

Jane Austen drew a line through most of this, and left the manuscript to read—

...and pained for Lady Russell, whose confidence in him had been entire.

The alteration obviously advances the interests of economy and brevity, but it also removes every hint of gleeful selfsatisfaction and aggressiveness from the passage, leaving intact the generous, affectionate sympathy that is the keynote of Anne's character.

Why, we might ask, did not revision of this kind repair some of the inconsistencies and weaknesses that strike us at many points in *Persuasion*? It is true that these might have been passed over had they occurred in the work of another, less careful writer, but since our standard of comparison must necessarily be Jane Austen's recent and fine performances in *Mansfield Park* and *Emma*, novels that had undergone careful revision before publication, they are weaknesses that are impossible to ignore. Revision by Jane Austen was in itself a process of artistic development, and even a few days' re-thinking and re-writing could make a great deal of difference, as we recognise if we examine her revision of Chapter 10 in Vol. 2. The alterations made there all tend to give the emotional side of Anne Elliot's character full play, and settings and incidents are changed in order to provide a sense of increasing tension that culminates in Anne's confession of her love in Wentworth's hearing.

Can we be certain that the rest of *Persuasion* was never subjected to Jane Austen's invariably purifying, brightening, corrective process of revision? We cannot, for the novel as we know it is very far from being a mere first draft. And yet, the reader is disturbed again and again while reading, by striking and uncharacteristic weaknesses. Look, for instance, at the absurd behaviour of the whole party when Louisa falls on the Cobb; or at the following description of Lyme Regis in Vol. 1, Chapter 11:

...as there is nothing to admire in the buildings themselves, the remarkable situation of the town, the principal street almost hurrying into the water, the walk to the Cobb, skirting round the pleasant little bay, which in the season is animated with bathing machines and company, the Cobb itself, its old wonders and new improvements, with the very beautiful line of cliffs stretching out to the east of the town, are what the stranger's eye will seek. . . The scenes in its neighbourhood, Charmouth, with its high grounds and extensive sweeps of country, and still more its sweet retired bay, backed by dark cliffs, where fragments of low rocks among the sands make it the happiest spot for watching the flow of the tide, for sitting in unwearied contemplation; the woody varieties of the cheerful village of Up Lyme, and, above all, Pinny, with its green chasms between romantic rocks. . .

The passage resembles nothing more than the descriptive prose of travel-guides to well known beauty spots. What, one might ask, is it doing in a novel? When we read, a little further on, that Charmouth, Pinny, and Up Lyme are beautiful, tranquil places that 'must be visited, and visited again, to make the worth of Lyme understood', we are tempted to ask 'By whom?' None of the party who travel all the way from Uppercross to Lyme visit any of these places, and it is difficult to see what functional role is played by this particular passage in *Persuasion*, with its super-fluity of irrelevant detail. If these passages were really intended to stand as they do now in the published novel, we cannot help feeling that such theatrical behaviour in hitherto sensible charac-ters and such pointless descriptive writing are faults and weak-nesses in the writer who created Sotherton Court in *Mansfield Park*, and who can rise in this very novel to the emotional heights of Anne's words to Captain Harville at the White Hart Inn.

Again, why is Dick Musgrove, a character who has died two years before the novel opens and can therefore play no important part in it, described so harshly, as

a thick-headed, unfeeling, unprofitable Dick Musgrove, who had never done any thing to entitle himself to more than the abbreviation of his name, living or dead—

why such bitterness, lavished by the narrator upon an insignificant character who never appears? 'Characters introduced only to be delineated' did sometimes occur in earlier work, but had no place in the closely organised, perfectly planned schemes of *Mansfield Park* and *Emma*. Besides, the passage standing as it does, we have to understand by it that Anne shares the narrator's opinion of Dick; and this would be quite as much at odds with her character as the passage just examined from the cancelled Chapter 10. Dick Musgrove enters *Persuasion* for one reason, and one only:

mutual amusement at similar recollections of him provides the first proof of those 'tastes so similar...feelings so in unison' that Anne believes herself to share with Wentworth. The estranged lovers react independently, yet alike, to Mrs Musgrove's 'large, fat sighings' for her dead son. It is hard to believe that Jane Austen's original sketch of Dick Musgrove would have survived a drastic revision of Chapter 6 in Vol. 1, and that some less startlingly offensive circumstance would not have been substituted for it that established better the signs of an unacknowledged *rapport* between Wentworth and Anne.

Another striking weakness in *Persuasion* is that Lady Russell does not impress us as an effective personality, although her influence over Anne is so decisive that it precipitates the action of the novel. A sufficient number of virtues and weaknesses are given, indeed, to equip this character with the outlines of a human personality: we learn of her intelligence, her honesty, and her sympathy, and find that these are counterweighted by a tendency to be swayed by social prejudice. What Lady Russell lacks is the illusion of life, which was spun about every character in *Emma* (even those, like Mr Perry or William Larkins, who never appear in person) by means of innumerable minute details which had the effect of brush-strokes filling in outlines on canvas. The reader of *Emma* achieves such perfect familiarity with the minds of its characters that he imagines he can predict what they are likely to think or do in a given situation. The admirers of Jane Austen's novels who amuse themselves by projecting visits from their relations, the Wickhams, to Mr Darcy and Elizabeth at Pemberley, or by imagining long winter evenings at Hartfield enlivened by conversation between Mr Knightley and his father-in-law, Mr Woodhouse, do not assist our better understanding of what Jane Austen actually wrote, but their efforts are evidence of the masterly manner in which she has given life—or the illusion of life—to the creatures of her imagination. Yet we are told very little about Lady Russell. That Elizabeth Elliot returns unread a book that Lady Russell 'would lend' her, or that Lady Russell leads a busy social life and takes an interest in the patterns of curtains, are not facts upon which the reader's imagination can build up a personality worthy of Anne's love and respect. If we did not see Lady Russell drawing up a sensible scheme for retrenchment at Kellynch-hall, we would have had to take her creator's word for it that she is what the novel requires her to be, for she is presented at any length in dialogue only when she is trying to influence Anne in Elliot's favour—and this interest on her part cannot give the reader a good impression of her 'sound abilities'. She lives even less in our imaginations than such comparatively minor characters in other novels as Mrs Gardiner and Mrs Weston.

A fourth feature of *Persuasion* that surprises and irks the reader is a certain inconsistency in Mrs Smith, Anne's invalid friend, who remains silent on the subject of Elliot's unsavoury past while she believes Anne is about to marry him, and opens Anne's eyes to his true character only when she is certain that no engagement is to take place. And again, how are we to regard the very long 'story of her life' that Mrs Smith tells Anne, slowing down the pace of the novel considerably in the process, and introducing many persons of whom we never learn more than their names? Colonel Wallis and 'my good friend Mrs Rooke', and even Charles Smith remain total strangers to the reader, even after the long story has been told. Such a clumsy piece of exposition might have been passed over in earlier work (we recall Willoughby's explanations to Elinor at Cleveland, and Colonel Brandon's similar confidences, besides Mr Darcy's letter to Elizabeth in *Pride and Prejudice*) but after the artistry of *Mansfield Park* and *Emma*, we cannot help being surprised by it.

In the light of our knowledge of the juvenilia and Jane Austen's earlier work, it is tempting to guess at intended alterations that were never made, to convince ourselves that revision would have filled in the shadowy outlines of Lady Russells' personality, excised or softened the portrait of Dick Musgrove, improved the scene on the Cobb, taken Mrs Smith out of her sickroom or in some other way made the story less dependent on gossip at second and third hand, and expanded the rapid notes descriptive of Lyme Regis—and especially of Charmouth, which seems, from Jane Austen's brief account of it, to have struck her as an appropriate spot for a scene involving Anne—into a more fitting setting for the events and discoveries that occur during the expedition to Lyme. The vocabulary of pictorial art is very relevant to the work of Jane Austen, who could not 'do any thing slovenly' when engaged in artistic creation of any kind, and whom we know to have been well versed in the rules laid down by experts in the art of design. She compared her own work to miniature painting on ivory,

on which I work with so fine a Brush, as produces little effect after much labour

a piece of self-criticism written a mere five months after her revision of Chapter 10 in *Persuasion*. In the light of the novelist's practice of revision over an extended period of time, and her own expectation, mentioned in her letters, that a year would pass before *Persuasion* was published, we would probably be right to consider this novel one that had advanced very near to its completion, a synopsis whose parts were in different stages of development, and that awaited a final and complete revision at the time of Jane Austen's death in 1817. Such an approach will help us to see the novel's 'weaknesses' in a proper light, as comparatively minor considerations that should not distract us from Jane Austen's major achievement in giving her writing a new direction.

Master craftsmen do not suddenly forget their tried methods and the individual, familiar ways of doing things to which they have won through after years of experiment, however sick, unhappy, or exhausted they may be—and ill health, family troubles, and physical or mental exhaustion have all been advanced as possible reasons for the faults in *Persuasion*, written a year before the novelist's death. It is therefore likely to be nearest to the truth to consider the portrait of Dick Musgrove an improvisatory sketch in strong, primary colours, that the artist would have returned later on to soften; Lady Russell an outline that would have been filled in with detail and subtly shaded; Mrs Smith a wrongly judged perspective that would have been corrected in revision; and the Lyme Regis passage a mere series of notebook jottings and personal recollections, awaiting selection and elaboration.

For Dick Musgrove and Mrs Smith, like the expedition to Lyme and even Lady Russell, are of small importance beside the character of Anne Elliot, to 'place' which as perfectly as possible Jane Austen revised Chapter 10. They are mere machinery, while Anne's sensitivity and intelligence together create the fabric and atmosphere of the novel, and could not therefore be allowed to suffer distortion or mis-statement. The personal reasons for the speed and urgency with which Jane Austen revised the part of *Persuasion* that forms the emotional climax of Anne's story we shall never know, but the obvious artistic one is sufficient: that she was dissatisfied with her management of that chapter, and felt compelled to rewrite and revise it. Other, minor, matters might await her leisure, but Anne Elliot, the novel's centre and her creator's chief artistic interest, could not be permitted to remain in any state short of perfection, or at any rate, of perfect and unambiguous clarity.

On many important points, such as this one concerning the perplexing inequalities in Jane Austen's last novel, we can only speculate. Yet we owe it to an artist of her ability that we should try to justly evaluate the words that *she* wrote, neither reading into and substituting for them a fabric of our own creation, nor resting content with a critic's 'interpretation' of what she has said herself with such skill and feeling. There is enough in *Persuasion* as it stands, without any need for speculation or interpretation, to indicate that its author has subordinated every earlier interest, notably her talent for satire and her inclination towards didacticism, to a new artistic problem, the psychological exploration of character. And although we cannot be certain whether a succeeding novel would have developed this interest further, or turned to a new one, we have in *Persuasion*'s Anne Elliot its justification and perfection. Incomplete and unrevised though it probably is, her achievement in *Persuasion* crowns a remarkable artistic career, reminding us that the skill and self-discipline that were part of Jane Austen's equipment as a writer and helped her to create works of art from the immediate problems of everyday life, were still with her when she began—in the shadow of her last illness—on a new journey of artistic exploration.

Jane Austen's work has had its share of every shade of critical opinion, the sympathetic, the appreciative, the fanatically affectionate, the objective, the irritable, the hostile. It is our pleasure, as individual readers who have directly experienced the spirit of her writing through the words that embody and communicate it, to make our own estimate of her achievement, and to reflect upon the meaning that her work holds for us.

# INDEX OF PASSAGES QUOTED